SAINTS AND ANIMALS IN THE MIDDLE AGES

SAINTS AND ANIMALS IN THE MIDDLE AGES

Dominic Alexander

THE BOYDELL PRESS

First published 2008

The Boydell Press, Woodbridge

ISBN 978–1–84383–394–9

The Boydell Press is an imprint of Boydell & Brewer Ltd
PO Box 9, Woodbridge, Suffolk IP12 3DF, UK
and of Boydell & Brewer Inc.
668 Mt Hope Avenue, Rochester, NY 14620, USA

website: www.boydellandbrewer.com

A CIP record for this book is available
from the British Library

This publication is printed on acid-free paper

Typeset in Perpetua by Word and Page, Chester, Great Britain

Printed in Great Britain by
CPI Antony Rowe, Chippenham, Wiltshire

CONTENTS

ACKNOWLEDGEMENTS

The origins of this book lie in an early postgraduate paper given to the Early Medieval Seminar at the Institute of Historical Research in the mid-1990s. First thanks therefore go to that seminar for many years of rigorous education in how to do medieval history. Particular thanks are due to Michael Clanchy, and especially Alan Thacker for a great deal of discussion, good advice and encouragement over the years, beginning as the final supervisor of my doctoral thesis, and generously continuing thereafter. I would like to thank the publisher's reader for many helpful suggestions, and the Isobel Thornley Bequest Fund for a grant towards the publishing of this book. I would specially like to thank Elaine Graham-Leigh, who had to live with the long gestation of this book, for her unstinting intellectual engagement with the project, for much work reading multiple drafts of the book, and for unfailing confidence and encouragement. I would also like to thank Angela Graham-Leigh for all her hard work proofreading, and to Anne Alexander for preparing the index. All mistakes remain my own.

ABBREVIATIONS

AASS	*Acta Sanctorum* (Brussels, Antwerp, Paris, 1643–1940).
MGH	Monumenta Germaniae Historica
MGH SS	Monumenta Germaniae Historica, Sciptores in folio (Hanover 1826–)
MGH SSRM	Monumenta Germaniae Historica, Scriptores Rerum Merovingicarum (Hanover 1884–).
PL	Patrologia Latina, ed. Jacques Paul Migne (Paris 1841–64).
Rolls Series	Rerum Britannicarum Medii Aevi Scriptores, or Chronicles and Memorials of Great Britain and Ireland during the Middle Ages (London 1858–96).

In memory of David G. Alexander (1939–1980)

CHAPTER 1

Reading the Lives of the Saints

IN 1097, Saint Anselm, then archbishop of Canterbury, upon leaving the court after a serious dispute with King William Rufus, saved a hare that was being hunted by the boys and dogs of his household. The hare 'fled between the feet of the horse on which Anselm sat', according to Eadmer, the archbishop's biographer. Eadmer goes on to describe how the saint ensured that the hare was safe, and then burst into tears as some of his men laughed at the plight of the animal, with the dogs still sniffing about, trying to get at the hare.[1] If taken as fact, and Eadmer claims to have been present at the incident, this story is plausible, since the dogs would have been frightened to run under the horse, while the rider would have been concerned to prevent his horse from panicking.[2] It could have been written as a miracle story, with the saint restraining the dogs by his saintly virtue, but Eadmer seems to play down any miraculous element to his story. The moral is clear nonetheless: Anselm says, 'You laugh, do you? But there is no laughing, no merry-making, for this unhappy beast. His enemies stand about him, and in fear of his life he flees to us asking for help. So it is with the soul of man . . .'. Anselm likened the peril of the hare to the peril of the soul after death, surrounded by demons, and desperately needing heavenly aid. The real question is why Anselm's hagiographer should wish to tell such a peculiar little story directly after recounting the saint's confrontation with the king, and immediately prior to his exile.

The vast corpus of medieval saints' lives (*vitae*) contains a very large selection of stories of saints and animals, of many very different types, but, understandably perhaps, modern historians have rarely taken them seriously as a form of evidence for medieval life and culture. However, the example of Anselm's hare is demonstration in itself that medieval people regarded such stories in a serious light. Why else does the story appear at such a pivotal point in Eadmer's account of the archbishop? The later account of Saint Anselm by William of Malmesbury gives the story a prominent place, and makes it clear, as Eadmer did not, that it was a miracle: 'he deprived the hare's open-mouthed pursuers of their bark and at the same time baffled their attempts to give chase'.[3] Eadmer himself did not stop with the story of the hare,

1 *The Life of St Anselm, Archbishop of Canterbury by Eadmer*, ed. and trans. R. W. Southern (Oxford 1962), bk 2, ch. 18, pp. 89–91 (hereafter Eadmer, *Vita Anselmi*).

2 I am indebted to Michael Clanchy for pointing out the plausibility of this story.

3 William of Malmesbury, *De Gestis Pontificum Anglorum*, ed. N. E. S. A. Hamilton, Rolls Series 52 (1870), 2 vols, at I, ch. 66, p. 123, and William of Malmesbury, *The Deeds of the Bishops of England*, trans. D. Preest (Woodbridge 2002), p. 80.

but followed it immediately with another story of a similar type. Here 'on another occasion', the saint saw a boy playing with a little bird by the road, having tied its foot to a string, and taking a childishly cruel amusement in the bird's attempts to escape. Observing this, Anselm hoped for the bird to escape, which forthwith it did, and then drew a spiritual moral similar to the one drawn for the hare.[4] The very next chapter details the beginning of the archbishop's exile from England. Clearly these two stories had some significance in the minds of medieval authors and their audience.

For ecclesiastical writers, William Rufus was a particularly oppressive king. The Anglo-Saxon Chronicle describes him as being 'very harsh and fierce', 'continually exasperating this nation with depredations and unjust taxes', and of course, 'he oppressed the Church of God'.[5] Later, Henry of Huntingdon claimed that the king's friends 'robbed and subverted everything', and that the king himself was 'most evil to God and to the people', mainly because of his treatment of Church positions and property.[6] These are later judgements, but if any such feeling existed during Rufus's reign, and there would always be some dissatisfaction which could be expressed in these terms, then Eadmer's stories of the hare and the captive bird would have fitted in neatly with such discontent. For those facing a predatory king, here is an archbishop of deep feeling for the sufferings of the weak. Where many may laugh at another's misfortune, this saintly man will at once weep and cast forth his holy power to save the hunted from the hunter.

The stories have the advantage of being metaphors: they can imply far more than they state directly, an advantage in a tense political confrontation between king and Church. If this context is accepted as plausible, one puzzling aspect of the stories may be explained. It is not clear why Eadmer seems reluctant to claim either story as a miracle as such, when there is no shortage of miracles in the *Vita* as a whole. The two stories were probably part of the original draft *Vita* that Eadmer drew up while he was one of Anselm's companions and that was later destroyed on the archbishop's orders, although not before Eadmer had made a copy. In these circumstances portraying the incidents as clear miracles might have been impolitic, but if they were intended to be spread about, the semi-miraculous formulation would still give the necessary message.[7]

This scenario depends upon the genre of the saint and animal miracle being familiar to a wide medieval audience, and for that audience to be ready to hear such tales in a metaphorical sense when appropriate. The hare story itself is part of a small tradition of miracle stories where a saint, usually a hermit, rescues a hunted wild animal from the spears or hounds of a hunting nobleman. The stories can be

[4] Eadmer, *Vita Anselmi*, bk 2, ch. 19, pp. 90–2.

[5] *The Anglo-Saxon Chronicle*, ed. and trans. G. N. Garmondsway (London 1953), the Laud Chronicle (E), p. 235.

[6] Henry of Huntingdon, *Historia Anglorum*, ed. and trans. Diana Greenway (Oxford 1996), ch. 22, pp. 448–9.

[7] For the writing of the *Vita*, see Southern's introduction to the *Vita Anselmi*, particularly pp. ix–xiii.

labelled the 'hermit and hunter' topos.[8] This type appears with some regularity in twelfth-century England, and thus Anselm's hare has good contemporary company, in a line of stories going back to Saint Martin of Tours in the fourth century.[9] It is a small part of the purpose of this book to show that the use of 'hermit and hunter' stories as metaphor, similar to that suggested here for Saint Anselm, is highly likely by the twelfth century. However, the tradition of saint and animal miracles contains many more types than this, and moreover it is unlikely that the stories were used or understood in exactly the same ways throughout the centuries, and across the different societies where Christian hagiography was written, creating or recycling the growing corpus.

If a beginning can be set to the whole tradition, then it can be found with the Egyptian Fathers of the fourth and fifth centuries, and from there it was transplanted into the burgeoning hagiographic literature of western Europe in the fifth and sixth centuries. By the seventh century the genre of the saint and animal story was fully formed, but variations and extrapolations, and even a few new themes, would be added later. In the transition to the central Middle Ages, the hagiographic literature of Ireland is a crucial case, showing how the genre was adapted to and by a society quite different from those post-Roman societies of western Europe. Having explored the main lines of the tradition, and the dominant messages to be found within it, it will be possible to assess some of the stranger stories, including the 'hermit and hunter' type. Also crucial to the full understanding of the genre is the cult of Saint Cuthbert in twelfth-century Durham and Northumberland, where numerous saint and animal miracles appeared towards the end of the twelfth century, in the context of a corpus of evidence from which it is possible to explore the full dynamic between ecclesiastical writers, popular belief and holy men, and to analyse the creation of these miracle stories. In the thirteenth century, the tradition receives its last major expression in the character of Saint Francis, where there is both strong continuity with past hagiography and indications of new conceptions. The social relations which had hitherto driven important strands of the animal and saint tradition were becoming less important in the more developed, institutional society of the thirteenth century.

Anselm's hare was a story from near the end of the span of centuries under consideration, and one that was relatively believable. Few of the miracles dealt with here can be so easily accepted as embellishments upon genuine incidents. Dragons and other mythical creatures show up in saints' *vitae* with some regularity from early on, showing saints at their most legendary. One of the earliest such appearances occurs in one *Vita* of the extraordinary fifth-century Syrian holy man, Saint Simeon Stylites. This is a strange story, carrying as it does the slight whiff of Origenist optimism over the possible redemption of even the most evil in creation. Thus that most demonic of creatures, the dragon, finding itself wounded in the eye by

[8] This is the phrase used in a discussion focused on Robert of Knaresborough by Brian Golding, 'The Hermit and the Hunter', in *The Cloister, the World: Essays in Medieval History in Honour of Barbara Harvey*, ed. John Blair and Brian Golding (Oxford 1996), pp. 95–117.

[9] This theme will be more fully explored in Chapter 6 below.

a piece of wood, and suffering for some time, drags itself out of its cave to lie in supplication before the entrance to the saint's enclosure. The branch falls out as the dragon becomes truly penitent, and presumably vegetarian, as it never harms anyone thereafter.[10] This is one of the earliest examples of a saint healing an animal, but it is also wholly symbolic, and a possible example of a miracle story being built up from biblical quotation. The branch is the beam in the eye which makes the sinner persecute his fellows.[11] The predator in the land ceases to be a predator when that blindness is cured by the presence of a saint, who is free of any mote in his eye, and acts as the conduit of grace for ordinary sinners. As if to underline the symbolic nature of the dragon, the following miracle, in the original Greek *Vita* by Antonius, recounts the conversion of a robber-chief from his evil ways to a life of religion.[12]

The dragon story may well have been intended to be understood as an allegory of sin and redemption, but it is also possible that the dragon was symbolic of a human being, an analogue to the robber-chief in the succeeding miracle. That the intended target of the symbolic dragon would be someone more important, and more official, than a bandit, is implied by the use of the metaphor itself. As with Saint Anselm's hare, the target of the metaphor cannot be identified directly, as that would be politically dangerous. Such a reading would accord with the classic analysis of late antique Syrian saints' *vitae* by Peter Brown, who argued that holy men were perceived by the laity as being trustworthy mediators in worldly conflicts because they were separated from the conflicting interests of society, being economically and socially independent. Their spiritual power gave them the miraculous ability to enforce their decisions when mediating conflicts, or so it was perceived. Thus the anchorite could act as a patron for local communities, who had lost their secular patrons to the political changes affecting their world. The picture Brown presents is of a society with fractured lines of authority, where many people turned to holy men for help. The very respect accorded to a holy man enabled him to act as a patron, influencing powerful men, and resolving quarrels.[13] In this picture, the healing of the dragon could represent a successful mediation between a powerful

[10] *Vita Sancti Simeonis Stylitae*, PL 73, cols. 325–34, ch. 10, col. 330. I have told the story here following the Latin text, which has slightly altered the sense from the original Greek version, where it is implied that the Dragon is pacific only when at the saint's shrine, and is silent on its subsequent behaviour; see Robert Doran, *The Lives of Saint Simeon Stylites* (Spencer, Mass., 1992), p. 95.

[11] Matthew 7:3–4; Luke 6:41–2; the Latin translation of the Simeon story does not appear to contain any direct biblical quotations, and uses *lignum* for the stick rather than the Vulgate's *trabes*, but the image is surely too close not to be conscious. Any direct allusion may have been lost in the translation from Greek to Latin.

[12] Doran, *Simeon Stylites*, pp. 95–6. The story of the robber chief is moved to a later point in the Latin version, *Vita Symeonis*, ch. 15, col. 331. Doran, *Simeon Stylites*, notes, p. 44, that the miracles involving animals harmful to humans, including the worms from the saint's festering leg sore, are partly intended to show that even these creatures have their proper place in creation. Moreover, the saint keeps the animal and the human apart in their proper places, and restores boundaries which had been violated.

[13] Peter Brown, 'Rise and Function of the Holy Man in Late Antiquity', *Journal of Roman Studies* 61 (1971), pp. 80–101.

human figure of some kind, whose presence in the area meant that 'no pasture grew in that spot', and the local people. The biblical admonition, to remove the mote in your own eye, would carry great resonance as a rebuke to powerful men oppressing the countryside. Normally the holy man's mediation is only revealed by his curse which marks a failed attempt at reconciliation, but in this story, the cursed dragon himself represents those powerful men rebuked by saints like Simeon Stylites.

Whether or not this suggestion for the dragon of Simeon Stylites is accepted, the story is a singular one in the appearances of dragons in saints' *vitae*. Generally speaking, the dragon is a creature to be defeated and destroyed, and is generally understood to represent sin in its most demonic manifestation. After all, dragons are but serpents, and the serpent was the original personification of sin. Perhaps the bulk of saints' stories involving dragons can be most safely understood to indicate the defeat of the powers of temptation and sin by the power of faith. Certainly the appearances of dragons in Jacobus de Voragine's thirteenth-century *Golden Legend* are easily read that way. Saint Matthew the Apostle in a contest with some pagan magicians confronts some dragons: 'The Apostle shielded himself with the sign of the cross and confidently went out to meet these beasts. The minute the dragons saw him, they fell asleep at his feet.'[14] This passage is steeped in standard Christian imagery of spiritual warfare, where spiritual efforts are exemplified by martial metaphors, although by the thirteenth century this vocabulary probably had a more literally warlike impact by virtue of the Crusades. Hence perhaps the popularity of the legend of one of the more famous saintly encounters with dragons.

Saint George may have been a genuine early martyr, but his early legend contains no dragon whatsoever.[15] It is only by the tenth century that the dragon-killing knight appears anywhere, but it seems to have been standard by the time the *Golden Legend* incorporated it.[16] Just like Saint Matthew, George when encountering the dragon 'arms himself with the sign of the cross', although he is aided somewhat by a lance.[17] The defeated dragon is led into the city by the sacrificial maiden whose girdle is tied around its neck, so that the tamed beast appears like a 'little dog on a leash', before being finally dispatched by the saint. It is only after this incident that the Saint turns fully towards the religious life. The legend thus takes the martial metaphor of the defeat of sin, which in this case has a distinctly sexual undercurrent, to its extreme. Later medieval artistic representations of the story would make the defeat of sexuality even more explicit.[18] Not all dragon stories make so much

[14] Jacobus de Voragine, *Legenda Aurea*, ed. T. Graesse (Dresden 1846), ch. 140, pp. 622–3; *The Golden Legend: Readings on the Saints*, trans. William Granger Ryan (Princeton 1993), 2 vols, at II, p. 184 (hereafter *Legenda Aurea*).

[15] *Acta Sancti Georgii*, *AASS* 23 April, pp. 117–22.

[16] For the development of the Saint George legend, see Samantha Riches, *Saint George: Hero, Martyr and Myth* (Stroud 2000), pp. 3–10. Note that Aelfric's version of Saint George, written in 998, contains no trace of the dragon-slaying saint; *Aelfric's Lives of the Saints*, ed. Walter W. Skeat (London 1881), pp. 306–19.

[17] *Legenda Aurea*, ch. 58, pp. 260–1; trans. pp. 238–40.

[18] On the sexual element in representations of dragons see Riches, *Saint George*, pp. 142–78.

use of martial imagery, but often do highlight the underlying metaphor of the suppression of sexual desire in a similar fashion. Saint Martha, of Gospel origin, in the *Golden Legend* meets a very richly described water dragon, that 'was half animal and half-fish, larger than an ox . . . with teeth as sharp as horns and a pair of bucklers on either side of his body'.[19] It is interesting here that the martial associations are attached to the dragon rather than to the female saint. In any case, this medieval version of Martha is allowed to go far beyond housekeeping. She sprinkles the beast with holy water when she finds it in the act of devouring a man, holds up a cross in front of it, and thus is able to subdue the beast by tying the girdle symbolising her virginity around its neck. The people, rather than the saint this time, dispatch the dragon with stones and lances.

If, by the thirteenth century, the dragon represented most often a specific form of temptation and sin, it was not always so simple a creature. Certainly, Saint Simeon's dragon cannot be interpreted in this fashion. The appearances of dragons in the fourth and fifth centuries are more likely to represent victory over paganism than over sexuality.[20] Such an interpretation, for example, would seem to make best sense of the apocryphal account of Saint Andrew and a huge serpent which coiled itself around a great oak tree in futile defiance of the Apostle's power.[21] As well as representing spiritual evil, a dragon could be used as a symbol of deadly disease, as in the first *Vita* of Gildas, where the saint, in killing the dragon, frees the people of Rome from a plague caused by its noxious breath.[22] Dragons were not even always demonic. In one eighth-century Irish *vita* the saint is shown that he must return to Ireland by a rather aggressive divine message: Saint Cainnech, on the point of promising to stay with an unidentified Italian king, finds himself in a circle of fire created by a 'fiery dragon' from heaven.[23] This exceptional story probably arose from the specifically Irish cultural context. Nonetheless, even with such obvious biblical imagery and precedent behind them, stories of saints and dragons were not fixed to one particular allegory, and it is important to be aware of other possible resonances that dragon and saint stories may have had before the twelfth century in particular.

Jacques Le Goff has advanced a very different symbolic role for dragons, arising not from Christian spiritual concerns but from folklore, in the case of Saint Marcellus of Paris. The dragon in this story is ambiguous, being either chthonic or aquatic, and the saint in banishing it gives it the choice of disappearing into the desert, that

[19] *Legenda Aurea*. ch. 105, pp. 444–5.

[20] Jacques Le Goff, 'Ecclesiastical Culture and Folklore in the Middle Ages: Saint Marcellus of Paris and the Dragon', in Jacques Le Goff, *Time, Work and Culture in the Middle Ages*, trans. Arthur Goldhammer (Chicago 1980), pp. 159–88, at pp. 168–9.

[21] *The Apocryphal New Testament*, ed. J. K. Elliott (Oxford 1993), p. 278.

[22] *Two Lives of Gildas by a Monk of Ruys and Carador of Llanrarfan*, ed. and trans. Hugh Williams (1899, reprinted 1990), pp. 33–5.

[23] *Vitae Sanctorum Hiberniae*, ed. W. W. Heist (Brussels 1965) (hereafter Heist), *Vita S. Cainnechi*, pp. 182–98, at ch. 9, p. 184.

is the wilderness, or the sea, which in the Parisian case is the river.[24] It is significant that the dragon is banished rather than killed. This story is not therefore primarily concerned with the vanquishing of sin but the establishment of boundaries, or the separation of chaotic nature from human settlement. Le Goff points out that the *faubourg* of St Marcellus was marshy in character, and speculates that the story represented the draining and clearing of land for settlement.[25] The dragon story in this reading is a foundation legend, where the *genius loci*, the dragon, is banished to make way for human construction. Other serpent or dragon stories may have also carried these meanings, argues Le Goff, but ecclesiastical authors did their best to diabolise the dragons in line with Christian symbolism.[26]

Le Goff's hypothesis can in fact explain other dragon stories. The *Vita* of the Norman Saint Vigor, a genuine sixth-century bishop whose existence was noted by Venantius Fortunatus, contains a story of the taming of the dragon of Cerisy. Although the *Vita* dates from the eleventh century, it contains local traditions, which may include the central dragon story, which date back much earlier.[27] Saint Vigor is invited to Cerisy to deal with an 'immense serpent' terrorising the people, and like Saint Marcellus, he does not kill the dragon but returns it to the sea, thus banishing the force of chaos to its primordial element. The hagiographer does his best to reconcile this story with Christian imagery, having the saint quote from the Gospels that Christ had given his disciples the power to tread on serpents and scorpions.[28] Then, before Vigor confronts the dragon he fasts and prays, crying a fountain of tears for God's mercy, and, like many a saint, defeats the dragon with the sign of the cross. However, it is the saint's young companion, Theudimir, who leads the dragon, 'as if a gentle sheep', away to the sea.[29] Here there are all the elements

[24] Le Goff, 'Saint Marcellus', pp. 169–71.

[25] Ibid. pp. 172–3.

[26] Ibid. p. 173.

[27] John Howe, 'The Date of the *Life* of Saint Vigor of Bayeux', *Analecta Bollandiana* 102 (1984), pp. 303–12, shows that the *Vita* as it exists now was written in the eleventh century, but also notes the details that indicate an earlier origin for some of its material. Also see G. Aubourg, 'Saint Vigor, évêque de Bayeux, VI siècle', *Bulletin de la Société des Antiquaries de Normandie*, part 1, vol. 57, pp. 317–75, part 2, vol. 58, pp. 127–73 (1965–6), particularly pp. 318–19, and pp. 343–5; *Vita Sancti Vigoris*, *AASS* 1 November, pp. 287–306.

[28] *Vita Vigoris*, ch. 5, p. 300; Luke 10:19.

[29] The use of the dragon miracle as a foundation story appears to have been endemic to the Breton and Norman regions, as the Vigor story is really part of a complex of dragon tales that make use, in different combinations, of various motifs. Wormonoc's ninth-century Breton *Vita* of Saint Paul de Leon broadly parallels Saint Vigor in a story where a dragon is banished into the sea. The dragon is significantly diabolised, but the episode is also a good candidate for the dragon miracle as foundation story: Wormonoc, *Vita Sancti Pauli Episcopi Leonensis*, ed. R. P. Plaine, in *Analecta Bollandiana* 1 (1882), pp. 208–58, at ch. 18, pp. 245–8. Howe argues, '*Life* of Saint Vigor', p. 311, that the Vigor story is drawn from the first *Vita* of Samson of Dol. However, there are crucially different details in the two stories. The two saints do have a young companion in each story, but in the Samson story the boy is merely an observer and does not lead the tamed dragon away. Moreover Samson flings the dragon from a height, and there is no mention of waters of any kind, in contrast to the sea in the Vigor story.

of the standard saint and dragon story, but the dragon neither stands for the defeat of paganism, nor of sin more generally. It is noteworthy that this story is also one of the earliest references to Cerisy, which may lend weight to the idea that it is a foundation story. The defeat of the dragon became the most important element in the cult of Saint Vigor, and other dragon stories were added to the *Vita*, probably in the eleventh century.[30]

Dragons can therefore be ambiguous motifs in hagiography. Dragon stories have clear biblical antecedents, and can therefore appear as Christian allegories of various kinds, and yet the same story could have had different meanings to different people, if the Le Goff hypothesis is seen to hold in stories like that of Saint Vigor. However, this discussion raises the thorny issue of ecclesiastical and popular culture in medieval Europe. The notion that there is really a folkloric element to such tales as Saint Vigor's dragon has been disputed. Dom Aubourg considered the motif of returning the dragon to the sea to be related to the leviathan in Job, who sleeps under the rule of the Lord, and the dragon which is cast out in Revelation, noting also, however,

Finally the dragon is commanded to die by Samson, while it is clearly left alive by Vigor: *Vita Sancti Samsonis*, *AASS* 28 July, pp. 568–91, at ch. 50, pp. 584–5. Saint Samson defeats another dragon later on, which he does fling into the sea, and charges to die in the name of Christ: *Vita Samsonis*, ch. 60, pp. 586–7. If the *Vita Vigoris* had built its dragon story from both these accounts in the *Vita Samsonis*, it would still not explain why Saint Vigor does not command it to die. Another of Saint Samson's dragon miracles follows the Le Goff model, in a mirror image of the Vigor story. Here Samson banishes a dragon, without killing it, but instead of flinging it into the sea, the saint commands it to cross the river Seine, and to remain under a certain stone, revealing this dragon as a chthonic figure: *Vita Samsonis*, ch. 58, p. 586. There is some doubt over the date of the *Vita Samsonis*, which was written some time between the seventh and ninth centuries: see F. Duine, *Questions d'hagiographie et vie de S. Samson* (Paris 1914), p. 42. The second *Vita* of Saint Samson, written at Pental in Normandy in the late ninth or early tenth century, simply modifies and adds to the dragon stories of the first *Vita*, and does not provide a template for the Vigor story: *Vita Antiqua Samsonis*, ed. R. P. Plaine, in *Analecta Bollandiana* 6 (1887), pp. 77–150, at bk 1, chs. 10 and 17, and bk 2, chs. 18 and 32; on its dating see Robert Fawtier, *La vie de Saint Samson* (Paris 1912), pp. 11–16. Even if these Samsonian dragon stories were considered to be the source of the Vigor story, a number of them could easily be interpreted also as foundation stories. Assuming that literary dependence accounts for these dragon stories does not explain the choice of different motifs within them; strong local traditions involving dragons could be the basis of most of the Breton and Norman stories, with literary dependence being a secondary factor in their composition and acceptance within various *vitae*.

30 Dragons appear with similar chthonic and aquatic symbolism in other types of medieval literature. Thus in the Welsh tale *Lludd and Llefelys*, composed perhaps in the late eleventh or twelfth century, dragons appear as chthonic spirits at the centre of Britain: *The Mabinogion*, trans. Gwyn Jones and Thomas Jones (London 1974), pp. 92–3. Equally the dragons at the bottom of Vortigern's tower are both aquatic and chthonic, clearly relating to the establishment of human settlement: Geoffrey of Monmouth, *Historia Regum Britannie*, ed. Neil Wright (Cambridge 1984), pp. 72–3. On the aquatic associations of dragons as a part of a Eurasian folkloric substratum to medieval culture, see Jacques Voisenet, *Bestiaire chrétien: l'imagerie animale des auteurs du haut moyen âge* (Toulouse 1994), pp. 174–8. The great serpent of the acropolis of ancient Athens also provides an example of a chthonic dragon functioning clearly as a foundation legend: Herodotus, *The Histories*, trans. Aubrey de Sélincourt, revised John Marincola (London 2003), bk 8, ch. 41, p. 514.

that the casting of the dragon into the sea goes back to the Babylonian Tiamat.[31] Such references could be seen in the connection between the dragon and the sea, but the hagiographer himself chooses to refer to Luke 10:19 instead, and to obscure the problematic motif of the sea beneath more traditional hagiographic imagery, as if aware that the story had non-biblical associations. Nonetheless, it cannot be proved absolutely that this dragon story had folkloric inspiration. The degree to which the argument is persuasive depends to a great degree on the approach taken to written hagiography which was created in a largely illiterate medieval society.

For many, the fact that a sophisticated ecclesiastical elite wrote hagiography would seem to rule out any serious likelihood of the 'contamination' of hagiography by popular stories. In many ways this assumption is a reaction to some earlier approaches. For some, even in the twentieth century, the miracle-laden, often grotesque and certainly fantastic, material to be found in saints' *vitae* demanded as an explanation that clerical writers, bereft of the sophisticated surroundings of classical civilisation, were veritably overwhelmed by a tide of rustic superstition. I am caricaturing here some views which were held often a good deal more subtly, but this is the background to a continuing effort to redeem medieval writers, and the medieval imagination more generally. It still seems difficult, to some, to credit that a sophisticated politician and theologian like Gregory the Great, for example, could have literally believed in the miracles he recorded in his *Dialogues*. In fact close attention to the justifications and explanations of the miraculous in such writers does reveal a theological approach, which while demanding witnesses and a certain level of proof, could accept the reality of the miraculous, through accepting the reality of God's presence in the world.[32] In this sense then, the reader of medieval hagiography must not be too quick to read the presence of pagan survivals, or rustic stories, into this material. Indeed, the story of Saint Simeon and the dragon is an example of how a fantastic tale could be built upon the foundation of biblical reference into a metaphorical story illustrating serious Christian themes.

Hagiography was also a form of literature which, in effect, developed its own rules, not necessarily having any regard to issues of factual verifiability or historical reliability. A saint's *vita* had to have certain elements, and should progress along a path recognisable within the tradition. If a saint's story states that people of all kinds, from near and distant places, came to visit the saint, this cannot be taken in any way as a reliable historical statement: it is a topos, a necessary and spiritually true 'place' in a standard hagiographic narrative. The classic example of the thinking behind topoi is the title of Gregory of Tours's sixth-century *Life of the Fathers*. This is a collection of different short accounts of various saints, but in Gregory's mind they only, in truth, have one *real* life, that in Christ. The continuities between them

[31] Aubourg, 'Saint Vigor', pp. 344–5; Job 41; Revelation 12. The Babylonian Tiamat is of course a prime mythological example of the dragon representing primordial chaos, tamed by the male hero; see Lise Gotfredsen, *The Unicorn* (London 1999), trans. Anne Born, pp. 14–15.

[32] See William D. McCready, *Signs of Sanctity: Miracles in the Thought of Gregory the Great* (Toronto 1989), for an analysis of this kind.

are more important than the differences.[33] Saints' *vitae* were in this sense composed of topoi, which were assembled in order to compare a saint to others, in rivalry or imitation, or to make certain arguments about the nature of a good bishop or abbot, for example. Thus, the story of Saint Anselm's hare is an example of a certain kind of topos, which Eadmer created simply because it was an acceptable and useful topos for his purpose.

It could easily be assumed therefore that hagiographers simply made up all their stories in the quiet of the cloister, with their main concern being their symbolic value in resonating with events in the Bible or in the hagiographic tradition. That hagiographers shaped their work around topoi is not in doubt. The question is rather to what extent they were manipulating existing stories, and even genuine events, into topoi, and to what extent they had entirely free rein. The answer to this question will be different for different times and places.[34] Equally, the answer will differ between the case of a long-dead saint, for whom little or no material survived, and that of a well-known contemporary figure. It is unlikely in fact that Eadmer could have entirely on his own cognisance created the story of the hare. Miracles can be more than literary fictions, and can be socially created. In the case of Saint Anselm, members of his household may well have turned a non-miraculous event into a morale-boosting reflection on their head of household in a time of conflict with the king. Later, with William of Malmesbury, it became a fully acknowledged miracle. Here, prior topos and minor anecdote are fashioned into a new miracle through a social process. If this can occur plausibly within an archbishop's household, how much more plausibly could it occur in society at large?

To assume that hagiography had no likely connection with tales told outside the cloister, by the secular elite, peasants, or townspeople, is, I believe, to imagine monastic writers as a caricature of the aloof academic. Certainly, the mass of people were illiterate and had no direct access to saints' *vitae*, but to suppose from this that there could be no interaction between a literate educated elite and general culture is to ignore how embedded monasteries were in medieval society. Monasteries controlled villages, had links with secular elite families, and very often with royal and princely courts. The concerns and interests of the outside world must have reached into the monastery, however much monks liked to claim spiritual isolation. Hagiography, in most circumstances, should be seen as intending to affect the beliefs and loyalties of certain people in society. Often, indeed, hagiography could be intended only to fix the identity of a particular religious house. Equally, the *vita* of a particular figure would have wider importance, precisely because of the importance of a monastery to a local area or even to a region. It is in this context that popular motifs can realistically be seen as influencing saints' legends, in addition to biblical quotation and existing literary topoi. If the expulsion of a dragon were a popularly understood motif for the foundation of a town, then using that motif and linking

33 Gregory of Tours, *Life of the Fathers*, trans. Edward James (Liverpool 1985), p. xiv.

34 For an analysis of the role of topoi and rhetoric in 'making' saints concerning whom little was known, see Thomas Head, *Hagiography and the Cult of the Saints: The Diocese of Orleans, 800–1200* (Cambridge 1990), particularly pp. 109–18.

it to a saint could be a powerfully political use of hagiography. Equally, such a tale could have existed among the people of a settlement, and a hagiographer wishing to mould local traditions, for all sorts of social and political motives, would need to adopt the story and adapt it to his own purpose.

In more recent years an old assumption about the nature of pre-literate cultures has also been reassessed. There is considerable scepticism now concerning the capabilities of oral societies in producing the complex epic narratives once thought the natural form of literature before writing made an impact.[35] Therefore, in the context of hagiography, it would not do to imagine that lengthy saints' legends could have existed in their entirety before a clerical writer happened upon them and recorded them for posterity. Nonetheless, early medieval Europe was not a purely oral society: writing was present and would therefore affect oral transmissions and traditions. The memory of an oral society is thought to be limited to three generations. Thus oral tradition and laws can always be subject to swift change.[36] However, it has been observed that a society with a literate elite, where the vernacular is not widely used for writing, may inadvertently encourage the formulation of oral, popular stories.[37] The literate presence within a society may thus paradoxically strengthen 'oral culture'. In considering possible popular influences upon the miracle stories recorded by hagiographers, it is also important to note the elements that are most constant in the long narratives made in oral societies. Among the west African LoDagaa, Jack Goody found that what is constant is not, by any means, the exact words of a passage, or any 'deep' symbolic structure. Rather, the constant element is the particular narratives of events, such as a story of a fruit bat which quarrels with its mate, a story which acts as a prompt for less memorable aspects of an account of a ceremony.[38] There is surely some similarity, on a formal level, between such short narratives and many miracle stories to be found in medieval Europe.

Given that social groups beyond the cloister must have created stories for various historical, political and social purposes, it is important to inspect hagiography for signs of where and when popular stories had an impact upon it. The term 'popular' in this cultural context cannot be given a neat empirical sociological content, and for this reason many object to its use, but it is nonetheless essential. In this context it expresses a pole in a *relationship* rather than a fixed social group. 'Popular' does not equate with peasant, nor on the other hand is it simply 'not-clerical' in a medieval European context: it refers to those elements in medieval culture which arose from the context of a rural, pre-industrial society rather than from the context of the literate cloister.[39]

35 See Jack Goody, *The Interface between the Oral and the Literate* (Cambridge, 1987), pp. 78–109.

36 Jack Goody, *The Logic of Writing and the Organisation of Society* (Cambridge 1986), pp. 4–8.

37 Goody, *Interface*, p. 93.

38 Ibid. pp. 172–3.

39 An important defence of research into popular ideas in pre-modern Europe, seeing peasant culture neither as autonomous, nor wholly dominated by elite conceptions, is in Carlo Ginzburg, *The Cheese and the Worms: The Cosmos of a Sixteenth-Century Miller*, trans. John and Anne Tedeschi (Baltimore 1992), note 58, pp. 154–5.

The Russian medievalist Aron Gurevich noted that the 'thoughts of the ruling class' become 'ruling thoughts', but argued that ruling ideas and concepts cannot eradicate other forms of social consciousness, which can be most conveniently described as 'popular'.[40] Patterns of time came to be amongst the most thoroughly controlled in medieval Europe, as the agrarian calendar became the liturgical calendar, the proper times for certain foods and for sexual activity were regulated, and even the day marked out by the church bells. Dissent and opposition to the social order thus most often took the form of chiliasm, the expectation of the millennium, a radical re-ordering of time and what might be expected from it.[41] However, the Church's social control varied greatly in different parts of Christian western Europe between the fourth and thirteenth centuries. The complete 'Christianisation' of time as described by Gurevich is something that only becomes dominant in most of the West in the course of the eleventh and twelfth centuries.[42] The Church as the dominant force in the lives of most people before then would probably be limited to those significant parts of the countryside held by monastic or episcopal landowners.

In areas where the Church was not strong, some peculiar elements could emerge in an otherwise Christian culture. The first substantial record of the cult of the seventh-century bishop, Saint Kentigern, around Glasgow emerges in the twelfth century, with two *vitae*. The first, now fragmentary, *Vita* was written for Bishop Herbert of Glasgow by an anonymous clerk of the new cathedral between 1147 and 1164, while the second, by Jocelyn of Furness, was written before 1185. The two are independent of each other and are based on two previous, now lost, accounts.[43] Both *Vitae* were the product of a process of colonisation of the area by the Scottish kings. The see of Glasgow had been re-established in the early twelfth century by the future King David I, along with a series of castles and lordships. In the words of a contemporary clerk of the cathedral, King Alexander sent David there 'to be their ruler and leader. He was able to punish them for their shameless and wicked practices, and through the honesty and unbending severity of his character, to bridle their outrageous rebelliousness.'[44] The two *Vitae* were needed to suppress disquieting aspects of the existing cult of Saint Kentigern, with the fragmentary account clearly failing to displant the earlier version of the legend. Jocelyn of Furness states that the now lost earlier version still used in the cathedral in his time opened with something 'contrary to healthy doctrine', while even his other source was tainted by elements that were 'perverse or opposed to the faith'. Consequently a new account with 'greater authority, with more evident truth' was needed.[45]

40 Aron Gurevich, *Categories of Medieval Culture*, trans. G. L. Campbell (London 1972), pp. 20–1.

41 Ibid. pp. 106–45. It should be noted that the really key aspect of life that the Church was able to determine through controlling time was labour, in particular that of the peasants.

42 See R. I. Moore, *The First European Revolution* (Oxford 2000), particularly pp. 52–5.

43 Alan Macquarrie, 'The Career of Saint Kentigern of Glasgow: *Vitae, Lectiones* and Glimpses of Fact', *Innes Review* 37 (1986), pp. 3–24, at pp. 3–4, 19–20.

44 Quoted in G. W. S. Barrow, *Glasgow Cathedral: King David I and the Church of Glasgow* (Glasgow 1996), p. 1.

45 Jocelyn of Furness, *Vita Sancti Kentigerni*, in *Lives of St. Ninian and St. Kentigern*, ed. and trans.

So what was so shocking about the legend of Kentigern current before Glasgow's colonisation by the kings? It was something to do with the saint's conception, of which the two surviving *Vitae* give entirely different accounts. The writer of the fragmentary *Vita* tells how Kentigern's mother wished to emulate the Virgin Mary by conceiving immaculately, but in fact is raped by a young man, deceitfully dressed as a woman. The rapist concludes 'weep not my sister, for I have not known you as a man is used to know a virgin. Am I not a woman like yourself?'[46] Thus, in a sense, there is no father in this conception. Tellingly, Jocelyn in contrast goes out of his way to show that the saint's mother could have been impregnated without her knowledge, while being drugged, for example. Jocelyn says that this long digression was necessary because of the 'stupid and foolish public' who believed that Kentigern was born of a virgin.[47] While the fragmentary *Vita* inserts into the story a man who could, however implausibly, claim not to have been a man at the time, Jocelyn chooses not to have any definite male agent. The contrast between the two *Vitae* raises the suspicion that the original legend was not simply one of an immaculate conception, but had its own supernatural agent of impregnation. This would not be unprecedented. Geoffrey of Monmouth's twelfth-century version of the legend of Merlin clearly describes his conception by an incubus figure, who could be present without his mother seeing him.[48] Such stories could pass in secular works but would be totally shocking in a saint's *life*. The legend of Kentigern's origins was therefore most likely the legend of conception by a supernatural creature that churchmen would see as diabolical, an incubus.

The legend of Kentigern's conception was a popular legend, and one that the Church found hard to eliminate, persisting as it did throughout the twelfth century. Yet this is not a simple story of the Church suppressing a peasant legend. Rather, it is to be suspected that in the eleventh century there was some kind of elite in place in the area, which used the cult of Saint Kentigern as the focus for its identity, and was able to support sufficient clerical skills either to compose or preserve the original version of the *Vita*. Thus, without a strongly organised Church presence, the culture of a secular elite could be drawn towards pre-Christian ideas and symbols, but as Jocelyn makes clear, it is the despised *populus* that is likely to persist in holding on to such stories. The persistence of the Kentigern story is also a warning that the power of the Church to eliminate beliefs that it did not like was far from complete even in a twelfth-century context.

The influence of popular culture on hagiography goes beyond the occasional appearance of folkloric motifs, because while the Church could in some degree impose its own measurement of time upon society, in its turn the agrarian economy would produce its own basic attitudes towards nature. Thus, according to Gurevich 'nature' does not stand in opposition to a separate human mind in medieval

Alexander P. Forbes (Edinburgh 1874), pp. 159–253, at p. 160.

46 Anonymous, *Vita Sancti Kentigerni*, in *Lives of St. Ninian and St. Kentigern*, ed. Forbes, pp. 243–52, at pp. 246–7.

47 Jocelyn of Furness, *Vita Kentigerni*, ch. 1, p. 162.

48 Geoffrey of Monmouth, *Historia Regum Britannie*, p. 72.

understanding, that conscious antimony being a modern conception.[49] Having said that, there are clear oppositions in medieval thinking between the social and the wild, but the point remains that the boundary between the human and other aspects of the natural was vulnerable, allowing for fluid transitions between the human body and the world. Thus hermits who become remote from society, and from Christian grace, are liable to transform into animal-like creatures, crawling on all fours and growing thick pelts of bodily fur.[50] Such stories appear in hagiography, but have their origins not in literate ecclesiastical culture but in popular consciousness of the thin boundaries between the human body and other forces in the world, a conception Gurevich dubbed the 'grotesque body', in a formulation that points to many a queasy miracle story of the Middle Ages.[51] However, if in the popular imagination the boundaries between human and animal could be relatively easily crossed, there is some sign that Church writers did not embrace this understanding with enthusiasm. Hagiographers rarely missed an opportunity to refer to the Bible, and so it is remarkable that there appear to be virtually no examples of a saint and animal miracle with an allusion to Balaam's ass, whom God makes speak in order to change the man's course.[52] In a sense, this ought to be a good example of animals obeying God's commands, in stark contrast to man. However, it seems that the image of God speaking through a donkey, a grotesquerie indeed, was not something that fitted the medieval hagiographers' theological agenda.[53]

The animals in miracle stories cannot be taken as straightforward representations of the natural world. They are apt to be associated with metaphors, whether theological or folkloric in origin. However, historians have in fact tended to treat the saint and animal story as uncomplicated evidence to determine medieval attitudes towards a 'nature' often conceptualised in essentially modern terms.[54] Nonetheless, perhaps only in England would a noted historian write a pamphlet

49 Gurevich, *Categories*, pp. 54–6. This analysis may be modified by the analysis of Saint Francis in Chapter 9, below.

50 See for example the early legend of the hermit with a 'terrible and hairy appearance' who when asked if he is a 'spirit' answers that he is just a sinning man: *Verba Seniorum*, PL 73, cols. 855–1062, at bk 7, ch. 12, col. 894. This subject is treated further in Chapter 6 below.

51 Gurevich, *Categories*, p. 62.

52 Numbers 22:27–30. For one isolated example, see Chapter 5, on Amelberga of Tamise, p. 101. Reference to Balaam's ass can occur in other contexts, as for example in the late Irish vernacular *Life of Saint Abban*, in which the saint cures a man who is dumb: C. Plummer, *Lives of Irish Saints* (Oxford 1922), 2 vols, at 1, pp. 3–10, at ch. 22 (38), p. 10.

53 Voisenet, *Bestiaire chrétien*, p. 199, considers the rarity of allusions to Balaam's ass to be the result of discomfort with a blurring of the boundaries between the human and the animal.

54 The subject has always fascinated historians. One nineteenth-century example is Charles F. R. Count de Montalembert, *The Monks of the West: From St. Benedict to St. Bernard* (London 1896), 6 vols, at II, pp. 185–237. Two ambitious books on the history of the interaction of 'culture' and 'nature', which both give some attention to the subject of saints and animals, are Clarence J. Glacken, *Traces on the Rhodian Shore: Nature and Culture in Western Thought from Ancient Times to the End of the Eighteenth Century* (Berkeley 1967), pp. 213–15 and pp. 288–318, and Francis Klingender, *Animals in Art and Thought* (London 1971), pp. 344–50.

for an animal rights interest group noting 'the early saints repeatedly laid stress on the fact that animals have their own rights, which should be respected'.[55] Beneath the light-hearted charm with which historians have often approached the subject, opinion seems, perhaps unsurprisingly, divided on whether the hagiographic tradition shows a delightful oneness with nature or a brutal western Christian attitude of domination. Rosalind Hill expressed one point of view that still can be heard in various forms: 'One of the most striking features of medieval hagiography is indeed the frequency with which saints are described as having a special care for or understanding of beasts and birds. This trait of sanctity, commonly but erroneously supposed to have originated with Saint Francis, is in reality very much older.'[56]

Probably few would now give Saint Francis the honour of being the one saint whose genius led him to discover an entirely new Christian sympathy for non-human creation and its creatures.[57] Indeed for some the 'love of birds and beasts, so evident in the bestiaries, despite their cumbrous didactic and allegorical form, also marks other strictly religious works of the Later Middle Ages'.[58] Thus, many historians seem to have fallen into the trap of trying to determine to what degree particular saints actually *liked* 'nature', on the basis of the saints' encounters with animals. Once again this approach neglects medieval mentalities and literary forms, imposing essentially modern categories on texts which will not bear such terms.

A much more nuanced view of these problems lies in Joyce Salisbury's work on medieval social or cultural perceptions of animals, and the boundaries between the human and the beastly.[59] Salisbury's contention is that the twelfth century saw a growing ambiguity towards the boundaries between the human and the animal, which during the previous centuries had been firm and stable. One interesting indication of rising anxiety concerning the interaction of human and animal is in the increasing penalties in penitential legislation for the sin of bestiality.[60] However, Salisbury's arguments lead her to posit a dramatic change around the twelfth century in saintly attitudes to animals. She writes that 'in the early medieval saints' *Lives*, the prevailing miraculous interaction between saints and animals was that

[55] Rosalind Hill, *Both Small and Great Beasts* (London 1953), p. 6.

[56] Ibid. p. 5. Jan Ziolowski, *Talking Animals: Medieval Latin Beast Poetry* (Philadelphia 1993), notes the 'happy consequences' of anthropomorphic understandings of animals in the *vitae*, pp. 32–4.

[57] The idea that Saint Francis stood outside Christian tradition in regard to animals was once axiomatic. One old textbook, Alan C. Bouquet, *Comparative Religion* (New York 1941), p. 39, states: 'To Hebrews man is the Lord of creation, ordained to have dominion over non-human organic life, and in this respect the Franciscan attitude – "our sisters the birds" – is not Hebraic. The gospels are perhaps neutral in this matter, and Saint Francis doubtless derives his friendliness towards animals and birds from eastern mysticism.' The discussion on Saint Francis has been developed much more systematically since, but even recently a degree of innovation for Saint Francis has been maintained: see Roger D. Sorrell, *Saint Francis and Nature: Tradition and Innovation in Western Christian Attitudes to the Environment* (Oxford 1988).

[58] Glacken, *Rhodian Shore*, p. 343.

[59] Joyce E. Salisbury, *The Beast Within: Animals in the Middle Ages* (London 1994), on saints see particularly pp. 168–76.

[60] Ibid. pp. 89–94.

saints frequently demonstrated the power to suspend the bestial nature of animals in their presence'.[61] But in the twelfth century, when animals were no longer seen to be so profoundly different from humans, saints' behaviour changed; there was now an 'inclination of saints to save animals' lives. This does not appear in the early Lives, and it would have been virtually inconceivable . . . to save the life of an animal without expecting a human return for it assumes that the animal's life has some intrinsic value beyond its service for humanity.'[62]

Salisbury's summary of the patristic tradition in this respect does include some central themes, such as obedience and the reversal of wild instincts. However, it is not as easy as all that to distinguish the early saints from twelfth-century and later saints. Saint Martin, not a saint particularly noted for his interactions with animals, is said nevertheless to have saved a hare exhausted by its long run from huntsmen's dogs:

> The blessed man through his pious judgement took compassion on it in its danger and ordered the dogs to leave off following it and let the fugitive get away. They pulled up at once, at the first words of the order . . . And so, with its pursuers pinned down, the little hare got safely away.[63]

There is no reversal of bestial nature here or any service rendered by the hare to the saint. Of course, this story represents one of the earliest appearances of the 'hermit and hunter' topos, which, as the example of Saint Anselm showed, has other possible purposes than demonstrating the saint's kindliness to animal life. Equally there is the story of Saint Columba in which he ordered a monk to tend to a tired crane, who was a 'pilgrim' from the 'land of our fathers'. The crane is tended for three days, with no reward for the humans. The question of its wildness or otherwise is not mentioned, and eventually it flies off back to Ireland, unmarked by saintly kindness.[64] The latter is a particularly atypical story, and the miracle in it concerns Columba's power of prophecy rather than his control of animals. Nevertheless, it must be admitted that, despite these two examples, it is far easier to find examples of early saints behaving in a fashion which would support Salisbury's argument.

One of the Greek *vitae* of Saint Simeon Stylites does contain, however, an apparent prohibition against the harming of animals, at least in the saint's name.[65] On one occasion some men call upon a pregnant hind to stand still in the name of the saint, and so it does, enabling them to kill and eat it. They immediately lose their human speech, and begin to 'bleat like dumb animals'. The men pray at Simeon's

[61] Ibid. p. 172.

[62] Ibid. p. 174

[63] Sulpicius Severus, *Dialogi*, PL 20, cols. 183–222, at Dialogue 2, ch. 9, col. 208; trans. F. R. Hoare, *The Western Fathers* (London 1954), p. 115. Otherwise Saint Martin's interactions with nature do indeed show him to be 'exercising power over nature, not sympathy with it': Clare Stancliffe, *St Martin and His Hagiographer* (Oxford 1983), p. 156.

[64] *Adomnan's Life of Columba*, ed. and trans. Alan O. and Marjorie O. Anderson (London 1961), bk 1, ch. 48, pp. 312–15.

[65] Doran, *Simeon Stylites*; Antonius' *Life*, ch. 15, p. 93.

pillar, until having done sufficient penance they are healed. Now the reason behind the saint's curse here is probably less to do with a regard for animal life, than with the misassociation of the saint with bloodletting, and perhaps even more with killing a *pregnant* animal. This associates the saint with more than one kind of spiritual pollution, from sexuality as well as violence, and so naturally the pollution falls back upon the men themselves. This story concerns the boundaries of the sacred and profane, not the miracle of a militant vegetarian saint, and demonstrates the dangers of attempting to sort saints' miracles into those kindly towards 'nature' and those not.

Turning towards later saints, it is easy to be misled by the surface appearance of a story if the hagiographic tradition is not taken into account. One of Salisbury's examples of the new twelfth-century saintly concern for animals is Gerald of Wales's famous story of the Irish Saint Kevin and the blackbird. Kevin was a 'great confessor of the faith, and abbot'. However, during Lent the abbot had a habit of fleeing 'the society of men', and was by himself in a hermitage:

> He was giving his attention to contemplation and was reading and praying. According to his custom he put out his hand, in raising it to heaven out through the window, when behold, a blackbird happened to settle on it, and using it as a nest, laid its eggs there. The saint was moved with such pity and was so patient with it that he neither closed nor withdrew his hand, but held it out in a suitable position without tiring until the young were completely hatched out.[66]

Gerald's story may well be felt to demonstrate a wonder for nature and a sense of the value of the animal life. However, this is a very modern reaction to the story, which does not take into account the possibility of allegory and the purposes of hagiographic rhetoric. It might be objected that Gerald of Wales was writing here as a chronicler, rather than as a hagiographer, and that the story could be a folktale. Certainly, Gerald himself claimed that none of the material in the first two sections was derived from written sources.[67] If we accept Gerald's word for this, there is still no reason to suppose that the story was not a piece of hagiographical literature in oral form, told to him by monks or clerics. There is no question that Gerald would have understood the rhetorical and spiritual devices in the story, and been able to record it much as it was told to him. In terms of hagiographic form the story is very effective in summarising key virtues of patience and pity, essential in an abbot dealing with all the irritating monks in his care. The story could thus even be seen as an allegory of the heroic qualities needed for an abbot.[68]

[66] Gerald of Wales, *Historia Topographica Hiberniensis*, ed. James F. Dimock, Rolls Series 21 (1867), at vol. 5, part 2, ch. 61, pp. 113–16; blackbird, p. 116; trans. John O'Meara, *Gerald of Wales: The History and Topography of Ireland* (London 1951), pp. 77–8.

[67] O'Meara, *History and Topography of Ireland*, p. 17.

[68] There is no reason to suppose that the *Rule* of Benedict was a direct source for these admired qualities, but nevertheless note, *The Rule of Saint Benedict*, ed. Timothy Fry (Collegeville, Minnesota 1981), ch. 4, p. 182, 'The Tools for Good Works', admonition 30, 'Do not injure anyone, but bear injuries patiently', and admonitions 14–19 on compassion for those in distress.

If we consider Saint Kevin as a heroic ascetic and hermit then there is further allegorical resonance. Firstly the story itself concerns the saint's heroic ascetic endurance, not his wonder for nature as such. The saint was so engrossed in contemplation and love of God that he was oblivious to the carnal world about him, and could thereafter endure the torment inflicted upon him. Of course, the torment of the carnal world is so lyrically described that this allegory does not exclude a sense of wonder for nature being part of the sensibility of the story. Secondly, however, the story should be seen in terms of hagiographic symbolism. Earlier animal stories provide some clues to the allegorical significance of the blackbird nesting in the praying hermit's outstretched hands: animals can be indications of a saint's own state of sin or grace. Thus one of the late-antique Egyptian hermits attempted to get himself eaten by a lion, because of his remorse for an earlier sin. The lion 'as if endowed by reason' leapt over the prostrate holy man, without even hurting him, thus showing the hermit that God, who controls animals, had forgiven him his sin.[69]

That story alone may not appear on the surface to have much to do with Saint Kevin. However, another story from that corpus of fourth- and fifth-century legend known as the *Vitae Patrum* highlights the mental landscape which informed the story of Saint Kevin. An Egyptian hermit lost grace in lusting after the daughter of a pagan priest. This loss was represented physically by a dove flying out of his mouth. In remorse for his sin the holy man redoubled his ascetic efforts, and after three weeks of continuous prayer and fasting was rewarded while at prayer by the return of grace. The bird landed first on his head, then perched in his hand, and finally flew back into the monk's mouth.[70]

The symbolism of the Saint Kevin story seems clear in comparison with the patristic tale: both are allegories of the reception of grace by a heroic ascetic. The meaning of Gerald's twelfth-century story lies in monastic rhetoric and allegory, and is by no means a clear example of a 'new attitude' of twelfth-century saints towards animals. If at some level there is still a sense of wonder for nature in the vivid picture of Saint Kevin and the bird, then the same sense of wonder cannot be denied to the patristic story. The wonder is itself part of the rhetoric which validates an allegorical tale. In fact it should hardly surprise the historian that examples can be found from any period of some sort of sympathetic, appreciative regard towards wild animals. However, if changes in a society's attitude towards nature are to be found through the deeds of saints, then closer attention must be paid to the literary traditions of hagiography and the spiritual and rhetorical depth of these stories. Animal miracles were not written to charm modern historians.

[69] John Moschus, *Pratum Spirituale*, PL 74, cols. 123–240, *Vita Pardi Monachi Romani*, ch. 101, cols. 169–70.

[70] *Verba Seniorum*, ch. 38, cols. 884–5. It might be objected that this is a rather obscure story from the *Vitae Patrum*, but it was in fact known and used at least once in England in the eleventh century: see Constance L. Rosenthal, *The 'Vitae Patrum' in Old and Middle English Literature* (Philadelphia 1936), p. 62. Also a story from the Apocrypha reveals a similar symbolic connection between a bird and the soul. In the *Acts of John*, possibly as early as the late second century, John, observing a partridge and in rebuke to a priest, said, 'the partridge is your soul': *Apocryphal New Testament*, ed. Elliott, p. 326.

Animal and saint stories are not therefore in any primary sense records of medieval attitudes towards nature. They make up a highly versatile genre capable of expressing theological and spiritual concerns, while perhaps being usefully employed for immediate political purposes, and also on occasion being influenced by the popular imagination. The degree to which folklore as such played a part in the development of the genre is difficult to assess, since the writing of the stories was always in the hands of literate ecclesiastics. Nevertheless, it has to be carefully considered, as the stories that turn up in western medieval hagiography are far from unique to that particular corner of the Eurasian and African continents. Early Buddhist myths, for example, have stories of wild animals becoming tame in the presence of holy men, ferocious beasts protecting them, birds feeding them, water animals ferrying them, dragons being tamed by them, and, like St Anselm and the hare, holy men protecting animals from hunters.[71] This does not mean that any such stories that appear in Christian material can be automatically considered to be folklore. Many of these motifs had been passed back and forth across the literatures of the ancient world, and so they may have arrived in hagiography by other means than the influence of popular culture. This, then, is the task of analysis: to determine the purposes of stories and the various influences upon the formation and development of the Christian genre of the saint and animal story. The place and time where this particular tradition began was in fourth-century Egypt with the sudden appearance of large numbers of Christian ascetics going out to the 'desert' to find spiritual perfection.

[71] R. S. Loomis, *White Magic: An Introduction to the Folklore of Christian Legend* (Cambridge, Mass., 1948), pp. 12–14.

CHAPTER 2

The Formation of the Tradition

THE Egyptian Fathers of the fourth and fifth centuries were much afflicted by the devil and his illusions, which frequently involved animals. Thus 'all the creatures of the desert' gathered threateningly around Saint Anthony's hermitage in the inner mountain. However, Anthony told them he would let them devour him, if they were there by God's will, but if they had been gathered by the devil, then they must flee, and so they did.[1] Another time, Anthony was able to cross the Nile safely despite the presence of many crocodiles.[2] Whenever Saint Pachomius needed to cross a river, crocodiles 'would carry him with the utmost subservience, and set him down at whatever spot he indicated'.[3] A monk of Sapsas was so full of grace that he was able to welcome lions into his cave and offer them food in his lap.[4] Saint Jerome, in his *Vita* of Saint Hilarion, claimed that his subject was able to tame animals who had gone wild, giving the example of a camel which had become possessed by the devil and trampled people to death.[5]

If some of the time wild animals were merely illusions of the devil, trying to play on the human fears of holy men, much of the time the animals were meant to be genuine wild beasts. The essential purpose of all these stories was to demonstrate that both the wild forces of nature and malign supernatural forces were subject to the authority of the Christian holy man. His power was derived through faith alone, or from another perspective, ascetic purity. In principle this power is open to any human with sufficient faith in Christ. If overall the *Vitae Patrum* were concerned primarily with spiritual lessons for Christian monks, the tales of saints and animals point to a potentially wider audience for earlier hagiographic literature. In these wonder tales, the Christian ascetic movement was claiming equality, if not superiority, with the exploits of heroes and holy men of pre-Christian Antiquity.

Classical legend certainly contributed to the stock of Christian legends, if not necessarily through direct borrowing, then certainly through general cultural

[1] Evagrius, *Vita Beati Antonii Abbatis*, PL 73, cols. 125–94, ch. 25, col. 149. The *Life* of Anthony was originally composed in Greek by Athanasius some time after 356, but Evagrius' translation was the medium through which Anthony was known to Latin Christendom for the rest of the Middle Ages.

[2] Ibid. ch. 14, col. 134.

[3] *Vita Sancti Pachomii*, PL 73, cols. 229–72; ch. 19, col. 241.

[4] John Moschus, *Pratum Spirituale*, ch. 2, col. 123. The *Pratum Spirituale* is an early-seventh-century work, but its miracle stories point back to the earliest accounts.

[5] Jerome, *Vita Sancti Hilarionis Eremitae*, PL 23, cols. 29–54, at ch. 23, col. 41.

continuity.[6] In a common type of Christian miracle, the saint rids a place, often an island, of vermin, snakes or other irritating creatures. There are a great number of classical parallels for this type of story, from Apollon Smintheus banishing field mice for his worshippers, to Pliny's note of a legend that Poseidon had destroyed the snakes which had made the island of Tenos uninhabitable.[7] In a sense this type of story does not need a model, but can spring automatically from basic material concerns of society, and it is in any case difficult to match any particular medieval Christian story or this sort with a classical precedent.

Nonetheless, in other cases specific stories might be the inspiration for hagiographic legend, as for example the story of Androcles' lion. This legend could, at one level, be the inspiration for Saint Simeon's dragon with the beam in its eye, even if biblical quotation is also at work in that story. A more direct imitation of the classical myth seems to appear in the seventh-century account of Eastern saints by John Moschus. A lion with a thorn in its paw came to Saint Gerasimus for help.[8] The saint removes the thorn, cleans and binds the wound, and the grateful lion insists on following the holy man as a disciple. The romance goes on from there, because one day the lion loses a donkey of which he was set to take care. Inevitably the holy man assumes his lion had eaten the poor animal, and as punishment the beast is forced to do the donkey's work. Later, by chance the lion finds the donkey and leads him back to Gerasimus. The lion would later die of grief at the passing of the old man. This narrative inspired the very similar story of Saint Jerome's lion, which first appears in the eleventh century.[9] While Androcles' lion is a possible model for these stories, the denouement of the classical legend, where the lion refuses to eat Androcles in the arena, is not used, apparently even in the early accounts of Christian martyrs.

It is as a more general influence that classical literature seems to have created a context which would encourage the proliferation of animal stories in hagiography. Greek heroes and even philosophers accreted legends of their marvels in relation to the natural world. Heracles strangled snakes in his crib, demonstrating that the presumption that heroes kill snakes is by no means limited to Judaeo-Christian mythology.[10] Thus the words of Pythagoras 'possessed an admonitory quality that prevailed even with animals, which confirms that in intelligent men learning tames even wild

[6] It has been argued that hagiography is dependent upon classical Greek biography for its structure; in particular, see Alison Goddard Elliott, *Roads to Paradise: Reading the Lives of the Early Saints* (London 1987), pp. 45–51, and J.-M. Picard, 'Structural Patterns in Early Hiberno-Latin Hagiography', *Peritia* 4 (1985), pp. 67–82, at pp. 70–1.

[7] See Alexander H. Krappe, 'Saint Patrick and the Snakes', *Traditio* 5 (1947), pp. 323–30, at p. 323. Krappe compiled a very impressive range of both classical and medieval variants upon this type of story, noting also early versions from as far away as Japan.

[8] For Saint Simeon see above, Chapter 1, p. 3, and for the lion see John Moschus, *Pratum Spirituale*, cols. 172–4.

[9] Elliott, *Roads to Paradise*, pp. 197–8. The same topos appears also in the probably eleventh-century *Vita* of Saint Aventin of Troyes, where the saint removes a thorn from a bear's foot: *Vita Sancti Aventini Presbyteri*, *AASS* 4 February, pp. 474–80, at ch. 8, p. 477.

[10] Elliott, *Roads to Paradise*, p. 80.

or irrational beasts', according to an account of around AD 300.[11] At one time the philosopher is able to talk to an ox to prevent it from eating green beans, a forbidden food for Pythagoras, and the author concludes that 'Pythagoras demonstrated that he possessed the same dominion as Orpheus over savage animals'. Where the Neoplatonic author saw such wonders as showing the power of reason, Christian writers would emphasise the power of faith, perhaps in conscious opposition to such precedents.

Indeed, legends of the first-century Neopythagorian Apollonius of Tyana drew direct Christian comment, with Justin Martyr in the second quarter of the second century concerned that 'if God is the maker and master of creation, how do the consecrated objects of Apollonius have power in the orders of that creation? For as we see, they check the fury of the waves and the power of the winds, and the inroads of vermin and attacks of wild animals.'[12] It is even conceivable that the early-third-century *Vita* of Apollonius by Philostratus could have been written partly to counter Christian claims to the exclusive possession of miracles. In any case, with so many claims to wonders in circulation, Christian writers had ample motive to start echoing existing stories with claims of their own. Christian heroes had to be able to compete with the miraculous capabilities of their predecessors. Hence perhaps the claim by Rufinus in the prologue to his *History of the Monks in Egypt*, written in the first decade of the fifth century, that the Christian monks had 'stopped the flow of rivers, and crossed the Nile dry-shod. They have slain wild beasts. They have performed cures, miracles and acts of power.'[13]

Another classical figure may have been one of the models for some of the stories of the Egyptian Fathers. The hero Pancrates swam with crocodiles, who fawned on him and wagged their tails, thus proving that he was a holy man.[14] This story recalls many of the stories of the Egyptian Fathers and crocodiles, including Pachomius' use of the animals as a ferry. However, a specifically Christian theme is being developed here in the *Vitae Patrum*. The crocodiles' obedience to Pachomius is evidence of the monk's exemplary faith, and the holy man thus prays to God to teach him to do His will. Whatever kind of continuity there may be between the classical and Christian stories, it is clear that considerable adaptation takes place within the context of Christian writing; with these kinds of legends, similar wondrous events can have quite different moral or social meanings.

If classical literature provided the context for the appearance of saint and animal stories, then the Bible should have been the direct source for many particular examples. Perhaps the two most ubiquitous biblical references in animal stories are Psalm 91:13, 'thou shalt tread upon the lion and adder; the young lion and the dragon shalt thou

[11] Iamblichus of Chalcis, *Life of Pythagoras*, trans. in K. S. Guthrie, *The Pythagorean Sourcebook and Library* (Michigan 1987), pp. 57–122, at ch. 13, pp. 70–1.

[12] Cited in G. R. S. Mead, *Apollonius of Tyana* (London 1901), p. 30.

[13] Rufinus, *Historia Monachorum*, PL 21, cols. 387–462; col. 390. For the dating of the work see *The Lives of the Desert Fathers* (Oxford 1981), trans. N. Russell, intro. B. Ward, p. 7.

[14] From Lucian's *Philopseudes*, cited in Stancliffe, *St Martin*, pp. 197–8. Another discussion of classical influence upon Christian stories of saints and animals is Maureen A. Tillery, 'Martyrs, Monks, Insects and Animals', in *The Medieval World of Nature*, ed. Joyce Salisbury (London 1993), pp. 93–108, at pp. 94–6.

trample under feet', and Luke 10:19, where Christ states 'Behold I have given you power to tread upon serpents and scorpions, and over all the power of the enemy'.[15] Saint Anthony's ability to keep his mountain hermitage free of wild beasts at one point receives scriptural explanation from Job 5:23: 'For thou shalt be in league with the stones of the field: and the beasts of the field shall be at peace with thee'.[16] However, it is not at all clear that the stories of Anthony's dealings with animals in the wilderness are created by the biblical image or whether the quotation was simply used to justify an existing legend. This is the methodological problem with most quotations from scripture, and each case needs to be judged on its own merits.

Another biblical reference open to hagiographic use, Balaam's ass, is, as we have seen, notable by its absence. However, the biblical episode may well lie behind a passage in the third-century apocryphal *Acts of Thomas*. Here, as the Apostle is speaking to the crowd, the colt of an ass comes to stand before him, and piously declaims a speech of praise of the Apostle.[17] The same text gives a long speech to a dragon also, in which it reveals itself essentially as a symbol of the devil.[18] Other apocrypha also contain talking animals. The *Acts of Peter*, written in Greek probably before 200, tells of Peter loosing a dog, which then 'received a man's voice' and asked the Apostle for his commands.[19] A later orthodox, if colourful, apocryphal text has both a leopard and a kid goat speak.[20] These stories serve to emphasise the different temper of the apocrypha from the main hagiographic tradition, which very rarely allows speech to animals.

Indeed, one argument on the rarity of references to Balaam's ass in hagiography suggests that it is discomfort with wonders where the lines between human and animal are crossed which inhibited hagiographers in this regard.[21] If so, this clearly did not apply to writers of some of the apocrypha. More spectacular in its transgression of the lines of human and animal than the talking animals above is a story which seems to have been in the original *Gospel of Thomas*. This is an infancy story of Christ where he changes some children into goats, which then frolic and play with him, which they had refused to do as humans. Soon the vengeful boy-Christ is persuaded to relent and changes the children back.[22] The only continuity with hagiographic tradition here is in the image of animals showing affection for the holy.

15 Psalm 91 (90 in the Vulgate), where it is the 'asp and basilisk . . . lion and dragon' that Christians are enabled to tread upon. For an analysis of the Old Testament's influence on medieval literature more generally see Ziolowski, *Talking Animals*, pp. 33–4. Many stories would also seem to invite quotation from Isaiah 11:6–9, but direct references seem rare.

16 *Vita Antonii*, ch. 25, col. 149.

17 *Apocryphal New Testament*, ed. Elliott, pp. 464–5.

18 Ibid. p. 460.

19 Ibid. p. 408.

20 Ibid. pp. 515–16.

21 Voisenet, *Bestiaire chrétien*, p. 199.

22 *Apocryphal New Testament*, ed. Elliott, p. 106. Although originally appearing only in Syriac and Arabic versions, this story later appears in medieval English and French versions: see *The Apocryphal New Testament*, ed. and trans. M. R. James (Oxford 1942), pp. 67–8.

A story from the *Vitae Patrum* which contains a transformation shows where Christian writers' concerns more usually lay. A girl who had consecrated her virginity to the Lord was transformed into a mare by the magic of an evil man. Macarius, a disciple of Saint Anthony, is called upon by the girl's parents, and he transforms her back after seven days of prayer and a rub over with oil.[23] There is a whiff of magic here even about the saint's miracle, but the role of the holy man is clear. Christian miracles restore the right boundaries between the human and animal, rather than disrupting them, as does pagan magic. The stories from apocrypha thus highlight the selectivity of early hagiography: there were many strange stories circulating among Christians in the fourth and fifth centuries that the early hagiographers chose not to use as models for their accounts of the saints, and not even biblical precedent could make some types of story acceptable.

If Balaam's ass was not a comfortable biblical image, then the story of Daniel in the lion's den (Daniel 6:16–23) ought in contrast to have been a fruitful image for hagiographers. Lions have a large presence in early hagiography, as they did in both the Bible and ancient literature in general. An early Christian legend of Saint Paul at Ephesus has the Apostle being thrown to the beasts, whereupon a lion lay down at his feet and licked him. The early-third-century Christian Hippolytus commented on this that if this was believed then 'how shall we not believe that which happened in the case of Daniel?'[24] However, other similar stories do not reference Daniel. The second-century *Acts of Paul* includes the story of Thecla. When the beasts attack Thecla in the arena, 'a fierce lioness ran up and lay down at her feet', and then proceeds to fight off the other beasts, before finally dying while killing another lion.[25] The only early *passio* story to contain an animal legend of this type is the influential narrative of Perpetua and Felicitas from the early third century. Here one of the Christians, Saturus, is matched with a wild boar, but the animal gores a gladiator instead. Then a bear refuses to leave its cage to attack the Christian. Later on the man is dispatched by one bite of a leopard, as he had wished.[26]

Despite some early references, hagiographers do not seem to have made much direct use of the Daniel story for the stories of the early Fathers. The Bible in any case has a host of references to lions, and beasts in general, all of which may have informed the formation of the early legends. Lions could be a symbol of the devil, as in one passage of the *Life of Anthony*. Here a reference to 1 Peter 5:8, 'your adversary

[23] Rufinus, *Historia Monachorum*, ch. 12, col. 432. Rufinus in his translation from the Greek text has added a comment here explaining that the transformation was just a diabolical illusion, not a reality. This is not necessarily the meaning of the Greek original, which may be why Rufinus interpolated his clarification; compare Rufinus to the text in *The Lives of the Desert Fathers*, trans. N. Russell, p. 110.

[24] *Apocryphal New Testament*, ed. James, pp. 291–2, and p. 574.

[25] *Apocryphal New Testament*, ed. Elliott, p. 370.

[26] *Passio Sanctorum Perpetuae et Felicitatis*, in *The Acts of the Christian Martyrs*, ed. and trans. Herbert Musurillo (Oxford 1972), pp. 106–31, at pp. 126–7. Nature does intervene in the *passiones* of some other martyrs, for example the dolphins which saved the bodies of fourth-century Donatist martyrs from destruction, or the wasps which guarded the body of a Syrian martyr: see Tillery, 'Martyrs, Monks, Insects and Animals', p. 94.

the devil, as a roaring lion, walketh about', helps to describe the saint's early trials with the devil, before he had gone out into the desert.[27] It is likely that this biblical reference was used to build another story of a solitary who lived near the Jordan. Going into a cave to escape the heat, he found a lion there, who 'began to gnash his teeth and roar' at the holy man. The hermit mildly pointed out that there was enough room for them both, and if the lion did not like it, he could always leave. The lion, or more likely the devil, thus left the cave.[28] There are more positive images of lions to be drawn from the Bible, indicating lions as symbols of strength and power, and the beasts often enough play a positive role in the stories of the early Fathers.[29]

The biblical image that spawned the largest number of stories in hagiography was Elijah and the ravens. While Elijah was hiding beyond Jordan, 'the ravens brought him bread and flesh in the morning and bread and flesh in the evening' (1 Kings 17:6). The original *Vitae Patrum* stories in fact tend to replace the ravens with mysterious human figures or literal angels. Abba Orr told a story of a holy man who was regularly brought heavenly food by angels, which gives the devil the opportunity to tempt him, appearing to him as an 'emperor' and offering to take him up to heaven 'like Elijah'. The hermit wisely resisted.[30] Even here, where the association of Elijah with miraculous feeding is acknowledged, no animal appears. Nonetheless, the motif of the saint fed by animals, as agents of God, even symbolic angels, was to appeal consistently to later writers. Saint Jerome's story of the legendary first hermit Paul is very likely the foundation story for those which follow later in the Middle Ages. Paul of Thebes was fed by a raven, which brought him half a loaf every day for sixty years.[31]

Later examples follow the model closely, but with some notable variations. The Irish *Voyage of Saint Brendan* introduces an anchorite named Paul, who has many similarities to Jerome's extreme anchorite, an island in the sea replacing the original desert cave. This Irish Paul is brought a fish every third day for thirty years by an otter, a more appropriate animal for the sea, perhaps.[32] Extensive use of the Elijah topos was made in the *vitae* of the seventh-century Northumbrian Saint Cuthbert. While on a preaching mission, Saint Cuthbert and a companion are brought food by an eagle, acting as a handmaid.[33] Cuthbert is unusual in leaving some of the food for the eagle: such stories do not usually contain any degree of reciprocity. In another

27 *Vita Antonii*, ch. 5, col. 130.

28 *Verba Seniorum*, col. 1003.

29 Elliott, *Roads to Paradise*, p. 203, makes the suggestion that lions, as ambiguous animals, were in fact ancient symbols of death, and that therefore victory over lions was a victory over death itself. This would be an appealing image for Christian writers to use, emphasising their faith as the religion of eternal life.

30 Rufinus, *Historia Monachorum*, ch. 2, col. 406; there are very many such stories in the *Historia*, the closest to the Elijah topos being ch. 7, col. 411; ch. 9, col. 425; ch. 10, cols. 428–9.

31 Jerome, *Vita Sancti Pauli Primi Eremitae*, PL 23, cols. 18–30, at ch. 10, cols. 25–6.

32 *Navigatio Sancti Brendani Abbatis*, ed. Carl Selmer (Notre Dame 1959), ch. 26, pp. 74–5.

33 Bede, *Vita Sancti Cuthberti* in *Two Lives of Saint Cuthbert*, ed. and trans. Bertram Colgrave (Cambridge 1940), pp. 141–307 (hereafter *Vita Cuthberti*), at ch. 12, pp. 194–7. The same story is told in the *Vita Sancti Cuthberti Auctore Anonymo* in ibid. pp. 59–139 at bk 2, ch. 5, pp. 84–7.

story involving the miraculous provision of food, the hagiographer, Bede, refers directly to the Elijah story: 'and from that day he became readier than ever to fast, because indeed he understood clearly that this food had been provided for him in a solitary place, by the gift of Him who once for many days fed Elijah in solitude, with food of the same kind, through the ministrations of birds, there being no man there to minister to him'.[34]

From twelfth-century Wales, another version of the Elijah topos appears in the *Vita* of the island hermit Elgar, who 'had nothing for food, except the supplies for him, through the will of God, of the protection of the divine creator, that is from the sea, and the eagles, or, as we may say, angels'.[35] It is notable that eagles, a more noble bird perhaps, seem to have replaced ravens as the angelic messenger of choice in both the Cuthbert and Elgar stories. When the eagles did not bring Elgar fish, he found a dead stag, which oddly enough God commanded him to eat, even though it was not his custom, and certainly was not the usual custom of ascetic hermits.[36] Although these examples all have their own eccentricities, their relation to the biblical story is fairly clear, even more so when it is noted that the common theme is very marked. The perfect anchorite's trust in providence and obedience to God's will is in each the moral or exemplary point.

The animals in the Elijah topos stories are purely ciphers for God's providence, with the partial exception of Cuthbert's eagle, whose animal needs are recognised and satisfied. Indeed, Cuthbert uses the incident for a sermon on the theme to his companion: 'Learn, my dear son, always to have faith and trust in the Lord; for he who serves God faithfully never perishes of hunger'.[37] This episode in Bede's *Vita* of Cuthbert is particularly suggestive of monastic literate culture. Even as an event occurs, the monk would seize upon literary precedents and thus reveal its spiritual significance, automatically making 'reality' into a topos. Of course, it is Bede who recorded the miracle, and Cuthbert's sermons in Bede and the anonymous *Vita* are very different in form, if not particularly so in their fundamental meaning. Nevertheless, while Bede was writing in the style of a Gregorian dialogue, it is reasonable to suppose that he was reflecting the mentality of the monks of his time. Two monks might, in a less formal and certainly less miraculous fashion, have the same sort of experience and discussion as did Cuthbert and his companion. Thus the topos operates as a means by which monks make sense of their own experiences, and give spiritual meaning to the myriad accidents of life.

That the Elijah topos was part of a living language of monastic culture is clear from the clutch of miracles in the two *Vitae* of Cuthbert which all relate to that story: the miracles of the eagle, the dolphin's flesh, and of Cuthbert's fasting and provision of food in the wild.[38] Specific reference to Elijah is made by the anonymous writer

[34] *Vita Cuthberti*, ch. 5, pp. 168–71.

[35] *Liber Landavensis*, ed. and trans. W. J. Rees (Llandovery 1840), p. 5. Elgar's *Vita* appears as the prologue of the Llandaff work, a combination of hagiography and charter material, pp. 3–7.

[36] Ibid. pp. 6–7.

[37] *Vita Cuthberti*, pp. 196–7.

[38] In *Vita Cuthberti*, chs. 12, 11, and 5 respectively; in anonymous *Vita Cuthberti*, bk 2, ch. 5; bk 2,

and by Bede at different points. Bede refers to Elijah in the chapter on Cuthbert's dedication to fasting. The anonymous author refers to Elijah in the chapter involving the three pieces of dolphin flesh, found while stranded among the Picts:

> And he glorified God because He then bestowed flesh upon the man of God with the same mercy as He had once bestowed it in the desert upon Elijah, and because, inspired by the same Spirit, Cuthbert foresaw the tempest and the calm, just as the Apostle Paul did in the Acts of the Apostles when he prophesied to the voyagers.[39]

Each had his own reasons to invoke Elijah for different miracles and stages in Cuthbert's life. The anonymous writer was concerned, in this case, simply to link Cuthbert's power of prophecy to biblical precedent. Bede, however, referred to Elijah in reference to Cuthbert's 'stricter course of life' and was clearly comparing the saint's activity to eremitical withdrawal, even as the saint is on a preaching mission. Elijah bridged the gap between Cuthbert's solitary ascetic tendency and his pastoral duties at this stage in his life. Neither hagiographer needs to refer to Elijah in the context of the eagle story; a direct reference is only needed to draw attention to a formal argument concerning the life of the holy man.

The Welsh legend of the hermit Elgar is a different case. The legend stays very close to the theme of the anchorite heroically obeying God's will, who 'led his life, present to the Lord, and unknown to man'. There is plenty of precedent within the *Vitae Patrum* for such a story, even apart from Jerome's Paul of Thebes. Nevertheless, a few elements of the Elgar story are suggestive of an origin outside a literate monastic context. As Elgar is so absolutely alone, he prepares his own grave in his oratory, and dies in it. Yet 'while the body was still warm, some sailors came to the little church, and what they found there prepared for burial, they buried'.[40] This stands in contrast to the stories of the *Vitae Patrum*, where extreme anchorites are discovered by other wandering holy men.

Jerome's story of Paul the hermit was probably deliberately fashioned to tame such myths, which he strategically dismissed at the beginning of his work, stating: 'Some tattle this and that. . . a man in an underground cavern with hair to his heels'.[41] These extreme anchorites recognise no social authority whatsoever, seeing human society as so irredeemably fallen that they can only seek salvation entirely isolated from human kind. The stories of these legendary anchorites would not sit well within the context of a hierarchical Church where salvation is dependent upon obedience to authority. Jerome's Paul thus concludes a genre of legend by representing it through a single manageable figure, whose authority is passed on to another great hermit, Saint Anthony. Paul the Hermit and Anthony represent a kind of apostolic succession of eremitical sanctity.[42] The Elgar story violates the implicit rules laid down by Jerome

ch. 4; bk 1, ch. 6 respectively.

39 Anonymous *Vita Cuthberti*, bk 2, ch. 4, pp. 84–5.

40 *Liber Landavensis*, p. 7.

41 Jerome, *Vita Pauli Eremitae*, col. 18; trans. Helen Waddell, *Lives of the Fathers* (London 1936), p. 30.

42 On the problem of authority among the loosely organised ascetics of Egypt, see Philip Rousseau,

about isolated anchorites. The closest the Elgar story comes to a legitimating Anthony figure as found in Jerome is the *magister* Caradog, who visits him and thus learns of his miraculous provisioning. However, it is laymen, not fellow religious, who are the ones to find and honour the holy man after his death. The legend of the extreme anchorite had been let loose again, despite Jerome.

Other elements also suggest a non-ecclesiastical origin for the Elgar story. The miraculous provision of food in the *Vita* is extended into a sequence of three repetitions. There is first the direct reference to Elijah, and there follows shortly thereafter the detail that in absence of food brought by eagles, the anchorite is provided with a 'great fish'. Finally, Elgar was directed towards eating a dead stag as the third instance of miraculous provision. This kind of repetition is a hallmark of orally transmitted folklore. It is possible that the second provision of food was inspired by the story of Cuthbert receiving the dolphin flesh in the land of the Picts. However, it need not be, since beach scavenging would be a normal seaside form of provision. Indeed, the twelfth-century English holy man Godric of Finchale found by providence a dead 'dolphin' on a beach where he was scavenging early in his life. God provided this meat for him to feed his very poor parents and siblings. The hagiographer, Reginald of Durham, gives an extended explanation of the morality of taking such food, finally having Godric remember that Christ himself ate fish. Reginald does not link the episode to Saint Cuthbert, which he might have been expected to do if that had been a reasonable justification in a twelfth-century context.[43] It looks less likely therefore that the dolphin flesh in Elgar was intended to function as a clear reference to Saint Cuthbert. There the triple extension of the Elijah topos does hint at a role for popular culture in the genesis of the anchorite's legend.

The status of Elgar's *Vita* as a whole strengthens this suspicion. The *Vita* opens the twelfth-century *Book of Llandaff*, a work containing the *vitae* of a number of important Welsh saints of the past, as well as a good deal of more recent charter material, in an effort clearly associated with the ambitions and prestige of the church of Llandaff. Elgar's *Vita* would be an oddity in this collection, unless it served a particular function related to the local or regional remembrance of the past. The anonymous author reports that in 1120 the relics of Elgar and Saint Dubricius, who was said to have been buried on the island, were translated by the bishop to the church of Llandaff, to 'the applause of all the clergy and people'.[44] This *translatio* is a moment of unity, or claimed unity, for the local society, but the prominent role given to ordinary secular people in Elgar's death and cult remains notable. Even more peculiarly, while Elgar presumably did exist, little indication of when

Ascetics, Authority and the Church (Oxford 1978), particularly pp. 49–55.

43 *Libellus de Vita et Miraculis Sancti Godrici, Heremitae de Finchale, Auctore Reginaldo Monacho Dunelmensi*, ed. Joseph Stephenson, Surtees Society 20 (1847) (hereafter *Vita Godrici*), no. 12, pp. 26–7. Bede links Cuthbert's dolphin to the desert experiences of the Israelites: *Vita Cuthberti*, ch. 11, pp. 192–5. For Reginald, however, the dolphin meat itself is less important than Godric's moral qualms; the point of the story is to demonstrate Godric's early attempts to imitate the actions of Christ even within a wholly secular life.

44 *Liber Landavensis*, p. 7.

he lived is given in the short *Vita*. The story of his life relates that he was born in Devon, taken prisoner by pirates and made a slave in Ireland. After his first master's death, he was forced to become an executioner, but gained his liberty and became a sailor. This narrative has the flavour of romance. He was then shipwrecked on the Welsh island of Bardsey, the site of the bodies of 'twenty thousand holy confessors and martyrs', and free from snakes, frogs and untimely death.[45] The curious mix of idiosyncratic detail, romance and legend of a patristic flavour suggests that little was known concretely about the actual hermit Elgar.

Much of the oddity of the *Vita* could be explained if the story of his life had been held in oral memory for some time. Some elements suggest there was some historicity in the story of Elgar at one time, particularly the role of the teacher Caradog.[46] Given the nature of oral memory, with its reach of three generations, and given how the *Vita* accords with an already deteriorating precise knowledge, the writer could have been in the third generation after the living witness to the real hermit. Since the work was written after 1120, this would, speculatively, place Elgar in the early to mid-eleventh century. Elgar was the only saint in the *Book of Llandaff* as a whole who could be said to exist within living memory. The church at Llandaff perhaps needed to acquire a recently remembered holy man for its present prestige. The purpose of the *Vita* was, then, to create, through this figure held in contemporary memory, a link to the other saints who had passed out of oral memory, but who were more central to the purposes of the *Liber* as a whole. Hence also arises the claim of 'twenty thousand' saints, placing Elgar in a kind of apostolic succession of holiness, providing a contact, however tenuous, to the saints of the sixth century.[47]

This is the hagiographic logic of the story, and the probable reason why the *Vita* was placed at the head of the *Liber*, but that makes it even more remarkable for common sailors to have been the church of Llandaff's link to the holy man's actual life. Perhaps important parts of the story were not open to hagiographic manipulation. In this context, the legend of Elgar is less likely to have been created in a literate ecclesiastical context than a popular one, and the oddities of the *Vita* reflect that origin, since the hagiographer could not wilfully depart from the remembered elements, such as the dead stag as provision for a Christian ascetic, or the sailors' discovery of the holy body. If this seems to have been a long digression from the topos of Elijah and the

45 Ibid. pp. 3–4.

46 Ibid. p. 4.

47 John Reuben Davies, *The Book of Llandaff and the Norman Church in Wales* (Woodbridge 2003), pp. 96, 124–8, identifies the Irish king whom Elgar served as executioner as Ruadrí Ua Conchobair, who first appears in 1076, and the master Caradoc, more tentatively, as Caradoc of Llancarfan. Elgar would then have been alive about 1098 to meet Caradoc, and would have been dead for only about twenty years when the *Vita* was written. However, neither of these identifications securely ground Elgar in history, since both could easily have been inserted anachronistically by the hagiographer, or earlier tellers of the story of Elgar. Nonetheless, if the late *floruit* for Elgar is accepted, the legend of the holy man could still have accreted in the manner suggested here in the first two decades or so of the twelfth century. Note also that Davies, *Llandaff*, p. 127, attributes to Elgar's *Vita* a role specifically related to authenticating the link with Saint Dubricius, or Dyfrig.

ravens, it does demonstrate a crucial point about the role of motifs whose original source is literary. The legend of Elgar is an example of a biblical topos having passed into the popular sphere and being used in the formation of a saint's story outside the control of the local literate elite. The purposes of the original popular story are lost within the written version in this instance, but its existence does demonstrate that simply because a story might have a distinguished literary lineage, the influence of popular culture cannot be ruled out of a role in its formation.

The Elgar story lies in contrast to Bede's equivalent stories of Cuthbert: those stories are clearly written by monks for monks, and move from detail to spiritual meaning in a way that the Elgar legend does not. Yet, if Bede's story of Cuthbert and the eagle is firmly within a monastic context, there is an element which legitimately gives pause for thought. This is Cuthbert's reciprocity with the eagle. The detail is not part of the topos, nor is it lyrical embellishment, as in the nesting of the blackbird on Saint Kevin's hand. Reciprocity with animals does not have a place within the Elijah topos, nor is it part of Bede's general attitude towards animal stories. Cuthbert's reciprocity may suggest the existence of some other layer of story or symbolism at work in seventh- or eighth-century Northumbria, but on its own the clue cannot be deciphered.

Indeed, Bede's very orthodox understanding of such stories is dominant. Bede commented on Cuthbert's animal miracles that 'if a man faithfully and whole-heartedly serves the maker of all created things, it is no wonder that all creation should minister to his commands and wishes'.[48] This was the moral of any animal–saint story for Bede, and it clearly reflects the meaning, for monks, of the Elijah topos, among other such motifs. Bede's theological, as opposed to hagiographic, work, certainly shows the same attitude. His commentary on Genesis describes how before the Fall there were no poisonous plants, no dangerous and predatory wolves or snakes, and all animals lived harmoniously on vegetation: in Eden everything was under man's dominion.[49] Within this theological context, Bede's statement concerning Cuthbert's control of animals exemplifies his belief that in the person of the saint, who is utterly obedient to God, the conditions of Eden are restored. This is the central meaning and motivation of nearly all the patristic stories of saints and animals, and is a dominant theme in the whole genre, irrespective of time and region.

The prelapsarian theme of the animal's obedience to the saint can be richly demonstrated from patristic and later hagiography. The snake as an animal has, of course, an unfortunate symbolism within this model. Thus, in a legend of Paul of Thebes, not used by Jerome, the saint 'used to take various kinds of snakes in his hands and cut them through the middle. The brethren made prostration before him, saying, "Tell us what you have done to receive this grace." He said, "Forgive me, Fathers, but if someone has obtained purity, everything is in submission to him, as it was to Adam, when he was in Paradise before he transgressed the commandment."'[50]

48 *Vita Cuthberti*, ch. 21, pp. 224–5.

49 See Glacken, *Rhodian Shore*, pp. 205–6 for Bede, and pp. 183–213 for the general patristic influence on views of nature in the Middle Ages.

50 Benedicta Ward, *The Sayings of the Desert Fathers* (London 1975), p. 171. Anthony also causes the

John Moschus states the same theme concerning Abbot Gerasimus. The astonishing obedience of the lion, and its death from grief after the death of Gerasimus, should not be considered to show that the lion had a rational soul, but rather to glorify God and to 'show how animals were submissive to the first man before he transgressed God's commandment and was driven from the paradise of delights'.[51] Pachomius learned to place his faith in God such that 'many a time he trod on snakes and scorpions, and passed unhurt through all'.[52] Thus also crocodiles obediently acted as a ferry for the holy man.

The centrality of power over the most disturbing of creatures, snakes and other fearsome predators, appears early in the western hagiographic tradition. Sulpicius Severus wrote at the turn of the fourth and fifth centuries: 'You have given instances of wild beasts with their ferocity subdued, obedient to the anchorites, but it was a very ordinary thing for Martin to vanquish the fury of beasts or the venom of serpents'.[53] The island of Lérins was uninhabited 'because of its utter desolation and unvisited for fear of its venomous snakes', but when Saint Honoratus came to the island, 'the terrors of the solitude were put to flight; the army of serpents fell back'. In the general scramble of early western hagiographers to mark out their saint as special, particularly in comparison to the Egyptian hermits, Honaratus' hagiographer, Hilary of Arles, manages to write: 'It is a fact, and one unheard of, and to be reckoned (I think) among the miracles to his credit, that not once was he ever in danger or even startled by an encounter with a snake, although encounters are so frequent in those arid wastes (as I can bear witness), especially when provoked by heavy seas'.[54]

Not all such stories are so stereotypical in their purpose, particularly where the hard treatment of snakes extends to the most fearsome snakes of all, the dragons. The various symbolisms carried by dragons have already been discussed, but one of the dragon stories of the Egyptian Fathers may help to explain some of the more idiosyncratic stories that appear in the early literature. A certain Ammon had a reputation as a slayer of dragons, and so when a dragon was ravaging the countryside and killing many animals, the people went to the holy man for help. In due course, the saint goes dragon hunting. On bent knees, Saint Ammon deals with the troublesome creature with the words 'may Christ the Son of God slay thee, even as He shall slay the Great Whale'.[55] The story, on the surface, seems to carry a standard spiritual symbolism where the destruction of the dragon exemplifies the redemptive power of Christ for the world.

However, like Simeon Stylites' dragon, this one may not be a simple spiritual

'creeping things', snakes, to flee from his mountain solitude: *Vita Antonii*, ch. 11, col. 133.

[51] John Moschus, *Pratum Spirituale*, *Vita Abbatis Gerasimi*, ch. 107, cols. 172–4.

[52] *Vita S. Pachomii*, ch. 19, col. 241.

[53] Sulpicius Severus, *Dialogi*, Dialogue 1, ch. 25, col. 199, trans. Hoare, *Western Fathers*, p. 97.

[54] Hilary of Arles, *Sermo de Vita Sancti Honorati, Episcopi Arelatensis*, PL 50, cols. 1249–73, at ch. 3, no. 15, col. 1257; trans. Hoare, *Western Fathers*, p. 260. Hilary also notes the two apposite biblical references for this miracle, Psalm 91:13 and Luke 10:19. Luke is also quoted by Rufinus, *Historia Monachorum*, ch. 8, col. 420.

[55] Rufinus, *Historia Monachorum*, ch. 8, col. 421.

symbol. The preceding chapter on the holy man Apollo contains a number of stories of monks' interactions with nearby villages. In one instance, he caused the destruction of a pagan temple and the consequent conversion of the inhabitants. On another occasion, Apollo has difficulty mediating in a quarrel between two villages because one has a bandit chief as its champion, and trusts to him. The holy man is the mightier and converts the man to a life of religion, amending his life 'as if he had been changed from a wolf into an innocent lamb'.[56] Both these stories could have been changed into a dragon allegory, and indeed Apollo is given a speech earlier in the chapter on sin and the crushing of the snake's head, so dragon symbolism is close to the surface.[57] To have a dragon story, which is already halfway to romance, immediately following the Apollo section in the original text, does suggest that the Ammon story should have an allegorical reading, the dragon representing some social terror rather than a purely spiritual one.

In the context of Saint Simeon, the dragon story appeared to be an allegory arising from the holy man's social function of mediation, and it seems clear from both the accounts of Apollo and Ammon that Egyptian hermits performed a similar social function. If Ammon's dragons may stand for bandits or politically powerful men, then other animals may also do so. A crocodile acted as a ferry for Abbot Helenus, and then obediently died on the saint's orders, apparently for its own sake; it would not then 'suffer the penalty for the slaughter of souls'.[58] It is hard to imagine what could be worse for an animal than being killed, since what other penalty could it suffer unless it had a soul to be punished after death? The story makes little sense if the crocodile is an animal, whereas if it was a symbol for a predatory human, the saint's action could be read as an allegory of conversion, and thus death to the old life of sin. Another crocodile in the Coptic account of the monks of Upper Egypt, by one Paphnutius, is also suggestive of allegory. Here a Nubian man loses his son to a crocodile and goes to Abba Aaron for help. The holy man instructs him to throw a piece of wood into the river where the crocodile had taken his son. The man does so and the crocodile appears, casting the boy on to the shore unharmed.[59] This could represent a folktale, and it does bear some similarity to stories that later appear in Ireland.[60] Alternatively, and not exclusively, it could be an allegory of kidnap or imprisonment, in which the holy man had negotiated the release of the man's son from some political or criminal power symbolised by the crocodile.

Thus while dragons and snakes carry particular symbolic resonance, other animals can carry allegorical meanings, and all creatures can illustrate conditions after the Fall. For example, a hippopotamus was laying waste the countryside, until a holy

56 Ibid. ch. 7, cols. 414–15. The order of the chapters in the PL text of Rufinus is somewhat different from the order of the Greek text, as translated in Russell, *Lives of the Desert Fathers*.

57 Rufinus, *Historia Monachorum*, ch. 7, col. 412.

58 Paladius, *Historia Lausiaca*, PL 73, cols. 1085–1218, ch. 59, cols. 1167–8; trans. Helen Waddell, *Beasts and Saints* (London 1934), pp. 20–1.

59 Paphnutius, *Histories of the Monks of Upper Egypt and the Life of Onnophrius*, trans. T. Vivian (Kalamazoo 1993), pp. 120–1.

60 See below, Chapter 4, p. 66.

man, at the behest of the local farmers, commanded it to go.[61] The theme of the control of animals does not rest, however, with domination stories. Many miracles involve the reversal of predatory or simply wild natures. Thus Abbot Gerasimus' lion, when it came to serve him, was fed on bread and pulses, demonstrating the reversal of its natural diet in the presence of the saint.[62] Some lions appear to be able to remain mostly wild, but are still helpful: the hermit Paemen did not notice the extreme cold of one night, to the astonishment of another monk; when pressed for an explanation, Paemen said that during the night a lion had slept beside him and kept him warm.[63] One Coptic story from Egypt falls within the theme of the reversal of wild natures. Here, Anthony's great disciple, Macarius, was praying in his cave when a hyena appeared and began to lick his feet, then 'taking him gently by the hem of his tunic, she drew him towards her own cave'.[64] The hyena brings the saint to her own cave and presents him with her cubs, which had been born blind. Macarius prays over them and returns their sight, and in return the hyena brought him the skin of a large ram, laying it at his feet. This is a very exceptional story, as the saint does not exercise control over the animal at all: it simply behaves according to human rules apparently on its own account. It is possible that this story should be taken as an allegory of the saint's spiritual services being given to all who might ask for his blessing. The blindness of the cubs could have a spiritual meaning, and this would then be a kind of conversion story. It does in any case represent one of the few early stories of reciprocity between a saint and an animal, to some degree parallel with Saint Cuthbert's allowance of food to the eagle.

Most western examples of the reversal of animal nature follow a more straightforward path. Sulpicius Severus carried the theme into the western tradition with two stories of ferocious predators being tamed. In one a hermit approached a palm tree, where a lion waited:

> the wild beast, in obedience to a divine command (as you could see), discreetly drew back a little and stood motionless while our host picked some fruit within reach on the lower branches. Then, when he held out his hand full of dates, the beast ran up and took them as naturally as any domestic animal could have done and when it had eaten them it went away.[65]

In the second story, the domestication theme is essentially similar, but the animal has become a wolf rather than a lion. A wolf always stood near a certain holy man as he ate, and would eat the bread he offered her. One day she stole a loaf of bread, and suffered guilt over the theft. Eventually, due to the hermit's prayers, the wolf came back and showed its penitence and was forgiven. Sulpicius' comments on this story are wholly predictable:

[61] Rufinus, *Historia Monachorum*, 'De Beno', ch. 4, col. 408.

[62] Moschus, *Pratum Spirituale*, *Vita Abbatis Gerasimus*, ch. 107, col. 173.

[63] Ibid. *Vita et Mors Abbatis Paemensis Solitarii*, ch. 167, col. 203.

[64] See Russell, *Lives of the Desert Fathers*, p. 110, and Waddell, *Beasts and Saints*, p. 149.

[65] Sulpicius Severus, *Dialogi*, Dialogue 1, ch. 13, cols. 191–2; trans. Hoare, *Western Fathers*, pp. 83–4.

> Now I ask you to consider the power that Christ manifested even in a case like this. In his service the brute creation displays intelligence and the savage beast grows meek. A wolf observes due ceremony, a wolf knows that theft is a crime.[66]

The notable element of this story is that the ubiquitous lion has been replaced by a wolf, a predator that would have had much more reality for a western audience. It might be that Sulpicius introduced a wolf in order to give the story some verisimilitude for those who were sceptical about the wonders effected by eastern ascetics. Postumianus, the foil to Sulpicius in this dialogue, and his journey to the East may both be fictions, but there is nothing in the stories themselves, except perhaps the wolf, that does not accord with other eastern accounts. These could easily have been stories in circulation about the Egyptian hermits, which Sulpicius heard and recorded, merely adjusting one for his audience. Nonetheless, whatever the status of Sulpicius' wolf, it is largely bears or wolves which feature as tamed predators in the western hagiographic tradition.[67] The theme itself remains very stable, such that a twelfth-century example could almost have been written in the sixth or seventh century. The founder of a new monastic order that would later merge with the Cistercians, Bernard of Tiron, was establishing his monastery when a wolf, as if it were tame, brought a lost calf back to the monastery.[68] The predator's natural instincts are reversed in the presence of the *virtus* of the saint. As the monks construct their Eden in the wilderness, so animals naturally come to serve, as they did before the Fall.

Saintly control of nature was not only a demonstration of the power of the Christian religion, but could also be used to reflect on the commitment of Christians themselves. This reflection can be found in the contrast between the faith of the saint and the fear of his followers in the face of dangerous animals. When Helenus trod on the back of the pliant crocodile, a priest who was with him was 'truly stricken with alarm when he had seen the monster'.[69] It is sometimes hard to commit oneself to God's will in the face of gaping jaws. Visitors to the desert monks are alarmed when they are required to follow the tracks of a dragon; even when reassured by the brothers, 'the frailty of our lack of faith made us more and more afraid'.[70] It is the superior faith of the saints which separates them from ordinary weak believers.

Sulpicius Severus picks up the same theme in the Postumianus dialogue. While visiting a hermit with a tame lion, 'my guide and I shook with fear at the sight of it but the holy man went up to it without pausing for a moment and, alarmed though we were, we followed him'. Of course, the narrator had nothing to fear: 'We who were watching all this, still shaking with fear, had no difficulty in realising how

66 Ibid. Dialogue 1, ch. 14, cols. 192–3; trans. Hoare, *Western Fathers*, pp. 84–5.

67 Gregory the Great favoured bears as the submissive predator: see Gregory the Great, *Dialogi*, ed. and trans. Adalbert de Vogué (Paris 1978–80), 3 vols, at bk 3, ch. 11, nos. 1–2, pp. 292–6; ch. 15, nos. 3–9, pp. 316–20; and ch. 26, no. 3, p. 366.

68 Geoffrey Grossus, *Vita Beati Bernardi Tironiensis*, PL 172, cols. 1362–1446 at ch. 8, no. 73, cols. 1410–11.

69 Palladius, *Historia Lausiaca*, ch. 59, col. 1168.

70 Rufinus, *Historia Monachorum*, ch. 8, col. 420.

strong was the faith of the hermit and how weak was ours'.[71] Jerome's Anthony was made of sterner stuff. As he was waiting with the body of Paul the hermit, two lions came bounding up to dig the legendary hermit's grave, and 'at sight of them he was at first in dread, then turning his mind to God, he waited undismayed, as though he looked on doves'.[72] These comments highlight part of the purpose of these stories: they are fables to encourage the faith and obedience of those in the religious life. If the narrators of these stories can endure the terrors they describe, or are shamed by their lack of faith, those of lesser stature can surely endure more mundane terrors. If wild creatures can show such devotion or obedience to a holy father, then surely monks should show such obedience to their abbot.[73]

However, there is another side to some of these stories, which is more pessimistic, and does not have a practical relation to monastic ideals. Thieves frequently stole the bread of the holy man Ammon, till one day he set out into the desert, and brought two dragons with him to guard the door of the monastery. When the thieves next came, they fainted in terror. The holy man revived them, saying: 'See how much harder you are than these beasts: indeed, they are obedient to us through God, yet you are not afraid of God, nor do you blush to disturb the life of the servants of God'.[74] Sulpicius Severus writes in the same vein. Saint Martin and friends were sitting pleasantly on a bank, when a snake started swimming across to them. He ordered the snake away: 'immediately, at the saint's words, the evil beast turned around and, as we watched it, swam across to the opposite bank'. A miracle to be sure, but not a cause for rejoicing: 'Martin sighed deeply. "Snakes", he said, "listen to me, and men refuse to listen."'[75] Saint Anthony, in search of Paul of Thebes, meets a satyr in the desert who asks the holy man to put in a kind word to God on behalf of his tribe. Anthony in wonder declares:

> Woe to thee Alexandria. . . who worships monsters instead of God. Woe to thee harlot city, in whom the demons of all the earth have flowed together. What have you now to say? The beasts speak of Christ and you worship monsters instead of God.[76]

Dragons and snakes, those most demonic of animals, show more obedience to saints and thus to God than do human beings. This theme may have inspired a passage in a late piece of apocrypha, which may date from the eighth or ninth century. The pseudo-Matthew gospel has the holy family going to hide in a cave during their flight to Egypt, when a number of dragons emerged from the cave. Everyone was understandably alarmed, but the infant Jesus stood in front of the beasts, which

71 Sulpicius Severus, *Dialogi*, Dialogue 1, ch. 13, col. 192; Hoare, *Western Fathers*, p. 84.

72 Jerome, *Vita Pauli Eremitae*, ch. 16, col. 28.

73 It is likely that many of the stories of animal obedience to the saint are also related to the more general problem of authority and obedience within the loosely organised early eremitical groups in Egypt. Obedience and authority are frequent themes even within the layers of the *Vitae Patrum* usually judged to be earliest: see Rousseau, *Ascetics*, pp. 49–55.

74 Rufinus, *Historia Monachorum*, ch. 8, col. 421.

75 Sulpicius Severus, *Dialogi*, Dialogue 3, ch. 9, cols. 216–17; trans. Hoare, *Western Fathers*, p. 132.

76 Jerome, *Vita Pauli Eremitae*, ch. 8, col. 24; trans. Waddell, *Lives of the Fathers*, p. 33.

then worshipped him: 'Then was fulfilled that which was said by David the prophet, "Praise the Lord from the earth, dragons and all you ocean depths". And the child Jesus, walking before them, commanded them to hurt no-one.'[77] Thus the human authorities who perpetrated the massacre of the innocents are more demonic than dragons themselves.

The topos of human frailty and animal obedience represents a deadly criticism of human virtue indeed, and it is also a symbolic core of the anchoritic motivation. It is the melancholy of the anchorite who has risen to a prelapsarian state. The anchorite is so much closer to God than his fellow humans that he is no longer the companion of human beings, but a companion of beasts, with their innate obedience to God's purpose. Thus there are such stories as of the holy man Theon of Oxyrhinchus:

> They said of him that at night he would go out to the desert, and a great troop of the beasts of the desert would go with him. And he would draw water from his well and offer them cups of it, in return for their kindness in attending him. One evidence of this was plain to see, for the tracks of gazelle and goat and the wild ass were thick about his cell.[78]

Theon was a recluse who lived near enough to people for them to flock to him for healing miracles. However there is a contrast between his contact with humans and with animals. With humans he would only reach a hand out of the window of his cell to touch the heads of the sick. Among humans, the saint is imprisoned, and has only the most tenuous physical contact with his fellows. At night, with the animals, he is free, and can engage, without fear of sin, in affectionate, sociable activities such as giving drink to his animal friends.

Theon with his animals is a companionable if melancholy image of the spiritual isolation of the saint, but the topos for this aspect of the desert experience is more familiar from Jerome's description of his own experience of the desert. Jerome was a 'companion of scorpions and wild beasts'.[79] For Jerome the desert was a place of horror and hallucinogenic temptations. The difference between Jerome and Theon is partly that Jerome was writing about himself, and must preserve humility. Even if he were inclined to do so, he could not describe such 'companionship' with animals in the same Edenic terms as a legend could. Nevertheless, the two sides of the topos illustrate the heroically unbearable conditions in which anchorites must live, in order to be pure enough for Edenic status. The topos of the saint's control over animals was thus at an early stage linked to the topos of the companionship between the two, where a saint could be affectionate or helpful towards his animal companions. This affection nevertheless remains firmly within the Edenic model where the holiness of the saint reverses normal hierarchies and boundaries, restoring the state

[77] *Apocryphal New Testament*, ed. Elliott, p. 94; Psalm 148:7.

[78] Rufinus, *Historia Monachorum*, *De Theone*, ch. 6, cols. 409–10, quotation col. 410.

[79] Jerome, *Ad Eustochium*, *Epistola* 22, PL 22 (1), cols. 394–425, at cols. 394–5. Jerome's comment seems to be inspired by Job 30:29, 'I am a brother to dragons and a companion to owls'. For Jerome's experience of the desert see John N. D. Kelly, *Jerome, His Life, Writings and Controversies* (London 1975), pp. 46–57.

of divine nature that fallen humans have lost. The 'companionship of animals' topos was created at a time when orthodox Christianity was still competing with other belief systems. The cry of Jerome's Anthony against Alexandria has to be put in the context of the conversion of the Late Roman world to Christianity.[80]

The fundamental themes of the Christian saint and animal story thus emerged from a late antique culture where many wonder stories of heroes and animals already existed, and in part was a response to existing traditions. The Christian hagiographic tradition adapted some ideas from classical tradition, while the Bible was a source both for certain motifs and of legitimation for these miracles. Whatever the origins of specific motifs, this type of wonder story was brought firmly within a Christian moral and theological framework, and it was to be the themes set in the early centuries of hagiographic writing which would dominate the genre as it appeared in saints' *vitae* in the centuries to come. Yet the saint and animal story was not merely a literary genre that followed a pattern set by theological rules. Whether in the miracles of a Syrian saint like Simeon Stylites or of the Egyptian Fathers, the saint and animal story had a social context which also was crucial in its original purpose and formation. It is not always possible to see the social problems and relationships which gave rise to particular miracle stories, but it should be borne in mind that such a context may have been crucial to many of the stories that appear otherwise as purely literary creations. When considering the development of the animal and saint genre in the west from the sixth century, the social and political as well as the monastic and spiritual contexts need to be considered.

80 These stories could also represent a reaction by ascetics to their troubles with the Church itself. Rousseau, *Ascetics*, p. 68, notes the development of bitter divisions between the monks and the bishops in Egypt at the end of the fourth century. Saint Martin's melancholy comparison of the obedience of humans and beasts could also have a context in the political troubles of ascetic circles in the West at the time of Martin and Sulpicius Severus.

CHAPTER 3

Monks and Animals in the Medieval Wilderness

THE Egyptian monks and hermits of the fourth and fifth centuries are commonly known as the 'desert fathers', a misleading phrase in a modern context, since 'desert' connoted 'uninhabited' from early on, and the monks of Egypt were frequently able to practise very fruitful agriculture in their 'deserts'.[1] In the West the 'desert' meant the wilderness, which produced its own difficulties for the development of agriculture in comparison to the Nile valley. Nonetheless, the fruitfulness of the uncultivated wilderness became established as a theme early on in the West. In the sixth century, Gregory of Tours described the 'recluse' Marianus as having 'no other food except the fruits of the field', and while sometimes people would bring him some honey otherwise he would subsist on what 'he could find in the woods'. He is eventually found dead 'lying beneath an apple tree'.[2] The context of the wilderness brings a contrast to the stories of the Egyptian Fathers, so many of whom were fed miraculously by angels. Certainly, Gregory of Tours was describing the bountifulness of nature in a way that is surely meant to reflect on God's providence, but not in a particularly miraculous fashion. It was just about possible, if somewhat heroic, to live off the fruits of the wilderness in the West, while this would have been impossible in Egypt.

Even so, the western saints sometimes required miraculous assistance. A Bishop Nicetius found his fish traps had been swept away by the force of the river, while he was in urgent need of supplies to feed a visiting king. The bishop nonetheless sent his men to empty the fish traps. After much unwillingness on their part, their poor faith is reproved when the traps were found so full of fish that ten men were barely enough to carry it all away.[3] The miraculous provision of fish became a common motif, also appearing in Jonas of Bobbio's seventh-century account of Saint Columban. Here a monk was sent to catch fish at a precise location, but caught nothing all day, because he was not in the exact place to which Columban had ordered him to go. Being sent back to the right place, his net filled up with an astounding amount of fish.[4] Both these miracles are in a sense less to do with nature as such than with the

[1] See Russell, *The Lives of the Desert Fathers*, intro. B. Ward, p. 15.

[2] Gregory of Tours, *Gloria Confessorum*, MGH SSRM 1(2) (1885), ed. B. Krusch, pp. 744–820, at ch. 80, pp. 798–9.

[3] Gregory of Tours, *Liber Vitae Patrum*, MGH SSRM 1(2) (1885), ed. B. Krusch, pp. 661–744, at ch. 17, pp. 731–2.

[4] Jonas, *Vitae Sanctorum Columbani, Vedastis, Iohannis*, MGH Scriptores Rerum Germanicarum 37 (1905), ed. B. Krusch, ch. 11, pp. 171–2.

obedience of monks in the context of productive labour: nature will provide so long as the monks obey their abbots without doubt or hesitation. The internal hierarchy of the monastery was not a primary question, at least in this form, in the early Egyptian monastic literature, but it quickly became so in the West. Nature miracles were thus one form of parable to reinforce the authority of the abbot.

In addition to the apparent difficulties in organising labour in the monastery, both nature and secular society provided additional difficulties. Gregory of Tours told the story of Saint Friardus, who was an object of ridicule to his neighbours on account of the prayers which accompanied his labours. When the harvesters were attacked by wasps in one part of the field, they mocked the saint further by suggesting that he should tame the insects with his prayers. Thus the saint did pray and made the sign of the cross over the wasps. With the stinging insects safely in their nest, Friardus was able to complete the harvesting, presumably also freed from human barbs.[5] The usual location of the western monks in the supposedly deserted 'wilderness' means that peasants are not normally as visible as they are in this story. Nonetheless, the wilderness was not deserted and would have been the site of extensive gathering and hunting activity, and monks were clearly determined to mark their possession of sylvan resources. Animal stories could serve once again as parables illustrating this possession. On one occasion, Saint Columban came across a bear devouring a stag, but the saint commanded it not to harm the hide, which he needed for shoes. Later, the saint's monks, sent to collect the hide, observed that no birds or beasts dared to scavenge the dead stag.[6] This story is thus not only a simple story of animal obedience, but a warning against poaching monastic resources.

Other encounters are less obviously utilitarian. Thus Gregory of Tours told the story of Saint Aemilianus' encounter with a young hunter called Brachio, who was chasing a boar of enormous size with his dogs.[7] The boar ran into the hermit's enclosure, and the dogs found themselves unable to enter, while the young hunter, sensing he was in the presence of the holy, went towards the cell. Talking with the holy man, he observed the boar to be unafraid and tame, later going off free into the forest. The hunter is the one who is caught, as he is convinced by Aemilianus to enter the religious life. An element of the miraculous protection of church property from noble infringement could be detected in Gregory's telling of this story, but equally the story had a precedent in Sulpicius Severus' tale of Saint Martin saving the hare from hunters.[8] Although these are two prominent examples of the 'hermit and the hunter' topos, it is in fact a rare story in the early centuries of western hagiography, indicating that its later popularity likely marks a shift in hagiographic concerns.[9]

5 Gregory of Tours, *Liber Vitae Patrum*, ch. 10, p. 706.

6 Jonas, *Vitae Sanctorum*, bk 1, ch. 17, p. 181. Ian Wood, 'The *Vita Columbani* and Merovingian Hagiography', *Peritia* 1 (1982), pp. 63–80, notes how animals play a significant part in emphasising the monastic virtue of obedience, p. 67.

7 Gregory of Tours, *Liber Vitae Patrum*, ch. 12, pp. 712–13.

8 See above, Chapter 1, p. 16.

9 This topos will be explored in Chapter 6 below.

Largely, animals needed to be prevented from damaging monastic property, rather than protected. Saint Columban one day found one of his gloves had been carried off by a raven, and declares that the bird would not be able to feed its young if it did not return with its booty. So it did, and 'forgetful of its wild nature, humbly in the sight of all, awaited its punishment'.[10] Later, Jonas tells another such story, this time of a fox with a fatal fondness for ecclesiastical grapes. A monk of Bobbio called Leubardus discovered the fox eating the forbidden fruit, and prohibited it from taking them any longer, but the animal was 'accustomed to live by theft', and upon consuming the grapes once more, died instantly.[11] Given the prior tendency for hagiography to represent humans as animals, it is possible to wonder whether the fox could equally well have been a needy peasant filching monastic property. Either way, this would have functioned as a powerful warning against taking the monks' resources. The miracle may be inspired partly by an earlier story in Gregory the Great's *Dialogues*. Here Boniface of Ferentia, as a boy, miraculously caused the death of a fox who had taken one of his mother's chickens.[12] Pope Gregory's miracle collection, taking the form of a dialogue between himself and his pupil, Peter, was one of the most influential western hagiographic texts for seventh-century and later writers. Thus while some new story variants had already appeared in the western tradition, the stories in the *Dialogues* were crucial to the literary development of the saint and animal story for the rest of the Middle Ages.

At the end of the sixth century, Gregory the Great was already writing with a very substantial inheritance of the Christian hagiographic tradition, but he was selective in his use of earlier themes, and had his own agenda in the recording of saint and animal miracles.[13] Just as for earlier writers, Gregory's immediate audience was the small elite of literate Christians. However, in Gregory the Great's work the presence of the mass of the uneducated is more marked even than in that of Gregory of Tours, and has a palpable effect upon his discussion of miracles. The people had to be guided by the Church, whose role by this time was as firmly political as religious.[14]

Gregory's pastoral concerns for the masses are particularly in evidence in his portrayal of Saint Benedict. The result is a visible compromise between the religion of those of 'infirm' mind and that of Gregory and his elite audience. Hence his pupil Peter needs a clarification at one point: 'What is the reason that in the patronage of martyrs we often times find, that they do not afford so great benefits by their bodies, as they do by other relics. And work greater miracles where they themselves are not

10 Jonas, *Vitae Sanctorum*, bk 1, ch. 15, pp. 178–9.

11 Ibid. bk 2, ch. 25, p. 293.

12 Gregory, *Dialogii*, bk 1, ch. 9, no. 18, pp. 90–3.

13 For the classical, biblical and patristic influences on the book of the *Dialogues* concerning the life of Saint Benedict see Maximillien Mahler, 'Evocations bibliques et hagiographiques dans la Vie de St. Benedict', *Revue bénédictine* 83 (1973), pp. 398–429.

14 For this latter aspect of Gregory's career, as well as the general context of the time, see Claude Dagens, *Saint Gregoire le grand* (Paris 1977) and Jeffrey Richards, *Consul of God: The Life and Times of Gregory the Great* (London 1980).

present?'[15] The story was of a woman being cured when she wandered into Saint Benedict's cave, after his death and burial elsewhere. Gregory replies to Peter's question that such things are necessary in order to reassure the weak faith of simple people. Perhaps people of 'infirm' mind were more interested in local sacred places than in distant official relic cults. The interest of this story is that it is recorded at all; healing miracles are among the most common, and Gregory is not making an important theological point about the nature of his subject's sanctity here. Rather, this miracle must have been of a type widely known, and Gregory had to make a special point of explaining it. As much as Gregory was influenced by the writers who came before him, he may have been using their authority to systematise general beliefs relating to miracles and saints, and bring orally circulating stories within the literary understanding of elite Christians.[16] The *Dialogues* could be seen as a dialectic between miracle legends and Christian intellectuals, as much as an educational exercise between Gregory and his real or fictional pupil.

Nevertheless, it seems clear that the miracle legends were, in Gregory's mind, entirely genuine, and thus had to be explained.[17] At any number of points in the *Dialogues*, after Gregory has told his tale, the pupil asks a question which enables Gregory to systematise a story and mould it into a framework of morals which suits his purpose. After the story is related, Peter or Gregory supplies the biblical quotations to contextualise the story. For example, there is a story of Abbot Equitatus whose rough clothing causes offence but which, miraculously, does not hide his spiritual worth. Gregory, explaining the moral, shows that God alone knows the truth of the heart, quoting Luke 16:15: 'And he said unto them, "Ye are they which justify yourselves before men; but God knoweth your hearts: for that which is highly esteemed among men is abomination in the sight of God"'.[18] Peter often sounds a sceptical note concerning certain miracles, but Gregory admonishes him to have faith, while providing biblical precedents.[19] Where Peter is sceptical, as in

15 Gregory, *Dialogi*, bk 2, ch. 38, nos. 1–5, pp. 246–8. On Gregory's agenda in this passage see Alan Thacker, '*Loca Sanctorum*: The Significance of Place in the Study of the Saints', in *Local Saints and Local Churches in the Early Medieval West*, ed. Alan Thacker and Richard Sharpe (Oxford 2002), pp. 1–43, particularly pp. 19–20.

16 McCready, *Signs of Sanctity*, argues that Gregory was consciously adapting oral stories at many points, see particularly pp. 128–35. This is the context in which to place Peter's scepticism, see ibid. pp. 206–11. A consequence of the adaptation of orally circulating stories is that 'literary' borrowings within the stories may well predate Gregory's accounts: see ibid. pp. 144–53. Thus also the *Dialogues* represent Gregory's *choice* of miracles from the oral pool, and he favours those which show biblical precedent: see ibid. pp. 241–2.

17 As recently as 1976, it seemed necessary to argue why Gregory could not have invented the figure of Benedict and the miracles in book two of the *Dialogues*: Adalbert de Vogué, 'Benoit, modèle de vie spirituelle d'après le deuxième livre des *Dialogues* de Saint Gregoire', *Collectanea Cisterciensia* 38 (1976), pp. 147–57, esp. p. 149.

18 Gregory, *Dialogi*, bk 1, ch. 4, no. 18, p. 54; for Gregory's exegetical and theological interest in the 'innerness' of the spiritual life see Carole Straw, *Gregory The Great: Perfection in Imperfection* (University of California 1988), particularly pp. 213–35.

19 For example, see Gregory, *Dialogi*, bk 2, ch. 22, no. 4, p. 204. Whether the story in question

the healing miracle at Benedict's cave, Gregory's moral seems clear. These may be legends which appeal to the unsophisticated, but God creates them for the benefit of the faith of those 'infirm' ones, not sophisticated men like himself and Peter. The *Dialogues* were clearly meant in the first instance for an educated clerical or monastic audience, rather than the people in general. But Gregory seems to have perceived a gap between the mentality behind miracle stories and the intellectual faith of others like himself. That gap is negotiated by the *Dialogues*.[20]

The systematisation of miracles is thus a recurrent problem. After another story, Peter wants to know whether miracles happen by prayer or by direct command of the living saint. Gregory replies that both are possible and supplies a convenient quotation from Saint John.[21] This problem, of miracles and the mentality of the simple, was a long-term conundrum for hagiographers. Given Gregory's prestige it comes as no surprise when later writers borrow his solutions for their own explanations of the miraculous. Early in the *Dialogues*, Peter wishes to know which holy man effected a resurrection miracle: the one who prayed to the saint or the saint himself. Gregory generously allows that the miracle happened due to the virtues of all: the deceased saint, the living monk and the mother, who was praying for her dead child.[22] Bede has a similar problem in the context of a posthumous miracle of Saint Cuthbert and allows for a similarly triple influence of virtue upon the miracle.[23] Bede's and Gregory's stories are very different and there is no obvious quotation from one to the other, but the abstract structure of the miracles and Bede's answer to the problem are identical. Bede used Gregory to find an authoritative way to explain a story that was circulated enthusiastically, but not explained intellectually. Thus, the animal stories within the *Dialogues* should be considered not just within the context of the literary tradition Gregory inherited. The other context lies in his own attempts to adapt stories which were already known outside the religious elite.[24] Equally, Gregory could choose stories that suited his purpose

actually was a popular legend is unknowable, but the idea that such a story could be was clearly not problematic to Gregory.

[20] The practical purpose of Gregory's *Dialogues* is a problem that has provoked many reactions. Firstly there is a clear contrast between the *Dialogues* and Gregory's other more formal exegetical works. Straw, *Gregory the Great*, p. 6, describes a 'baffling' contrast between the exegetical works and the 'more popular spirit' of the *Dialogues* and homilies on the Gospel, where Gregory uses his 'learned ignorance' to teach his audience. Straw seems to be implying here a less sophisticated audience for these works in comparison to the monastic audience of the exegeses. Francis Clark, *The Pseudo-Gregorian Dialogues* (Leiden 1987), 2 vols, even sees the contrast between Gregory's work as a reason to question the authenticity of the *Dialogues*. However, it seems quite clear that the work was meant for a similar audience as was his exegetical writing, but with a different purpose: as a resource for pastoral work among the general population; see Dagens, *Saint Gregoire*, pp. 45–55 and pp. 198–201, and McCready, *Signs of Sanctity*, pp. 47–57, for discussions of the audience and pastoral intentions of the *Dialogues*.

[21] Gregory, *Dialogi*, bk 2, ch. 30, nos. 2–3, pp. 220–3.

[22] Ibid. bk 1, ch. 2, no. 7, pp. 28–30.

[23] *Vita Cuthberti*, ch. 46, pp. 300–7.

[24] On Gregory's general hagiographic argument see de Vogué, 'Benoit, modèle de vie spirituelle', pp. 147–57, and Marc Doucet, 'Pedagogie et théologie dans le "Vie de Saint Benoit" par Saint Gregoire

and ignore others that were in circulation.

One important topos in earlier hagiography was the 'companionship of animals' theme, which contrasted the disobedience of men with the compliance of animals to God and his saints. The difficulty with this theme is its tendency to question human authority in general, particularly in the context of the legends of the extreme anchorites. Even the authority of Church leaders could be undermined by these legends of independent ascetics whose rejection of human society was total. It is probably for this reason that the theme is muted in the *Dialogues*: Gregory was greatly concerned with issues of Church authority in general, and specifically of abbots within a coenobitic context. One appearance of the theme, concerning a bishop cast to a bear, illustrates how Gregory could nevertheless use the 'companionship' theme to promote ecclesiastical authority. The bear intended to devour the saint, but 'suddenly forgetting its wildness, with a bent neck and humbly lowered head, he began to lick the feet of the bishop: visibly to give all to understand that men have bestial hearts towards the man of God, and the beasts as if hearts of men'.[25] The moral of this story certainly accords with the melancholic message of the anchoritic legends, yet there is a political dimension to the story. This bishop was cast to the bear by a 'false king', the Gothic King Totila, and so the story of the submission of an animal to a dominant saint shames the rapacious secular power.[26] As this is a parable directed at strengthening Church authority, a full lyrical elaboration of the companionship theme does not appear. Another writer with a different purpose might have embellished the theme, but Gregory's story is terse for a reason.

The topos appears in more fully developed form in a monastic story. Here a bear is sent to Florentius, a man of God, 'whilst he lived alone', and shows no trace of wildness, being able to tend the sheep of the 'man of God'. In his great simplicity, Florentius often called the bear his brother.[27] Monks jealous of the holy man, on behalf of their abbot who had not done such miracles, kill the innocent bear and are struck down with leprosy. Gregory allows the 'companionship of animals' theme to appear here, but seems to have turned the story into a parable of the problems of authority and obedience in the monastery. Furthermore, Gregory's and Peter's discussion of the miracle focuses on the gravity of Florentius' sin in cursing the jealous monks. The holy man spent the rest of his life atoning, and Gregory refers to Saint Paul's statement that *maledici* are excluded from the king-

le grand', *Collectanea Cisterciensia* 38 (1976), pp. 158–73. In the general context of Gregory's writings and his conception of the *vir dei*, see Straw, *Gregory the Great*, pp. 66–89.

25 Gregory, *Dialogues*, bk 3, ch. 11, nos. 1–2, pp. 292, on Cerbonius, bishop of Populonium.

26 Totila was, of course, an important political and military figure for a brief period in the mid-sixth century. An account of his career can be found in John Julius Norwich, *Byzantium: The Early Centuries* (London 1988), pp. 234–43, and pp. 248–52. Totila also had an encounter with Saint Benedict, probably in 542: see Philip J. McCann, *St. Benedict* (London 1937), pp. 206–9. See also P. A. Cusack, 'Some Literary Antecedents of the Totila Encounter in the Second Dialogue of Pope Gregory I', *Studia Patristica* 12 (1975), pp. 87–90.

27 Gregory, *Dialogi*, bk 3, ch. 15, nos. 3–6, pp. 316–18.

dom of heaven.[28] It seems unlikely that the original story focused so much on the 'sin' of Florentius, but rather was a story of the ambiguous thaumaturgic power of the hermit, and of his preference for the companionship of animals rather than humans.

Gregory's ambivalence about the companionship theme seems to be confirmed in the story of Saint Benedict and the crow. Gregory's presentation of Benedict shows him as a reforming abbot, yet also possessed of the same grace ascribed to the anchorites. Indeed, Benedict is the quintessential coenobitic holy man. Benedict's difficulties in reforming the monks are thus set against his control of animals. Benedict's pet crow, which habitually took food from the saint's hand, is commanded to dispose of a poisoned loaf. The bird, having to take the bread in its mouth to do so, indicates his difficulty by bouncing up and down on the loaf and flapping its wings. Having been assured by the saint that it would come to no harm, the crow obeys his orders.[29] From one point of view this story could be seen as a reversal of the Elijah topos: the bird is fed by the saint rather than *vice versa*, and removes dangerous food rather than bringing food in a context of privation. Also, of course, there is again the quandary of the saint: animal creation will obey him, because of his purity and grace, yet sinful humanity cannot see this grace.

The poisoned loaf was an attempt by an enemy, in this case a priest, to dispose of Benedict himself. Yet the story lacks the usual moral reflections, particularly in contrast to the story of Florentius and the bear. The bird is described as a 'wild raven', yet Gregory does not describe a reversal of its wild nature, as he did in other stories. In comparison with earlier stories of the affectionate relationship between dominant saint and obedient animal, Gregory makes very little of the 'pet' relationship between Benedict and the bird, yet the image is unmistakable. Perhaps Gregory was working with a famous contemporary legend which he had to include, but removed the elements which clashed with his own conception of the holy man. Thus he concentrated on the theme of obedience, perhaps adding the flourish of the crow's dismay at his task, to the exclusion of any other. Gregory was presenting a picture of a pastoral holy man and could not therefore allow the pessimistic symbolism of a 'companionship of animals' motif to contradict his picture.

The anchorites enjoyed their Edenic relations with animals in a state of isolation from human society. In contrast, Gregory's concern is for the pastoral role of Saint Benedict and his other saints. Their sanctity shines in the world and helps to reconstruct the shattered polity of their time, through their example of Christian holiness. Consequent upon this conception of the saint is his role in preaching within a hierarchical and organised church, and Gregory is therefore ambivalent about holy men being free from the authority of other men, in contrast to the anchoritic legends of the *Vitae Patrum*.[30] Gregory's conception of the holy man may actually

[28] Ibid. ch. 15, nos. 8–10, p. 320; 1 Corinthians 6:10.

[29] Gregory, *Dialogi*, bk 2, ch. 8, nos. 3–8, pp. 162–6.

[30] For a discussion of Gregory's conception of the holy man see Straw, *Gregory the Great*, particularly p. 95, and pp. 73–4 on Gregory's opinion that there are few men for whom pure anchorism is safe, and his concern to place saintly power firmly within the Church's hierarchy.

owe something to Benedict himself, through the latter's *Rule*, where the monk must receive full coenobitical training before embarking on the spiritually dangerous life of the hermit.[31]

Gregory's ambitions for a Church very much involved in ordering the world created an insoluble contradiction between his conception of the role of the holy man and motifs of the saint alone in his own Eden, enjoying the companionship of obedient animals rather than irredeemable humans. The anchoritic legends were evidently popular in hagiographic literature, and there is no reason to suppose they did not circulate in various forms in sixth-century Italy. Gregory's treatment of animal stories is thus an indication that there could be competing versions of certain miracle stories at this time. Other clerics may have held different views of the role of the Church and told these stories differently. Indeed different social groups may have found different versions appealing. In any case, it is clear that if the social purpose of hagiographic agendas changes, then the kind of animal legend recorded will also change.

Gregory's model of the saint and animal story thus bequeathed a strict structure for the genre to later centuries. Firstly, Gregory defined saint and animal topoi around the notion of control of nature, as had Sulpicius Severus. Secondly, for example with Benedict's crow, Gregory forced the anchoritic legends of the 'companionship of animals' topos into the model of sanctity for the western abbot. An ambivalent role for the theme can also be found in Bede's account of Saint Cuthbert, and it is very likely that the English hagiographer was working with Gregory's models in mind.[32] The stories involved have been interpreted as representing Cuthbert's 'kindness' towards animals, but there is clearly a more complex agenda involved in Cuthbert's miraculous discovery of food on one of his journeys.[33]

In the anonymous hagiographer's version of the story, Cuthbert's horse is incidental to the miracle: its role is simply to pull at the thatch of a house, inadvertently revealing the hidden human food. It is Bede's version of the story in which sentimental topoi are employed; Cuthbert refers to the horse as his *comes*, or comrade, and shares the bread with his horse. In these two details Bede draws the story he has inherited from the anonymous author into the patristic tradition: the two topoi are the companionship of animals, and the reversal of animal nature, enabling it to share human food. These two elements are directed less towards a generalised 'kindness' to animals than to the theme of the humanisation of an animal in the presence of the saint. It is of further significance that the horse is a domestic animal: the hierarchical Edenic order is in full view with the horse as a servant in harmony with its kindly

[31] *Rule of Benedict*, ch. 1. Straw, *Gregory The Great*, notes Gregory's ambivalence concerning the anchoritic life, pp. 19–20.

[32] For the notable marks of the *Dialogues* on Bede's Cuthbert in general terms see Colgrave's notes: Colgrave, *Two Lives of Cuthbert*, pp. 341, 347, and 350. See also Paul Meyvaert, 'Bede and Gregory the Great', in Paul Meyvaert, *Benedict, Gregory, Bede and Others* (London 1977), pp. 1–26.

[33] Note Colgrave's comment on these stories, *Two Lives of Cuthbert*, p. 320. The story itself appears in both accounts: anonymous *Vita Cuthberti* bk 1, ch. 6, pp. 70–1, and *Vita Cuthberti*, ch. 5, pp. 168–71, and has already been mentioned above, in the context of the 'Elijah' *topos*, Chapter 2, p. 26.

but absolutely superior master. The miracle is in fact a chance for Bede to illustrate his saint's pastoral qualities and the exchange of obedience and care within a social hierarchy. In both Bede and Gregory, the 'companionship of animals' story concerns the animals' obedience to the saint, or the saint's pastoral virtues, rather than the loneliness of the isolated anchorite.

It is the context of the 'companionship of animals' theme in which the famous story of Saint Cuthbert and the otters should be seen.[34] Cuthbert, at that point a monk of Melrose, steals away from the monastery of Coldingham, which he is visiting, to observe his private ascetic practices away from the dubious atmosphere of that house. The monk who observes the saint sees Cuthbert up to his neck in the sea, 'singing praises'. When the saint emerges from the sea, two otters approach him, warming his feet with their breath and drying him with their fur. The story clearly invokes the Edenic obedience of animals to their true superior, the saint. The service the animals render to the saint lies in contrast to the sinful monk who 'was stricken with deadly fear and weighed down with such distress, that he could scarcely reach home with faltering footsteps; and in the early morning he approached Cuthbert and, stretching himself on the ground, tearfully entreated his pardon for the guilt of his foolish daring'.[35] Of course Cuthbert blessed the otters as they left: the good servants had discharged their duty to their master, the saint. Cuthbert is also forgiving to the implicitly disobedient monk; the story is thus an allegory of the gentle yoke the saint lays upon those who recognise his spiritual authority. At the core of the story, in terms of animal miracles, is the symbolism of divine hierarchy, rather than any mystic connection to or affectionate regard for animals. Bede's concern, as was Gregory's concerning Benedict, was to show the holiness of the pastor, as opposed to the isolated individual virtue of the Egyptian hermits.

Indeed, for a saint so often commended for his kindliness to animals, Cuthbert in his two *Vitae* shows remarkably little unprompted acknowledgement of animal activity. A series of chapters on Cuthbert's phase as a hermit on Farne Island makes the patristic emphasis clear. Two ravens, which had inhabited the island before Cuthbert, tear up the material of the saint's roof for their own use, and are commanded to leave. They return begging forgiveness, each bringing a gift of lard. They are forgiven and allowed to remain in their home.[36] Bede's spin on the anonymous version is to reprise his Gregorian theme at the beginning of this story: thus 'human pride and contumacy are openly condemned by the obedience and humility of the birds'. Cuthbert, according to Bede, recounted this story 'in order to give mankind an example of correction'. Bede adds another miracle, lacking in the anonymous *Vita*, to emphasise the theme of creation's obedience to the saint. Cuthbert drives off the birds which are eating his crop of barley, and they 'thenceforward refrained

[34] Anonymous *Vita Cuthberti* bk 2, ch. 3, pp. 78–83; *Vita Cuthberti*, ch. 10, pp. 188–91. For the native context of the story see Colgrave's notes, pp. 319–20. There are no serious differences between the two versions of the story for the present purpose. For a different, but not incompatible, interpretation of the story, see Benedicta Ward, *The Spirituality of Saint Cuthbert* (Oxford 1992), pp. 10–11.

[35] *Vita Cuthberti*, pp. 190–1. Ward calls the man the 'third otter', *Spirituality*, p. 11.

[36] Anonymous *Vita Cuthberti*, bk 3, ch. 5, pp. 100–3; *Vita Cuthberti*, ch. 20, pp. 222–5.

altogether from attacking his crops'.[37] Of course, the model for this story is Saint Anthony's conflict with the wild animals in his own desert plot, as Bede himself says: 'in driving the birds away from the crops, he followed the example of the most reverend and holy father Anthony, who with one exhortation restrained the wild asses from injuring the little garden that he himself had planted'.[38]

The other major hagiographic work that was certainly influenced by Gregory's agenda is Jonas of Bobbio's account of Saint Columban and his successor abbots. The focus of the animal stories here is firmly on obedience, as an example to the monks of their debt of obedience to the abbot. Nonetheless, most of the main topoi of late antique hagiography are used by Jonas. It should also be noted here that as Columban was Irish, it has sometimes been assumed that his animal miracles represent the influence of Irish hagiography, but in fact nothing in any of these miracles goes beyond patristic precedent, and none of the more specifically Irish motifs appears. However Irish the saint was himself, his *Vita* is continental rather than insular in character. Thus Columban contemplated whether it would be better to be slain by 'the rage of wild beasts' rather than men, since the men would lose their souls because of it, a danger not relevant to the animals.[39] As he was thinking this, twelve wolves appeared around him, but the saint remained steadfast in his obedience to God's will, even as the beasts seized at his clothing. The wolves then wandered back into the woods, the holy man having passed the test. Thus Columban's power over nature is confirmed, and animal miracles are frequent after this incident. Directly after this first story, Jonas inserts another miracle where the saint banishes a bear from a cave, for it never again to return. Most spectacularly, when Columban and his monks are in danger of starvation, a whole flock of birds appears and waits obediently to be gathered as food.[40]

Not all of Columban's animal miracles are quite so brutal in their treatment of wild animals, and indeed the 'companionship of animals' theme appears in a highly developed and lyrical form. The saint was often seen wandering and praying, and calling on wild animals: 'The beasts and birds joyfully played, frisking about him, just as cats frisk about their mistresses'. Squirrels had even been seen coming down from the tops of trees, being taken in the saint's hand, and let 'go into and come out from his bosom'.[41] However much more lyrical this story is than any of Gregory's in the *Dialogues*, the moral remains centred on abbatial authority. Jonas introduces the story warning, 'do not wonder that the beasts and birds thus obeyed the command of God'. Just as in the story of Cuthbert's otters, the 'companionship of animals' theme had been adapted from its Egyptian context, where it signalled alienation from humanity, to a context where it exemplified the perfect social relations of a good monastery where the abbot could rule absolutely. Moreover, the stories of the saints' control of animals had gone beyond the domination over animals expressed

37 *Vita Cuthberti*, ch. 19, pp. 220–3, and Colgrave's note, p. 350.

38 *Vita Cuthberti*, ch. 19, pp. 222–3.

39 Jonas, *Vitae sanctorum*, bk 1, ch. 8, pp. 166–7.

40 Ibid. bk 1, ch. 27, p. 215.

41 Ibid. bk 1, ch. 17, pp. 185–6.

individually, to a claim of property over the 'wilderness' and its resources. The monks were colonising their deserts.

The desert or the wilderness was not always perceived as a place of fruitfulness and abundance. Instead, particular hermitages were portrayed frequently as places of horror and demonic infestation. Most often in the stories of the Egyptian Fathers, it seems they stayed that way, but one exception was to influence medieval hagiography profoundly. Saint Anthony's little plot in the desert is the first appearance of a major theme in hagiography, the colonisation and transformation of places of horror: 'he came to a deserted fort, through time and solitude, full of poisonous creatures, in which, making himself into a new guest, he lived. Immediately at his coming, the monstrous crowd of serpents, as if suffering persecution, fled.'[42] This story is obviously parallel to the many stories of saints driving away snakes from their chosen hermitages. Nevertheless, the theme is developed beyond the message of the saint's power over individual animals. Here the saint colonises a place, turning it from a place of horror to a place of sanctity.

Once Anthony flees to the inner mountain, and makes the garden that provides him with bread, there takes place the second miracle which laid the basis for the 'colonisation' topos. Anthony embraces his new hermitage, as if it were offered by God, with its 'fountain of sweet water' and its date palms.[43] But soon, to avoid dependence upon the brothers who send bread out to him, he begins to grow crops to make his own bread. The wild animals who try to eat his crops are given a saintly speech similar to Cuthbert's. Both saints ask the animals why they do this damage to the saint's plot.[44] Bede, in modelling Saint Cuthbert's period as a hermit on the adventures of Saint Anthony, conflates the latter's two main periods as a hermit. In Anthony's first period, his hermitage is essentially a place of horror, inhabited by the snakes he banishes. In the second, a place he loves immediately, there is a fountain and a date palm, and there he curbs the attentions of the wild animals. Cuthbert drives the demons from Farne, and by a succession of miracles transforms it from a place of horror to a place which human labour can cultivate.[45]

It may be that Bede was working directly from the account of Saint Anthony in his description of Cuthbert's colonisation of Farne, but it is also possible that he was influenced by Gregory of Tours. In the story of Saint Caluppa, Gregory also seems to conflate the two hermitages of Saint Anthony in a seamless story of the transformation of a place of horror. Caluppa found a refuge so remote and difficult that 'even wild beasts can only get there with some trouble. He put together a small oratory, where, as he used to tell us with tears, snakes often used to fall on his head while he was praying, and twist around his neck, filling him with terror.'[46] The saint is able to resist his fear, but the devil, not giving up that easily, sends two enormous

42 *Vita Antonii*, ch. 11, col. 133.

43 Ibid. ch. 24, col. 148.

44 *Vita Antonii*, ch. 25, cols. 148–9; *Vita Cuthberti*, ch. 19, pp. 222–3.

45 See *Vita Cuthberti*, chs. 17–21, and compare with anonymous *Vita Cuthberti*, bk 3, chs. 1–5.

46 Gregory of Tours, *Liber Vitae Patrum*, ch. 11, no. 1, pp. 709–10; trans. James, *Life of the Fathers*, pp. 77–8.

dragons in response. The saint, although terrified, says the Lord's Prayer to himself, and, gradually recovering his confidence, is able to banish the dragons and the snakes alike. This place of horror is thus transformed, as neither dragon nor snake ever appear again, and now fish in the nearby river come to the saint by God's will. Moreover, since it was difficult for water to be brought to him from the monastery, Caluppa asks God to provide, and instantly a spring appears in the rocks, just as it would do for Bede's Cuthbert on Farne Island.[47] The stories of Anthony, Gregory of Tours's Caluppa and Bede's Cuthbert are the major early examples of the colonising topos, which would reappear in many other later saints' *vitae*.

In the twelfth century, the colonising theme becomes a pervasive mentality in the hands of writers from the new Cistercian order of monks. In the *Vita Prima* of Bernard of Clairvaux, the colonisation ideal is spelt out: 'Clairvaux . . . had once been a hide-out of robbers and was formerly known as the valley of Wormwood . . . It was in that place of horror and desolation that these righteous men established themselves and turned a den of iniquity into God's temple and a house of prayer.'[48] In a traveller's description of Clairvaux, all of the harmony and obedience of nature to human needs and the aesthetic beauty of creation are held up as a proof of the Cistercians' grace and ability to recreate a kind of Eden: the sight of the place 'brings to mind the heavenly bliss to which we all aspire, for the smiling face of the earth with its many hues feasts the eyes and breathes sweet scents into the nostrils'.[49] This lyricism has been interpreted as expressing a mystical love of nature.[50] However, it should be seen within the context of the colonisation topos: what is valued here is not nature in and of itself, but the impact of human labour upon nature. Nature was not itself admired in the patristic tradition, where cultivated land, not wild landscape, had aesthetic value.[51] This same mentality seems to colour the Cistercian rhetoric of nature.

There are other animal stories that frequently form a part of the colonisation theme. One of the most common is the story of the monastic founder who, while labouring to bring new land under the plough, employs wild animals as if they were domesticated oxen.[52] In the Cistercian Jocelyn of Furness's *Vita* of Saint Kentigern, the saint, in 'sowing sand' and bringing forth a crop of wheat, puts a wolf and a stag under one

47 Gregory of Tours, *Liber Vitae Patrum*, ch. 11, no. 2, pp. 710–11.

48 *Vita Prima Sancti Bernardi Clarevallensis*, *Liber I*, PL 185 (1), cols. 225–68, at ch. 5, no. 25, cols. 241–2; trans. Pauline Matarasso, *The Cistercian World* (London 1993), p. 26.

49 *Descriptio Positionis seu Situationis Monasterii Clarae-Vallensis*, PL 185, cols. 570–4, at cols. 571–2; trans. Matarasso, *Cistercian World*, p. 290.

50 See Sorrell, *Francis and Nature*, pp. 29–31. Note however that Giles Constable, *The Reformation of the Twelfth Century* (Cambridge 1996), pp. 140–2, puts such 'mysticism' in the context of both Bernard's anti-scholasticism and the Edenic divine order.

51 David S. Wallace-Hadrill, *The Greek Patristic View of Nature* (Oxford 1968), particularly pp. 87–91; also Jean Leclercq, *The Love of Learning and the Desire for God*, trans. Catherine Misrahi (London 1961), pp. 164–5, emphasises the role of labour in Cistercian nature rhetoric.

52 For references to early medieval examples of this topos, see Montalembert, *Monks of the West*, II, pp. 212–27.

yoke of a plough.[53] Jocelyn combined the motif of the taming of wild animals with the idea of the transformation of a desert, the sandy soil, into a garden for holy monks. As such this is a very developed expression of the 'colonisation' theme.

Among English hermits, there are two related stories involving Robert of Knaresborough, who died in 1218 and whose first *Vita* was probably written by a Cistercian. Robert went to the local lord asking for a cow to provide for his needs and those of the indigent for whom Robert cultivated his land. The lord had a 'certain most wild cow' in his forest, which he gave to Robert. The hermit dealt with this ungracious gift by placing his arms about the wild animal and leading it away, 'as if it were a most gentle lamb'.[54] This was not the end to Robert's troubles with animals, however. Certain wild stags 'invaded' his fields, 'trampling and consuming' his crops. The same lord gave Robert permission to do what he liked with the wild animals. So Robert chased the wild stags, also compared to 'gentle lambs', into a barn. Thereafter Robert harnessed the stags and put them to the plough as if they were cows.[55] As so often, Robert's miracle is a reproof to the powers of secular society, specifically a lord in this case, showing how much more fruitful the wilderness can be when it is cultivated within monastic conditions, with proper faith in the providence of God. The topos in general emphasised the superiority of religious over secular society.

An original example of the colonising theme, again in a Cistercian context, is Caesarius of Heisterbach's story of the obedience of the storks, in his early-thirteenth-century *Dialogue on Miracles*.[56] At the house of Cîteaux itself, 'where is the head of our Order, many storks nest. This is permitted by the brothers of the Order, because by them not only the monastery but all the places around are cleared of foul worms.'[57] The storks are only permitted at Cîteaux because they aid the monks in turning the place from a desert place of horror, full of worms, to a place of Edenic

53 *Vita Kentigerni*, ch. 22, pp. 193–5; trans. p. 66. Jocelyn's *Vita* was based on earlier *vitae*, which are now lost. Jocelyn was therefore probably adapting an earlier story, although his treatment still shows the Cistercian approach to such material. See Chapter 1, p. 12.

54 '*Vitae Sancti Roberti Knaresburgensis, Vita Recentior*', ed. Paul Grosjean, in *Analecta Bollandiana* 57 (1939), pp. 375–400, ch. 15, pp. 389–90. Although this second *Vita* was not written by the Cistercians, it follows closely the surviving parts of the original, probably Cistercian, *Vita*: '*Vitae Sancti Roberti Knaresburgensis, Vitae Antiquioris Fragmenta*', ed. Paul Grosjean, in *Analecta Bollandiana* 57 (1939), pp. 365–74.

55 *Vita Roberti Recentior*, ch. 16, pp. 390–1.

56 Caesarius of Heisterbach, *Dialogus Miraculorum*, ed. Joseph Strange (London 1851, reprinted 1966), 2 vols, at II, bk 10, ch. 58, pp. 256–7; *Dialogue on Miracles*, trans. Henry Scott and Charles Bland (London 1929), bk 10, ch. 58, pp. 218–19. For a detailed discussion of Caesarius' sources, oral and literary, and his themes and organising principles, see Brian P. McGuire, 'Written Sources and Cistercian Inspiration in Caesarius of Heisterbach', *Analecta Cisterciensia* 35 (1979), pp. 227–82, and 'Friends and Tales in the Cloister: Oral Sources in Caesarius of Heisterbach's *Dialogus Miraculorum*', *Analecta Cisterciensia* 36 (1980), pp. 167–247.

57 'immundis vermibus'; this choice of words contains a notion of spiritual uncleanliness. The notion of an Eden, purified of the sin symbolised by the worms, would have been obvious to Caesarius and his audience.

beauty and obedience. The storks emphasise the degree of their obedience to the monks by flying up to the prior at migration time, clearly asking for permission to depart, 'that they might not be thought ungrateful for the hospitality granted them'. The prior gives his permission by blessing the birds. In the master's discussion of this miracle he notes that the obedience of the birds puts men to shame, quoting Jeremiah: 'The turtle dove and the swallow and the stork watched for the time of his coming; but my people knoweth not the judgement of the Lord its God'.[58] Caesarius no doubt intended sophisticated readers to understand this story as a demonstration of the Cistercian's complete consummation of the monastic ideal. The Edenic conception of monks and animals had reached its peak in the Cistercian literature of the twelfth and thirteenth centuries.

All the major themes arising from the early hagiographic tradition have now been explored, but one important issue remains, which is the role, or the lack of it, of female saints. The Edenic conception of the saint and nature may be inherently inhibiting towards that type of thaumaturgic display by female saints, as it was Adam to whom obedience was primarily due. Moreover, in a social context, it might be assumed that women in late-antique or early-medieval society were not in a position to live on their own in the desert or the wilderness, and so would in a practical sense be shut out of the locus for saintly and animal interaction, or the plausible creation of such stories. In fact, while female ascetics appear to have been largely an urban phenomenon, there were some female hermits in Egypt. Palladius told of one *amma* who lived in a tomb like Saint Anthony, although this was a fully enclosed space.[59] Overall, there were no absolute bars, of either a theological or social nature, to female sanctity having power over nature. Thus the apocryphal *Acts of Paul* has a fierce lioness defend Thecla from the other beasts in the arena.[60] It is perhaps notable that the saint and animal are gender-matched here, but this is nonetheless an early example of female sanctity benefiting from the Edenic principle. Curiously, however, in the early *passio* story of Perpetua and Felicitas, it is a male martyr who is defended from the beasts, while this particular aspect of the miraculous seems to be denied to the female Christians.[61]

[58] Jeremiah 8:7. Sorrell, *Francis and Nature*, p. 31, interprets this story as showing 'a general feeling of affinity with the rest of creation', and being comparable to Saint Francis's feeling for nature. In the light of the story's obvious links with topoi of domestication, colonisation and obedience of creation, it seems hard to sustain Sorrell's interpretation. The other animal stories in Caesarius, which surround the story of the storks, give no support to Sorrell's argument: see *Dialogus*, bk 10, chs. 57, 59, 62, 64, and also bk 1, ch. 15, p. 22, and bk 5, ch. 17, p. 337, for animals in various, usually antagonistic, relations with humans. McGuire considers some of these stories to be secular folklore rather than monastic stories: 'Friends and Tales', p. 239. The story of the storks is unusual among Caesarius' animal stories in having a 'cloister' context.

[59] *Heraclidis Paradisus*, PL 74, cols. 251–342, at ch. 1, col. 255; see also Joan M. Petersen, *Handmaids of the Lord: Holy Women in Late Antiquity and the Early Middle Ages* (Kalamazoo 1996), pp. 31–3.

[60] *Apocryphal New Testament*, ed. Elliott, p. 370; the story of Paul and Thecla is a text which is generally associated with an important and wider role for women in early Christian communities than later became the norm: Bart D. Ehrman, *Lost Christianities* (Oxford 2003), pp. 33–7.

[61] *Passio SS. Perpetuae et Felicitatis*, in Musurillo, *The Acts of the Christian Martyrs*, pp. 126–7.

Among the hagiographic accounts of female ascetics from the east, there is an account where animals do appear, namely the *Vita* of Mary the harlot, written *c.*600. This story was written using the legends of the extreme anchorites, but in order to make salvation more accessible the legend was based upon a very great sinner. If the heroism of the desert fathers made it appear almost impossible for ordinary Christians to achieve grace, the example of Mary the harlot showed that salvation was truly open to all.[62] As an inhabitant of the deepest desert, Mary, once an enthusiastic prostitute, was now a naked anchorite, entirely beyond the sight of any human, until the holy man Zossima happened upon her. Her physical beauty had long since been destroyed by the desert, and her body is blackened and shrivelled as if she were a walking corpse, although Zossima thought initially that she was a demonic phantasm sent to tempt him.[63] In a sense Mary's ordeal simply parallels the extremes of asceticism in which the male anchorites engaged, although the emphasis on the destruction of the sexual body is much more marked. She is also afforded miraculous powers of clairvoyance and the ability to walk across the waters of the river Jordan.[64] Nonetheless, it is only at her death that animals appear, in marked contrast to the desert fathers. A lion comes and licks her dead feet and helps Zossima to bury her body.[65] Thus the wild does serve this female saint, but only after her death: she is apparently not able to achieve the Edenic state while still alive.

Mary of Egypt may represent a sort of limit beyond which patristic women generally could not go in their miracles. This is illustrated by the late-antique story of Melania the younger, who had an estate where there was a pool, on one side of which there was a wood in which 'various kinds of beasts and game' made their home while bathing there.[66] This lyrical image is not, however, an opportunity for an Edenic topos to illustrate the qualities of the holy woman; rather the place affords the devil the opportunity to tempt her to avoid giving away her wealth. On another occasion, Melania advises sailors during a great storm simply to commit the ship to the prevailing winds, and therefore to God's will.[67] While a male saint might have demonstrated a thaumaturgic ability to lead the ship out of the storm, Melania's *virtus* here is essentially passive.

Late Antiquity did not bequeath a model of female sanctity to the early-medieval West, and subsequent *vitae* are very various in form for that reason.[68] Nonetheless, the social power of aristocratic women seems to allow for a greater range

[62] *Vita Sanctae Mariae Aegypticae Meretricis*, PL 73, cols. 671–90; see also Lynda L. Coon, *Sacred Fictions: Holy Women and Hagiography in Late Antiquity* (Philadelphia 1997), pp. 84–94.

[63] *Vita Mariae Aegypticae*, ch. 7, col. 677, and ch. 11, col. 679.

[64] Ibid. ch. 22, col. 687.

[65] Ibid. cols. 688–9.

[66] Gerontius, *Vitae Sanctae Melaniae Junioris*, in *Analecta Bollandiana* 8 (1889), pp. 16–23, at bk 1, ch. 18, p. 33.

[67] Ibid. bk 2, ch. 2, pp. 42–3.

[68] Julia M. H. Smith, 'The Problem of Female Sanctity in Carolingian Europe c.780–920', *Past and Present* 146 (1995), pp. 3–37, at p. 12.

of miracles, including the occasional animal miracle. The second *Vita* of the sixth-century Merovingian queen and monastic founder Radegunde, written by the nun Baudonivia, makes the central claim that 'birds and beasts rightly obeyed Radegunde, for she never neglected to obey the teaching of the Lord'.[69] This claim is illustrated by the story of a 'night bird' who hoots during the chanting of the offices. Radegunde sends one of the nuns to order it to depart without returning, while making the sign of the cross over it. This banishment of the bird as a demonic pest does represent a certain power, but also perhaps a certain conservatism in the choice of miracle type. Nature is sent away, so that the nuns remain undisturbed within their enclosure. Another time some sailors on an important voyage for Radegunde herself are caught in a storm, and appeal to heaven in her name for aid. A dove then comes and circles around the ship, and one of the queen's servants is able to pull three feathers from its tail, which when dipped in the sea, calm the storm.[70] Radegunde thus does demonstrate some power over nature, but it is perhaps significant that the animal miracle appears in an account written by a woman, rather than the earlier *Vita* by Venantius Fortunatus.[71]

Possibly in imitation of Radegunde, the seventh-century *Vita* of the Merovingian Saint Gertrude has a shipping miracle where the saint is invoked by sailors, but this time to drive away a sea monster.[72] The probably early-sixth-century *Vita* of Saint Genovefa of Paris contains a number of wonder-working stories, where the saint rights some ships in danger of capsizing, saves a harvest from a rain storm and quells a storm at sea, yet there are no animal miracles as such.[73] Thus it is possible for female saints to demonstrate power over animals in the early-medieval West, but it is the exception rather than the rule. In fact, the majority of Carolingian *vitae* of female saints lack miracles altogether, let alone animal stories, and those miracles that do occur are focused on the internal problems of female religious houses, rather than being engaged in the wider world.[74]

There is one major exception to the cloistered confinement of early-medieval female saints, and this is Saint Brigit of Kildare. There are abundant animal and nature miracles in her tradition, from the earliest accounts onwards, and these will be discussed in the next chapter. However, it is useful to comment here on the impact of Saint Brigit's legend. Within Ireland, it seems that Brigit's wonder-working allows subsequent female saints to exercise power over nature also. Thus the originally eighth-century *Vita* of Saint Samthann, although existing now only in

[69] Baudonivia, *Vita Sanctae Radegundis*, MGH SSRM 2 (1888), ed. B. Krusch, pp. 377–95, at ch. 19, pp. 390–1; trans. Joan M. Peterson, *Handmaids of the Lord*, pp. 400–24, at p. 419.

[70] Baudonivia, *Vita Sanctae Radegundis*, ch. 17, pp. 389–90.

[71] Venantius Fortunatus, *Vita Sanctae Radegundis*, MGH SSRM 2 (1888), ed. B. Krusch, pp. 364–77. Venantius does include a shipping miracle, which Baudonivia may have used as a basis for her more developed story, at ch. 31, p. 374.

[72] *Vita Sanctae Geretrudis*, MGH SSRM 2 (1888), ed. B. Krusch, pp. 447–74, at ch. 5, pp. 458–9.

[73] *Vita Sanctae Genovefae Virginis*, *AASS* 3 January, pp. 137–53, at ch. 7, no. 39, p. 141, and ch. 10, nos. 49–50, p. 142, respectively.

[74] Smith, 'Female Sanctity', pp. 29–31.

a late form, does include a terse note that 'this virgin through the power of her prayers restrained beasts in a local lake. Prior to this they were dangerous to men and livestock, but afterward they harmed none.'[75] Another time, Samthann gave a leper a cow and a calf, which were miraculously replaced, in a type of miracle common in Irish hagiography.[76] The late *Vita* of Saint Monenna, again probably based on an early text, also reproduces some miracles common in the Irish tradition, resurrecting a calf that had been eaten, and another time compelling a wolf to bring back a calf which it had taken from the pasture.[77]

These Irish examples are true animal miracles, equal in nature to the male Irish animal miracles, in a way that the continental examples seen thus far are not. The appearance of such miracles in the Irish *vitae* can be explained partly by the different social structure of Ireland in the seventh century. The household-centred pattern of property and social hierarchy probably afforded women a more prominent public role in the seventh century, in comparison with the more developed aristocratic societies of the continent. Also the influence of Saint Brigit on later Irish hagiography allowed this initial pattern to survive even as a true class society took shape. Once a female saint had been allowed such powers, it was easier for similar miracles to appear in later saints' *vitae*. Yet, while Saint Brigit's legend spread widely and robustly outside Ireland it apparently had a minimal influence upon continental female saints, so literary precedent is itself not enough to establish a tradition.[78]

In the early Middle Ages then, despite the exception of Ireland, female sanctity was not much associated with power over nature. This seems to start to change in the tenth and eleventh centuries. The tenth-century German *Vita* of the Ottonian Queen Mathilde (d. 968), while modelled on Venantius Fortunatus' account of Radegunde, adds a miracle of control over a doe which had come into the cloister.[79] This is a very rare thaumaturgic act in Ottonian female hagiography, and it is notable that the miracle is within the settled cloister rather than the wilderness, where male saints are able to demonstrate their power. Later, Goscelin of Saint Bertin in his *Vita* of Saint Edith, a tenth-century Anglo-Saxon nun of Wilton, describes her garden enclosure, where wild animals from doves to wolves and bears live in docility, and are fed by hand by the saint.[80] This is the full Edenic topos, expressed for possibly the first time in an account of a female saint. Goscelin compares this garden

[75] Charles Plummer, *Vitae Sanctorum Hiberniae* (Oxford 1910), 2 vols: II, *Vita Sanctae Samthanne*, pp. 253–61, at ch. 8, p. 255; translation in Thomas Head, *Medieval Hagiography* (London 2001). p. 104. On the dating of this life see ibid. pp. 97–101.

[76] *Vita Samthanne*, ch. 3, p. 254.

[77] *Vita S. Darercae seu Moninnae Abbatissae*, in Heist, pp. 83–95, at ch. 15, pp. 87–8, and ch. 22, p. 90.

[78] Smith, 'Female Sanctity', p. 13, note 33.

[79] See Patrick Corbet, *Les saints ottoniens: sainteté dynastique, sainteté royale et sainteté feminine autour de l'an mil* (Sigmaringen 1986), p. 35 and pp. 142–4.

[80] Goscelin of Saint Bertin, *Vita Sanctae Edithae Virginis*, ed. Andre Wilmart, in *Analecta Bollandiana* 56 (1938), pp. 5–101 and 265–307, at ch. 10, pp. 65–8.

'solitude' to the hermitages of the desert fathers, Saint Anthony in particular, and emphasises the traditional wonder that all these ferocious creatures submit to the saint. Nonetheless, Edith's miracle does carry a whiff of the patristic reluctance to allow female sanctity out in the world: it is enacted in the privacy of the cloister, unlike the open-air miracles of Saint Brigit and her Irish compatriots.

Nonetheless, Edith begins to look less like an exception, and more the start of a significant shift. In the eleventh century, the 'Vulgate Legend' of Saint Catherine of Alexandria appears; while imprisoned, the martyr is deprived of food, so a white dove from heaven brought her celestial food.[81] Thus the Elijah topos is allowed to a female saint. The late legend of Saint Martha and the dragon has also been discussed earlier.[82] Seemingly late also is the more famous story of Saint Margaret of Antioch who, having been swallowed by a dragon, makes the sign of the cross thus bursting the dragon apart from inside.[83] An eleventh-century account of the posthumous miracles of Saint Faith of Conques tells the story of the girl saint resurrecting a donkey.[84] The probably eleventh-century *Vita* of the Anglo-Saxon Saint Milburga recounts a story where the saint finds great flocks of wild geese eating the corn of her fields. She commands them to leave, and the geese never return or damage her crops again.[85] This later miracle in particular certainly does not conform to patristic or Carolingian models of female sanctity: the saint's *virtus* is exercised over the animal world in an economic and public context. Eleventh- and twelfth-century accounts of Saints Wereburga, Amelburga, Opportuna and Pharailde include miracles similar to Milburga's that equally shatter all previous models of female sanctity, beyond that of the Irish *vitae*.[86]

Given the absence of hagiographic precedent for this apparent explosion of female thaumaturgy, some other reason must be found. One explanation might lie in the changing social roles, purposes and inspiration for hagiography in the eleventh and twelfth centuries. It is likely that the influence of popular culture on hagiography drove this surge of female holy power, as will be explored further in Chapter 5. Another, apparently simpler, explanation would be to claim that Irish hagiography had become influential in the eleventh century. This is plausible, but raises the question of why the legend of Saint Brigit, for example, had not been influential outside Ireland between the seventh and eleventh centuries. In either case, before considering those miracles of male and female saints of the eleventh and

[81] *Seinte Katerine*, ed. S. R. T. O. d'Ardenne and E. J. Dobson, Early English Text Society ss 7 (Oxford 1981), pp. 144–203, at p. 186.

[82] See above, Chapter 1, p. 6.

[83] See Head, *Medieval Hagiography*, pp. 675–708, for three English accounts of the legend, and *Acta Sanctae Margaritae seu Marinae*, *AASS* 20 July, pp. 33–9, at p. 37, where the miraculous swallowing and bursting is absent and the dragon merely a diabolical illusion.

[84] *Liber Miraculorum Sancte Fides*, ed. Luca Robertini (Selestat 1994), pp. 91–2.

[85] The *Vita* of Milburga only survives in John of Tynemouth's fourteenth-century summary: see *Nova Legenda Anglie*, ed. Carl Horstman (Oxford 1901), 2 vols, at II, *De Sancta Milburga Virgine*, pp. 188–92, and for the relevant miracle, p. 191.

[86] These miracles will be discussed in Chapter 5 below.

twelfth centuries which seem to depart from hagiographic tradition, the particular tradition of the saint and animal story in Ireland needs to be considered.

CHAPTER 4

The Irish Variant

THE western Christian tradition has come under criticism in recent times for having been interested in nature only as a foil to theology, an approach which has been thought to allow the growth of a destructive anti-environmental culture. Our present troubles are, in this argument, at least partly the result of a theology which regarded the natural world as fallen, and essentially separate from a transcendent God. Irish, or 'Celtic', culture has often been held to be the exception, and learning from it could restore something lost to western culture. Something in the spirituality of Ireland or its Celtic culture attuned its saints and writers to a more appreciative sense of the place of nature in God's Creation.[1] A famous example of Irish natural spirituality is the probably tenth-century poem in praise of a hermit's hermitage:

> . . . I have a hut in the wood, none knows it but my Lord;
> An ash tree this side, a hazel on the other, a great tree on a
> mound encloses it . . .
> Tame swine lie down around it, goats, young pigs, wild swine,
> tall deer, does, a badger's brood.
> Peaceful, in crowds, a grave host of the countryside, an assembly at my house;
> Foxes come to the wood before it – it is delightful.[2]

This can be read, and it has been, as an example of an author taking 'nature' as a 'subject' rather than an 'object': appreciating nature for its own characteristics rather than for purposeful human needs.[3] This may well be the case, but the interpretation ignores the contemporary theological context. The theme of this piece is the earthly paradise, where there is no antagonism between the social (human) and the wild. The hermitage is a miraculously peaceful Eden, and a contrast to the sin and violence of human society as well as of the unblessed wilderness. It is not a celebration of nature as it is, but as it is idealised in God's grace. Human society

[1] A recent defence of the 'green credentials' of Irish Christianity can be found in Mary Low, 'The Natural World in Early Irish Christianity: An Ecological Footnote', in *Celts and Christians*, ed. Mark Atherton (Cardiff 2002), pp. 169–203.

[2] Translation of the 'Hermit's Hut', otherwise known as 'Marbán's Hermitage', from Kenneth Hurlstone Jackson, *A Celtic Miscellany* (London 1951), pp. 68–70.

[3] See Low, 'The Natural World', p. 190: 'it can be seen as a celebration of the natural world in all its beauty and biodiversity'.

and the effects of the human Fall on the world are actually very much the subject of the poem. In this sense, there is not a peculiarly 'Irish' spirituality evidenced here: rather it is a skilful adaptation of mainstream western Christian themes to the vernacular literature.

Just as standard Christian themes lie at the basis of this poem, early Irish hagiography was fully a part of the existing hagiographic tradition, and was clearly concerned to show Ireland's saints reproducing all the essential characteristics of the established Christian saints. However this does not mean that Irish hagiography needed to be a carbon copy of existing literature. It had to be adapted to Irish conditions, and it had to be convincing to an Irish audience, even if the immediate audience of the Latin hagiography is assumed to be clerical. One striking difference between the Irish stories and the early hagiographic tradition is the great number of domesticated animals that feature. Cogitosus' Brigit in early childhood is required to perform numerous female labouring tasks 'in the same way as other women were required to do'. Of course, in other accounts, Brigit is an illegitimate daughter of a bonded woman, and in that situation her labours would not therefore be remarkable.[4] Nonetheless, Cogitosus, in suppressing Brigit's illegitimacy, must be assuming that it remained plausible for the daughter of the head of the household to have to perform such duties as churning butter, at least when being fostered. Her father Dubtach and mother Broicsech are 'Christian and noble parents', according to Cogitosus, so the fact that Brigit should need to churn butter and milk cows is a strong indication of the household rather than class character of the Irish economy in the seventh century.

The butter Brigit makes she gives away to the poor, so when called to present the results of her labours to her 'mother', Brigit is 'in dread'. Rescued by God in this instance, the other miracles recounted by Cogitosus early in the *Vita*, although not necessarily early in Brigit's life, are based upon the miraculous supply of food, and her power over nature is placed firmly within a female division of labour. She is able to provision a group of bishops by milking the same cow three times in a day. Although Cogitosus has removed this story from any clear context, the implication here is that while Brigit is directly responsible for hospitality, she is again also required to perform labour herself.[5] In one sense these miracles are firmly within the traditional Christian view of the saint and nature, in that the problems of scarcity in a fallen world are overturned. However, these are not stories, as told by Cogitosus, that would have been at all appropriate to a Merovingian abbess. Indeed, it is a sign of the sanctity of Queen Balthild, widow of Clovis II, that when in the

4 Cogitosus, *Vita Sanctae Brigidae*, *AASS* 1 February, pp. 129–41, at ch. 1, no. 4, p. 129, and 'Cogitosus: Life of Saint Brigit', trans. Sean Connolly and J.-M. Picard, *Journal of the Royal Society of Antiquaries of Ireland* 117 (1987), pp. 5–27, at ch. 1, p. 13 (hereafter Cogitosus and trans. Brigit, respectively). The story of Brigit's illegitimate birth does not appear in Cogitosus, but first in the probably eighth-century *Vita I*. Nonetheless, if *Vita I* was based on an earlier *Life*, that earlier *Life* probably carried the story, and so Cogitosus is suppressing the information in his *Vita*.

5 Cogitosus, no. 8, p. 136; trans. Brigit, ch. 5, p. 15.

monastery of Chelles, she engages in lowly work, such as cleaning the latrines.[6] For Saint Brigit the work itself is not a sign of sanctity to Cogitosus. Further, the triple-milking motif seems most likely drawn from Irish secular stories.[7] It is noteworthy that while Cogitosus does not indicate anything unusual in Brigit's milking of the cow, a much later Irish vernacular *Vita* does seem to single that out for attention, noting 'Brigit herself milked the cows'.[8] The social structure of Ireland had changed by the time of this later *Vita*, and it was now surprising for an elite figure to engage directly in labour.

Thus the social context of Ireland affected the transmission of hagiographic themes to the Irish tradition. It is noteworthy also that while very many miracles in the European tradition emphasise the saint's disruption and reversal of normal relations between humans and nature, Cogitosus' presentation of Brigit here has a different theme altogether. Despite her miracles, Brigit fitted into the sexual division of labour, and was in no danger of disrupting the gender hierarchies of society through her saintly power. In distributing butter to the poor, she had indeed usurped the role of her mother and father, but God's grace here allows this usurpation to be covered up, and social hierarchy within the household is restored. Brigit miraculously *performs* female functions, she is not disrupting them. This is surely a deliberate part of Cogitosus' portrayal of Brigit: whatever may follow in the *Vita*, his saint is not to be seen as a danger to a crucial part of the social system.

Saint Columba of Iona naturally lends his fruitful blessing to the cattle herds of those giving him hospitality, in a miraculous *quid pro quo*.[9] Columba himself is not required to engage in labour, but his closeness to the daily tasks of agricultural labour is shown often. Columba is called upon by a young man to bless a pail of milk. It turns out that the young man has been negligent in his work, allowing a devil to hide in the bottom of the pail.[10] Of course, in a sense this story simply shows that the monks of Iona lived up to the monastic ideal that monks should live from their own labour. Nonetheless, western hagiography rarely shows such close interest in the dairy work of male monks in particular. Other stories show a similarly unusual proximity to the regular tasks of agricultural life, even highlighting the occasional difficulties of reconciling strict monastic principles with the rough nature of such work. Columba is asked to bless a knife which had actually been intended to be used for slaughtering cattle. The contradiction is revealed when it is found that the knife cannot now be used to kill. When Columba finds out the purpose of the knife

6 *Vita Sanctae Balthildis*, MGH SSRM 2 (1888), ed. B Krusch, pp. 475–508, at ch. 11, pp. 496–7.

7 Felim Ó Briain, 'Saga Themes in Irish Hagiography', in *Féilscríbhinn Torna*, ed. Séamus Pender (Cork 1947), pp. 33–42, argues that triple milking miracles, of which the earliest is in Cogitosus, were probably adapted *by* saga writers from hagiography, p. 38. This might be the case but it raises the question of the origin of the motif. It did not come from patristic hagiography.

8 *Life of Brigit*, in *Lives of the Saints from the Book of Lismore*, ed. Whitley Stokes (Oxford 1899), pp. 182–200, at line 1685, p. 197.

9 *Adomnan's Life of Columba*, ed. A. O. and M. O. Anderson (Edinburgh 1961), bk 2, chs. 20–1, pp. 366–71.

10 Ibid. bk 2, ch. 16, pp. 358–61.

he declares, 'I trust in my Lord . . . that the implement I have blessed will not harm man or beast'.[11]

In a society such as Ireland's the unit of production would largely have been the household. Most labour was owed to the head of the family, and affective relations were thus closely bound up with productive relations. The holy monastery, as a model of the nearest to perfection human society could come, reflected those relations even down to the animals. Thus, a white horse, which had been a loyal workhorse, approached Columba as he was dying and 'put its head in his bosom, inspired, as I believe, by God, before whom every living creature has understanding . . . it began to mourn, and like a human being to let tears fall freely on the lap of the saint, and foaming much, to weep aloud'.[12] While this story could find echoes in patristic stories of affection shown by animals to saints, the remarkable aspect of this story is precisely that it is a domestic animal that is shown with human traits in the presence of the saint, where the hagiographic tradition had normally stressed miraculous emotion being shown by deadly wild animals. The intention of Adomnán's story here is rather to stress the bonds of love and perfect harmony of the productive family within the saint's realm, in no doubt stark contrast to normal secular households. It is not *nature* that is being depicted here, it is *society*.

It might be objected that Brigit, being female, is an exceptional case, and Columba does not directly engage in agricultural labour. However, among a group of *vitae* that are very probably of eighth-century date, there are a number of further examples of elite individuals having to engage in agricultural labour as a matter of course.[13] In the *Vita* of Saint Cainnech, as a boy he is put to work along with the son of a king in minding a herd.[14] Then, put in charge of two wild oxen, he is able, miraculously, to tame them.[15] Saint Luguid is sent to fetch a pail of milk, but his horse stumbles and the milk pot is smashed. Fortunately, the young saint receives angelic assistance to undo the accident.[16] Saint Fínán Cam as a boy is sent to care for the calves, and to control them and their mothers he draws a line in the ground with his staff, a line which both cows and calves obey.[17] Once again, while the theme of miraculous control of animals is clearly related to the traditional hagiographic theme, the emphasis in this story is not on the transformation of nature, but rather the miraculous enforcement of social boundaries. The miracle presages the saint's social power later on in life where his role is to restrain undesirable human behaviour.

11 Ibid. bk 2, ch. 29, pp. 390–3.

12 Ibid. bk 3, ch. 23, pp. 522–5. The detail that the horse was white is interesting, given that in other *vitae* white animals with red ears have clearly supernatural associations.

13 There are eight *Vitae* that Richard Sharpe, *Medieval Irish Saints Lives: An Introduction to 'Vitae Sanctorum Hiberniae'* (Oxford 1991), pp. 238–97, has convincingly argued must be eighth-century. The *Vitae* appear in Heist; the saints are Aed Mac Bricc, Ailbe, Cainnech, Colmán Élo, Fínán Cam, Fintán of Clonenagh, Fintan/Munnu of Taghmon, and Luguid/Molua.

14 *Vita S. Cainnechi* in Heist, pp. 182–98, at chs. 2–3, p. 182.

15 *Vita S. Cainnechi*, in Heist, ch. 4, p. 183.

16 *Vita S. Luguidi*, in Heist, pp. 131–45, at ch. 21, p. 135.

17 *Vita S. Finani*, in Heist, pp. 153–60, at ch. 3, p. 153.

This type of animal and saint story carries on appearing into twelfth- and thirteenth-century *vitae*. By that time, the range of animals on display may owe more to established literary convention than to anything more profound. However, for the seventh- and eighth-century stories, the number of miracles involving domestic animals does seem to reflect particular aspects of Irish society and the particular concerns of Irish hagiographers, rather than being a straightforward adaptation of the western European hagiographic tradition. In the aristocratic societies of fifth- to seventh-century Francia and then England, the ruling elites probably rarely had to deal directly with domestic animals: that was the job of the *rustici*. It would therefore have seemed out of place for an aristocratic saint to have dealings with pigs or sheep.

Two exceptions may be shown to prove the rule. Bede refers in passing to the youthful Cuthbert having some flocks committed to his care. However, all the saint's animal miracles are connected with wild animals, or his horse, a perfectly respectable animal for an aristocrat to be associated with after all. Moreover, there is a hint of embarrassment in Bede's treatment of Cuthbert as a shepherd. The chapter-heading presents Cuthbert as being 'with some shepherds', and the text speaks of the flocks being in Cuthbert's care, as if Cuthbert was the overseer of the shepherds. He was the man in charge, not the man doing the rustic labour.[18] More explicitly, Gregory of Tours's account of Saint Patroclus notes that as a youth he was set to 'watch over the sheep', while his brother was sent to 'study letters'. Gregory admits here that 'they were in truth not of the highest nobility, but nevertheless they were free'. Moreover, it is made clear that entry into the clerical sphere marks a clear class difference, as Patroclus says: 'Sit further from me, you peasant. You herd sheep, while I study letters; the care of such a task ennobles me, while you are made common through your work.'[19] There is no similar discomfort in the Irish *vitae* about saints' rural labours. It seems that in seventh- and early-eighth-century Ireland, despite the existence of a warrior elite, there was not yet a fully developed class society.[20]

18 *Vita Cuthberti*, ch. 4, p. 165.

19 Gregory of Tours, *Liber Vitae Patrum*, pp. 702–3; trans. James, *Life of the Fathers*, ch. 9, p. 66.

20 Chris Wickham, *Framing the Early Middle Ages: Europe and the Mediterranean, 400–800* (Oxford 2006), argues that Ireland at this point was a ranked peasant society, without a developed aristocratic class: see particularly pp. 354–64. It might be objected (see Chapter 3, p. 45) that here, early English hagiography, specifically Bede, is characterised as being part of the aristocratic western European tradition, while Wickham argues that English society did not have a fully developed aristocratic class in the seventh, or even eighth, centuries: ibid. pp. 314–26, 428–34, but see also pp. 342–3. However, in England the Church was from the beginning part of a state-building process that was crucial in developing such a class. This process marks out Bede and other early English hagiographers from the very different social relations in which the Church was embedded in Ireland. Nonetheless, there was no doubt always some pressure throughout the seventh to eleventh centuries in Ireland too towards the differentiation of the elites into a true ruling class, and the Church played an important part in this, particularly with the gradually increasing power of the *coarbs*: see Richard Sharpe, 'Some Problems concerning the Organisation of the Church in Early Medieval Ireland', *Peritia* 3 (1984), pp. 230–70, at pp. 264–5.

This is not meant to downplay the complexity of Irish society or the important extent of Irish kings' authority. Indeed, Kim McCone comments on the powers of the king of Leinster in Cogitosus, where he is able to issue an edict through all *plebes et provincias* for the building of a road.[21] However, respected central authorities can exist without there being a fully differentiated property and class system or without a landholding aristocracy having fully emerged. An indication of the precarious position of emerging aristocratic landowners may be revealed in the eighth-century *Vita I* of Saint Brigit. Here a 'noble and rich man' sent to Brigit for aid as he was seriously ill. When Brigit came, a herdsman (*armentarius*) revealed that the rich man's peasants (*agricolae*) had collectively cursed him. Brigit declares that the solution is to gather everyone together to bless him in reverse.[22] Revealed here is the Church's role in supporting aristocratic rights over peasants, and the urgent need such men had for the support of an outside institution, in this case the Church, against their own peasants.

Elites then certainly existed in seventh-century Ireland, but as individuals they still often had a direct role in production. With wealth based on cattle, it might be no shame indeed for an elite figure such as a saint to have dealings with cows. To the extent which Irish hagiographers would have reflected the concerns of Irish elites in general, the recurring concern that saints maintain rather than disrupt social roles and boundaries is significant. The typical pattern of the saint and animal story in the western hagiographic tradition finds the saint in a state of alienation from his society, and in that liminal state he is able to reverse normal boundaries and rules of human and natural relations. This pattern reveals a criticism of a fallen human society from a traditional Christian theological perspective. This is not what is found in these Irish stories; rather the concern is to show how the saint fits harmoniously into human society, and is able to maintain and strengthen boundaries both natural and social. It is very likely that the relatively weak position of Irish elites is at the root of this shift in hagiographical concerns as the tradition was adapted to an Irish context. That process of adaptation carried on as Irish society developed, so that the more conventional theme of the isolated religious in an 'earthly paradise' could be more comfortably used in an Irish context in the tenth-century poem of the idealised hermitage discussed above.

[21] Kim McCone, *Pagan Past and Christian Present in Early Irish Literature* (Maynooth 1990), p. 9. McCone also notes that people came by kindreds and families and divided up the work amongst themselves, drawing the conclusion that *túath* were functioning as 'subordinate links in an efficient chain of provincial command rather than as loosely federated independent units owing little more than nominal allegiance to an over-king'. However, this seems to push the interpretation of the passage further than it warrants. Firstly, Cogitosus would have had an interest in maximising the authority of the king, since monasteries generally need royal protection for security. Secondly, the fact that the *túath* organised *themselves* is surely an indication that while the king may have had the *authority* to call for public works to be done, he did not necessarily have the power to compel labour. If local communities had not thought the road was a worthwhile project, would it have been built, and would a king risk his authority demanding the people do something they did not wish to do?

[22] *Vita I Sanctae Brigidae*, *AASS* 1 February, pp. 118–34, at no. 57, p. 126.

Nonetheless, despite the differences in the Irish social context, seventh-century hagiographers were clearly deeply influenced by the patristic tradition, and most of the key patristic topoi are represented in the earliest surviving *Vitae* of Columba, Patrick and Brigit. Adomnán is particularly concerned to show that Saint Columba shared in all the essential miraculous powers and virtues of the established saints. Power over animals is signalled as a key category in the first chapter, where the types of Columba's miracles are outlined: 'with Christ's help, he checked the raging fury of wild beasts, by killing some and strongly repelling others'.[23] The miracles follow later, after a section of stories demonstrating Columba's power to take vengeance against violent human enemies. The opening story rather brutally sets the tone for this section. Columba encounters a boar in a dense wood, having gone there to pray alone. The saint prays aloud, commanding the boar to 'approach no further' and to die on the spot. So it does, and the power of the saint is confirmed.[24] Any argument that Irish literature shows a qualitatively different attitude towards nature, compared to the rest of the Christian tradition, must acknowledge this story. Here the powers over nature, lost to humanity since the Fall, and restored in the person of the Christian saint, are confirmed as if by conquest.

In the two stories which follow, Columba's power over animals is confirmed again in largely traditional manner. Columba controls a water monster, and then blesses the land of Iona so that 'from this moment of this hour, all poisons of snakes shall be powerless to harm men or cattle', so long as the inhabitants of the island obey Christ.[25] The latter miracle, in asserting power over snakes, clearly recalls many patristic miracles, not least of Saint Martin.[26] The former story is more intriguing as it involves a water monster in the River Ness. Inevitably the question has been raised whether this story has anything to do with our Loch Ness Monster. The connection has been discounted, largely on the grounds that the miracle happens on the river rather than the loch, and that the monster is not directly described as large. That Adomnán structured the story to echo a miracle of Saint Martin where he repelled a serpent is quite probable. Equally, the probably twelfth-century Irish *Vita* of Colum Cille (Columba) turns the monster into a snake in an entirely standard hagiographic move.[27]

Nonetheless, the monster in Adomnán is clearly meant to be fearsome, and there seems no reason why a monster legend could not migrate up into the loch in the course of time. Furthermore, one aspect of the story should make us pause before dismissing a 'Nessie' connection out of hand. The result of the miracle over the monster is to impress the observing pagan Picts and to cause them to praise the

[23] *Columba* bk 1, ch. 1, pp. 194–5.

[24] Ibid. bk 2, ch. 26, pp. 384–5.

[25] Ibid. bk 2, chs. 27–8, pp. 386–91.

[26] Sulpicius Severus, *Dialogi*, Dialogue 3, ch. 9, cols. 216–17.

[27] Jacqueline Borsje, 'The Monster in the River Ness in the *Vita Sancti Columbae*: A Study of a Miracle', *Peritia* 8 (1994), pp. 27–34, at pp. 29–30. For the St Martin miracle see Sulpicius Severus, *Dialogii*, Dialogue 3, ch. 9, cols. 216–17, and for Colum Cille see *Book of Lismore*, ed. Whitley Stokes, *Life of Colomb Cille*, pp. 168–81, at lines 1031–5, p. 179.

'God of the Christians'. The story is a conversion miracle, where the Christian saint defeats a terror of pagan culture. If there is a conscious echo of Sulpicius Severus' Martin in this story, there may be parallels to more than one story. Saint Martin is well known for destroying pagan sites of worship, not least by cutting down holy trees;[28] this story may be an example of a similar event. It begins with Columba and his monks coming across the Picts burying a man on the bank of the river, which implies that there was something solemnly ritual about this particular point on the River Ness. The man had been killed by the monster in the water, according to Adomnán: 'When the blessed man heard this, he ordered notwithstanding that one of his companions should swim out and bring back to him, by sailing, a boat that stood on the opposite bank'.[29]

Reading between the lines of the story, Columba is here deliberately setting out to ignore or break some particular ritual prohibition: to do something equivalent to Martin's cutting down of holy trees. Just as trees could be sites of worship to pagans, so bodies of water are well known for having attracted cultic attention.[30] Within this interpretation, the terrifying monster which attacked Columba's monk 'with gaping mouth and with great roaring' is a metaphor for pagan cultic practices. The story is therefore a 'monstering' of a pagan funeral rite. In this reading, a legend of a dragon-type beast in the Ness waters could be the *result* of stories of Columba's victory over pagan religion, rather than an existing monster legend being the inspiration for the Columba story. The legend would then neither be an autonomous pre-Christian survival, nor a creation simply of a literary saint and monster miracle, but the result of the Christianisation process itself.

Closing the section on animals is the story of Columba's blessing of the knife, which then is unable to be used as a slaughtering tool. The emphasis in the three previous stories had been on the saint's commanding power over nature, which served to show Columba's equivalence to other Christian saints, but also very likely was intended to show the saint's powers in relation to heroes of vernacular stories. The final story thus serves to distinguish him firmly from these 'pagan' heroes. Adomnán is showing the reader a clearly Christian hero, and Columba's powers should not be mistaken as mere parallels to those of the heroes of the pagan past: they are of a different quality altogether.

The story of the blessed knife brings the account of Columba's miracles back from the realm of the wild into the ordered human world. However, the first story involving a wild animal appears in the first book, where Adomnán tells of Columba's powers of prophecy. Here Columba predicts that a 'pilgrim' will arrive on Iona exhausted from its travels, and that this pilgrim will be a crane, which should be tended gently and fed until strong enough to carry on its journey. The crane

28 Sulpicius Severus, *Vita Beati Martini*, PL 20, cols. 159–76, at ch. 13, cols. 167–8.

29 *Columba*, bk 2, ch. 27, pp. 386–7.

30 For example, see Gregory of Tours, *Gloria Confessorum*, ch. 2, pp. 749–50, where rustics offer libations and sacrifices to a lake. Also see Bernadette Filotas, *Pagan Survivals, Superstitions, and Popular Cultures* (Toronto 2005), pp. 145–8, for related examples.

arrives and stays for three days, as the saint predicted.[31] Adomnán appears not to take this story entirely seriously, saying it is a 'lesser one' showing the saint's 'pleasant foreknowledge', and clearly does not consider it as an 'animal' miracle as such. Indeed, the story does not fit within the patristic paradigm: the saint demonstrates no control over the crane, the animal's nature is not changed by contact with the saint, nor does it serve the saint in any way – quite the reverse: the crane is treated as a human guest. This is then a specifically Irish contribution to the corpus of saint and animal miracles, and reflects a key Irish institution of the period: the solemn duty of hospitality to travellers. Here the saint is revealed as a transcendent practitioner of that social virtue, treating an animal as if it were a human guest. Adomnán's refusal to treat this story as anything other than a prophetic miracle, despite the obvious implications of the story, is an indication that he is reluctant to allow non-patristic influences to colour his treatment of Columba.[32]

The overriding concern of Muirchú's seventh-century *Vita* of Saint Patrick is the conversion of Irish at the hands of Saint Patrick, and it is in this context that the saint's miraculous powers are pressed into service. Control over the forces of nature is, however, important in Patrick's demonstration of the superiority of the Christian God over those of pagans. Thus when he is about to be attacked by a pagan king's followers, Patrick asks God to scatter his enemies; a 'great earthquake' arises causing the chariots and horses to career away over the plain.[33] In Patrick's contest with the 'wizard' Lucetamil, whose power is only to disorder nature by bringing unseasonal snow or darkness during the day, Patrick's role is to reaffirm the natural order, by banishing the pagan's illusions.[34] Muirchú is concerned to show patristic and biblical precedent for all Patrick's miracles, comparing this contest to that between Peter and Simon Magus, but the underlying concern here differs from standard patristic themes. While the patristic tradition concentrates on the saint's reversal of animal nature and restoration of Edenic status, the Irish hagiographer is again more concerned to show that the saint's power is used to defend or restore the natural order, and, by implication, the social order. In this Muirchú's presentation of Patrick is thematically in line with the stories involving domestic animals discussed above.

[31] *Columba*, bk 1, ch. 48, pp. 312–15. Mary Low, 'The Natural World in Early Christianity', p. 177, adduces this story for the case that Irish saints showed a specially tender regard for animals, and notes in addition the domestic white horse's grief for Columba's passing, *Columba*, bk 3, ch. 23, pp. 522–3. However, the crane story should be treated as the metaphor for a social institution, and the horse's grief is simply an adaptation of the patristic idea that in the presence of the saint, Edenic conditions are restored. Neither story demonstrates any sentimental regard for animals in themselves.

[32] For the argument that Adomnan was indeed concerned to remove awkwardly syncretic elements in the stories told about Columba, and to remodel his saint on entirely safe patristic lines, see John Carey, 'Varieties of Supernatural Contact in the Life of Adamnán', in *Saints and Scholars: Studies in Irish Hagiography*, ed. John Carey, Máire Herbert and Pádraig Ó Riain (Bodmin 2001), pp. 49–62, at pp. 61–2. Carey notes Saint Wilfrid's criticism of the cult of Columba, which implied there were unorthodox elements in the tradition of the saint.

[33] Muirchú, *Vita Sancti Patricii*, in A. B. E. Hood, ed. and trans., *St Patrick: His Writings and Muirchu's 'Life'* (London 1978), pp. 61–77, at ch. 18, p. 69, trans. p. 90.

[34] Ibid. ch. 20, pp. 70–1, trans. pp. 91–2.

Where Muirchú tells a story directly concerned with Patrick's power over animal life, the same theme of the defence of boundaries is explicitly at work. Here a rich man called Daire has given Patrick and his followers some land on which to live, but then sends a prize horse to graze on the Christian's field. The horse dies during the night, and Daire, after commanding his servant to kill Patrick in revenge, is himself struck dead. The man's wife perceives the situation accurately and sends to ask for the saint's blessing. The water blessed by Patrick restores both the horse and the man. Subsequently, Daire gives Patrick 'as far as it is mine to give, that piece of ground which you once requested', and the place becomes Armagh.[35] Property rights were likely far from absolute when Muirchú was writing, and this story is meant to show how dangerous it is to take liberties with land dedicated to the Church. The extremity of the saint's vengeance and the remarkable restoration of a horse as well as a man is testament to the Irish Church's need to make grand claims to protect itself.

The story has a clearly symbolic coda: Patrick and Daire go up to the high ground Daire has given to the saint and find there a deer and her fawn, which Patrick's companions wish to kill. The fawn is lying upon the site of the future altar of the north church of Armagh. Patrick forbids its killing and instead carries the animal upon his shoulders, while the deer 'followed him like a very gentle docile ewe'. Here is an image probably influenced by patristic stories of the saintly taming of wild animals, but the import of the story is about Patrick's transformation of Irish society, from bloody paganism to pacific Christianity. Patrick's power over animals is not Muirchú's key concern, but the Daire story introduces a motif which does not appear within the mainstream patristic tradition, the resurrection of animals. It is possible that Muirchú was using a pre-existing story which placed the resurrection of the horse in a more prominent position, and he relegated it here to a minor matter. This is not the case in the many other Irish stories which feature animal resurrection.

Resurrection stories are themselves perfectly mainstream in hagiography, bearing the obvious biblical precedent of the raising of Lazarus, and the symbolic meaning of the convert's new life in Christ. It is appropriate, therefore, that human resurrection stories should attach themselves to Patrick; by the time of the probably ninth-century *Tripartite Life of Patrick* there are a very large number. The unusual aspect here is that Patrick is able to revive people while he is still a child.[36] Startlingly, his first resurrection is not of a person, but of several animals. Like other Irish saints, Patrick is required to tend animals in childhood, but on one occasion a wolf carried off one of the sheep. Patrick is blamed by his foster-mother, but the next day the wolf returns, apparently regurgitating the sheep whole. It is not entirely clear that this is meant to be a full resurrection of the animal, but the immediately following story is far less ambiguous. A cow goes mad and kills five

[35] Ibid. ch. 25, pp. 74–5, trans. pp. 95–6.

[36] *Tripartite Life of Saint Patrick*, ed. and trans. Whitley Stokes, Rolls Series 89 (1887), see for example his resurrection of his foster-father, p. 15.

others, which Patrick brings back to life, while also curing the madness of the first.[37] These miracles fall clearly within a specifically Irish group of topoi. Another human resurrection story gives details that can be found in some of the animal resurrection stories that predate the *Tripartite Life*. A boy devoured by pigs is resurrected by the saint, who orders his bones to be gathered together to effect the restoration.[38] These resurrection stories may have become attached to Patrick to show he was capable of the same wonders attributed to saints like Brigit, whose resurrection stories will be discussed below.

Other examples of Patrick's interactions with nature in the *Tripartite Life* seem to reveal local traditions explaining the landscape with reference to persons of power. The saint is able to both bless and curse, producing fruitfulness and barrenness, as in the rivers blessed to produce the finest salmon in Ireland, or another which was cursed for being the site where two of his young companions drowned.[39] Another story's purpose is the standard warning against encroaching on ecclesiastical property: some men steal and eat two goats that carry water for Saint Patrick. The goats alert him by bleating from the stomachs of the men, and Patrick duly curses the men.[40] The milking of hinds, albeit by a female companion of the saint, shows more of a structural similarity with patristic miracles, as it represents the domestication or taming of a wild animal for the benefit of the saint.[41] The story of the fawn and doe at the site of Armagh is repeated largely unchanged in the *Tripartite Life*, with an addendum, where the deer, placed in a forest by Patrick, is credited with being the source of further unspecified wonders in the service of Patrick. This appendix can be explained by reference to patristic stories in which tamed animals serve their saintly masters; the extension of the story thus may simply have served to round it off in a satisfying fashion.

Subsequent Irish eleventh- and twelfth-century redactions of the *Vita* of Patrick remain remarkably true to the versions of the animal stories found either in the *Tripartite Life* or in Muirchú. The story of the wolf and the apparently regurgitated sheep is made somewhat clearer, but not less grotesque, in one later Irish *Vita*.[42] At most, some stories are elaborated slightly, but there is no discernible attempt to alter the emphasis of any of the stories which reappear, nor does there appear to be any pattern to the stories which are sometimes omitted.[43] This conservative approach in the later *vitae* seems in marked contrast to the earlier more creative

37 Ibid. p. 13.

38 Ibid. p. 199.

39 Ibid. pp. 143, 147.

40 Ibid. p. 181.

41 Ibid. p. 73.

42 *Four Latin Lives of Saint Patrick*, ed. Ludwig Bieler (Dublin 1971); *Vita II*, written perhaps in the eleventh century, p. 57.

43 Compare, for example, the wolf and sheep miracle and the mad cow miracle in Bieler's *Vita II*, pp. 56–9, and *Vita III*, p. 120, written anywhere between 800 and 1130, to that of the *Tripartite Life*, pp. 56–9, 120. The story of the boy eaten by pigs is omitted in *Vita III*, but this could be for a host of reasons which do not reflect on the status of the miracle itself.

period in Patrick's legend, in the substantial differences between the seventh-century accounts of Muirchú and Tírechan, and the later *Tripartite Life*. It seems that by the eleventh century the saint's legend had become essentially fixed; once the episodes had become generally known it was less possible to omit or reinterpret them. For this very reason it becomes more difficult to assess the meaning the stories would have had in an eleventh- or twelfth-century context.

Given this hagiographic stability, it is remarkable that Patrick's best-known miracle should enter the corpus as late as the twelfth century. Patrick is famous today for having banished snakes from Ireland, a miracle which is a stupendous enactment of biblical and patristic precedent where the saints' power over snakes reflects their power over sin. The legend appears for the first time in Gerald of Wales's twelfth-century *History and Topography of Ireland*, which contains a number of discussions of the island's lack of poisonous reptiles, and briefly notes that 'some indulge in the pleasant conjecture that Saint Patrick and other saints of the land purged the island of all harmful animals'.[44] This comment implies that the story did not have much authority behind it at this stage. Nonetheless, it appears in hagiography for the first time in Jocelyn of Furness's presentation of Patrick. Here, Jocelyn might well have intended the snakes as the demonic creatures Patrick battled with on a mountain, as narrated in the *Tripartite Life*, where the demons were in fact birds.[45] It could be suggested that the story is a reaction to Columba's miracle where he banished snakes from Iona.[46] However, if this were the case, it would not explain why the reaction was so late: if competition between the cults of Columba and Patrick were the origin of the story, it should have emerged at least by the time of the *Tripartite Life*, if not before.

The significance of the story and its invention may lie in the very obscurity of its origin. Most *vitae* are concerned to attach a saint to a particular monastery, or to demonstrate through the saint the rights and prestige of that monastery. Thus Muirchú's *Vita*, for example, was particularly concerned with the superiority of Armagh. The story of the banishment of poisonous snakes need not have had an origin in the agenda of any particular church, but could have arisen from the widespread popularity of Patrick among the Irish in general in the twelfth century. In this case, Jocelyn of Furness's version of the story was a reaction to a popular legend. It seemed essential to include the legend in his version of Patrick, but Jocelyn wished

44 Gerald of Wales, *Historia Topographica Hiberniensis*, ch. 28, p. 62; trans. O'Meara, *History and Topography*, ch. 21, p. 50.

45 Mary Donatus, *Beasts and Birds in the Lives of the Early Irish Saints* (Philadelphia 1934), pp. 115–19, and Stokes, *Tripartite Life of Saint Patrick*, p. 115. On this story see also Patrick K. Ford in 'Aspects of the Patrician Legend', in *Celtic Folklore and Christianity: Studies in Memory of William W. Heist*, ed. Patrick K. Ford (Santa Barbara 1983), pp. 29–49. Ford notes the extensive use of serpentine imagery in Muirchú's Patrick, pp. 30–1, but locates the proximate origin of the story of the banishment of snakes with the battle with demons on Crochan Acla mountain in the *Tripartite Life*: see Ford, 'Aspects', p. 39. However, the lateness of the legend casts some doubt on whether Muirchú or even the *Tripartite Life* was really the direct inspiration for the story.

46 *Columba*, bk 2, ch. 28, pp. 388–91.

to show it as a symbolic story rather than the literal truth, which according to Gerald of Wales some believed it was. The story of Patrick and the snakes of Ireland would then be an example of the creation of a story, otherwise clearly patristic in character, from outside the literate ecclesiastical context.

In both the seventh-century *Vitae* of Columba and Patrick, there is a very strong influence of patristic hagiographic tradition, but some elements in both which appear to come from a particularly Irish context. This could, in some cases, represent the Irish hagiographers' own inventions of new motifs, but equally could represent the influence of pre-existing stories and motifs in Irish culture. The third great figure of seventh-century hagiography is Saint Brigit. The earliest surviving text for this saint, and probably the earliest of the seventh-century Irish *vitae* considered here, is Cogitosus' *Vita* written in Kildare in the second half of the seventh century.[47] Cogitosus' purpose here is not to provide a biography of the saint, but simply to prove her saintly powers and defend the superiority of her monastery, Kildare. The biography probably already existed in a now lost *Vita*, which was the basis for subsequent *vitae* of Brigit.[48] Cogitosus provides many more animal miracles in his account of Brigit than were present in either the *Vitae* of Columba or of Patrick, which marks Brigit out as a saint with a speciality in nature miracles. This is in itself highly unusual for a female saint, but as noted above, Cogitosus does make efforts to show gendered roles being respected by his wonder-working subject. Nonetheless, Brigit in the seventh century was not a real contemporary figure, so the extraordinary was less problematic than it would be in the life of a sixth-century Merovingian abbess.

Brigit has sometimes been considered to represent the Christianisation of a pagan goddess, but Cogitosus himself was concerned to demonstrate Christian theological and monastic values through the *Vita*. Thus the themes of faith, charity and obedience are stressed throughout.[49] Brigit's gift of bacon to a hungry dog exemplifies the virtue of charity, and her power over the weather, saving the harvest, could be seen as an example of the power of faith.[50] However, the ability of a hagiographer to link such wonder stories with Christian virtues and biblical references does not necessarily explain the stories in themselves. Other models can be used to explain the content of Brigit's career. Kim McCone notes Saint Brigit's virtues of hospitality, particularly through her miraculous provision of food and drink. The suggestion

47 Kim McCone, 'An Introduction to Early Irish Saint's Lives', *The Maynooth Review* 11 (1984), pp. 26–59, at pp. 29–30.

48 Picard, 'Structural Patterns in Early Hiberno-Latin Hagiography', pp. 72–3. Also see R. Sharpe, '*Vitae S. Brigitae*: The Oldest Texts', *Peritia* 1 (1982), pp. 81–106, on the view that the Bollandist *Vita I* and the Irish *Bethu Brigte* are dependent upon a lost seventh-century text. Cogitosus was an ecclesiastic of Kildare in the second half of the seventh century, and wrote probably before Muirchú, and not later than 700: McCone, 'Brigit', p. 86.

49 See Cogitosus pp. 6–8. For a full exploration of the question of Saint Brigit's origin, see Elva Johnston, 'The "Pagan" and "Christian" Identities of the Irish Female Saint', in *Celts and Christians*, ed. Mark Atherton (Cardiff 2002), pp. 60–78.

50 Cogitosus, nos. 6–7, p. 136; trans Brigit, chs. 3–4, pp. 14–15.

is that Brigit is partly based upon a mythical female hospitaller.[51] Brigit's possible pagan past cannot be resolved either way here, but certainly these discussions highlight the need to consider multiple sources of influence for the animal miracles of Cogitosus.

Certainly, patristic themes can easily be found in Cogitosus. In one story, where Brigit's generosity is being tested once more, a leper demands the best cow of her herd be given to him along with the best of all the calves. Brigit accedes to the request, sending along her own chariot for the transportation of the calf; the cow follows obediently after the chariot for the whole journey: 'You see, dearest brethren, how even the brute beasts, contrary to their custom, used to do her bidding'. Cogitosus' conclusion to the story could come from any patristic story exemplifying the obedience of animals to saints.[52] However, it is possible to suspect here that Cogitosus was trying to make this story conform to a patristic model, where the point of the story might have been somewhat different in an earlier version. The ninth-century vernacular version of the *Vita* of Brigit, the *Bethu Brigte*, offers some indication that this might be the case.[53] The story appears considerably altered in this account, with the leper's demand for a cow countered with Brigit's request that she be allowed to heal him of his leprosy. The leper refuses, on the grounds that he makes a better living through begging than he would if able-bodied. He is subsequently tricked into washing in water blessed by the saint, and is thus cured, and becomes her servant.[54] Another version of the story appears in the probably eighth-century so-called *Vita I* of Saint Brigit, where this time Brigit does not have a cow to give, but the leper rather more graciously accepts her offer to heal him.[55] With so many versions of the story existing, it is very possible that variants already existed in Cogitosus' time, and perhaps the hagiographer, confronted with a version similar to the one in *Bethu Brigte*, felt it was not sufficiently dignified for his saint, and therefore suppressed it. It was noted above that Adomnán in his treatment of Columba seems concerned to exclude non-patristic elements, and here it seems that one of Cogitosus' motives in writing was also to reconcile the legend of Brigit more closely to patristic precedent.

A more conventional animal miracle occurs slightly later, where 'a lone savage wild boar' comes rushing at Brigit's herd of pigs. Brigit sees it and blesses it, and it then tamely remains with them. Again, Cogitosus underlines the point in patristic style: 'even brute animals and beasts were unable to resist her words and will,

[51] McCone, *Pagan Past and Christian Present*, p. 162.

[52] Cogitosus, no. 18, p. 137; trans. Brigit, ch. 15, p. 17.

[53] *Bethu Brigte*, ed. Donncha Ó hAodha (Dublin 1978), pp. xxiv–xxvi; for its date, and for its dependence on earlier traditions, dating at least to the eighth century, see pp. xiv–xx. Nonetheless, it is widely thought that all the Brigitine traditions have a source earlier than Cogitosus: see p. xxii.

[54] Ibid. ch. 23, p. 25.

[55] *Vita I S. Brigidae*, no. 19, pp. 120–1. Another story may have grown from the same source, this one of two lepers, one 'arrogant' and the other humble. Both are given cows, but the arrogant one is punished, drowning alongside the cow he was given: ibid. no. 78, p. 129.

but became tame and submissive and served her'.[56] Wolves can act in surprisingly unnatural ways for Brigit, in a parallel to the lions of the Egyptian fathers. A man offers Brigit some pigs, but when messengers are sent to help collect them, they discover the herd of pigs coming along the road, being driven by wolves. The 'wild wolves . . . out of the utmost respect for blessed Brigit . . . as competent herdsmen . . . left the pigs unharmed, acting with wonderful intelligence and contrary to their habits'.[57] Another time Brigit sees some ducks swimming 'according to their natural instinct' and she commands them to come to her: 'In winged flight and with remarkable zeal for obedience, they began to fly to her in flocks without any fear, familiar with her calls as if domesticated'. Brigit touches them and takes them in her arms before allowing them to fly away again. This is an image of the Edenic status of the saint, where 'the whole of nature, beasts, cattle and birds, was subjected to her power'.[58]

If these stories make Brigit's miracles appear to conform very closely to the patristic model, others show more unusual characteristics. The story of the cow that is milked three times certainly shows power over nature, but has no precedents among patristic stories.[59] This relates to Brigit's miraculous hospitality and her fruitfulness, which are themes entirely compatible with Christian hagiography, but which arise from Irish social concerns rather than directly from patristic literature. Similarly, the two stories of bacon given to dogs, one of which eats the bacon, but without diminishing Brigit's supply at all, and the other which carefully guards the meat, are both stories of the miraculous abundance of the saint, but have no direct inspiration from patristic literature.[60]

Two important stories remain in Cogitosus' account of Brigit, both of which stand entirely outside patristic tradition and seem best explained by a tradition of native Irish story. A king has a tame fox, which amuses his court with its tricks, but an 'uneducated' man at court kills the fox, not realising it is a pet.[61] The furious king intends to have the man killed, and his wife and sons reduced to slavery, unless he can produce another talented pet fox. Showing the saintly virtue of compassion towards the powerless, Brigit prays to God for a solution, and so God sends 'one of his wild foxes to come to her', which it does, jumping into Brigit's chariot, and nestling under her cloak. Coming to court, Brigit pleads for the life of the poor man, and finally, in the face of the king's obduracy, produces God's fox: 'in the presence of the king and the whole crowd, it showed all the traits and the docile subtlety of the other fox and performed before everyone tricks in the same way as the previous one'. The poor man's freedom is thus secured, but once Brigit leaves the court, the cunning fox 'ran away to wild desert places where he had his den, outwitting the many horsemen and dogs which were in pursuit and, fleeing across the open plains, escaped unharmed'.

56 Cogitosus, no. 21, p. 137; trans. Brigit, ch. 18, p. 18.

57 Ibid. no. 22, p. 138; trans. Brigit, ch. 19, pp. 18–19.

58 Ibid. no. 24, p. 138; trans. Brigit, ch. 21, p. 20.

59 Ibid. no. 8, p. 136; trans. Brigit, ch. 5, p. 15.

60 Ibid. no. 6, p. 136, and no. 16, p. 137; trans. Brigit, ch. 3, p. 14, and ch. 13, p. 17.

61 Ibid. no. 23, p. 138; trans. Brigit, ch. 20, pp. 19–20.

Now this story, it can be argued, exemplifies Christian morality: the saint shows compassion, and the king, who does not, is therefore tricked and punished as a result. Yet the story violates basic patristic parameters when it comes to animal miracles. The animal is obedient to God and the saint up to a point, but its wild nature is clearly in no way compromised by the service it renders the saint. Indeed the proverbial cunning of the fox provides the punch-line of the story. This story looks very much more like a secular morality tale than one that would have emerged directly from the ecclesiastical context of hagiographic writing. It implies that there were other cultural forces acting upon the legend of Brigit than simply the agenda of a hagiographer like Cogitosus.

Cogitosus gives a rather prim conclusion: 'And all admired what had taken place and venerated saint Brigit who had the power to perform ever greater exploits by virtue of the privilege of her sanctity'. This conclusion seems to contradict the plot, since it implies that the trick that was played on the king became known to all. Surely this would result in the king's displeasure with both the saint and the poor malefactor. However, clearly the hearer is not meant to raise those questions. Cogitosus' conclusion shows the hagiographer as somewhat uncomfortable with a story that, due to its popularity perhaps, he had to include in the *Vita*. This seems to be confirmed by the version of the story in *Vita I*, as there is almost no difference between the stories in plot or emphasis. However, *Vita I* does not include anything like Cogitosus' conclusion, ending more naturally with the fox's escape back to the wild, making no attempt to moralise.[62] A twelfth-century *Vita*, based upon *Vita I*, similarly ends with the fox's escape, but describes the king's hunt for the fox, which is found in Cogitosus' version, but not in *Vita I*.[63] Thus where the twelfth-century version does not slavishly imitate its model, it chooses not to add a moralising conclusion like Cogitosus', accepting the natural end of the story.[64]

Given the likely origins of the story of the untamed fox from outside a strictly hagiographic context, it is possible that other stories in Cogitosus have similarly unorthodox origins. One possible candidate is the story of the restored calf. Here Brigit receives the hospitality of a poor but faithful woman, who uses the wood of her loom to make a fire and kills her only calf to supply a meal. In the morning the hostess finds that her loom has been restored, and that her cow has a calf of the same kind as the one she has killed. This story, while in one respect being a provisioning miracle like others in the *Vita*, is probably a resurrection and restoration miracle

[62] *Vita I S. Brigidae*, no. 110, p. 134.

[63] *Vita IV Sanctae Brigidae*, *AASS* 1 February, pp. 141–71, at no. 76, p. 171; Sharpe, *Medieval Irish Saint's Lives*, p. 391, considers *Vita IV* to be a revision of *Vita I*.

[64] The other difference worth noting here is that the man who kills the pet fox, described simply as 'uneducated' ('nulla suffultus scientia') in Cogitosus, is described in more directly class terms in *Vita I* as a 'rustic'. The two twelfth-century Brigitine *Vitae*, both dependent upon *Vita I*, accentuate the class undercurrent in the story, emphasising how out of place the rustic is at court: *Vita IV S. Brigidae*, no. 76, p. 171, and Laurence of Durham, *Vita V Sanctae Brigidae*, *AASS* 1 February, pp. 172–85, at nos. 60–3, p. 180. These changes are a good indication that the importance of social status was becoming more marked after Cogitosus wrote.

like others in the Irish tradition. Indeed, the resurrection motif is clearer in *Vita I* of Saint Brigit. In this version the calf is 'restored' (*restitutus*) to the poor woman, just as her loom is *renovata* so that 'they were as before'.[65] This formulation implies the resurrection of the animal, rather than replacement as Cogitosus would have it. That this is not simply an incidental difference in vocabulary is suggested by another miracle in *Vita I*, where it is made clear that a cow given away by Brigit is miraculously replaced by a cow 'resembling the others'.[66] As was noted in the discussion of Patrick's animal resurrection miracles, this type of story does not arise from patristic tradition, and that may have provided Cogitosus with reason to disguise a resurrection miracle as one of simple miraculous replacement.

While the relationship between Muirchú's *Vita* of Patrick and the later *Tripartite Life* is relatively close, it is clear that Cogitosus is not the direct source for the so-called *Vita I* of Saint Brigit. Nonetheless, almost all of the animal miracles in Cogitosus are to be found in *Vita I*, often with little difference in theme or content. Thus the story of the triple milking of a cow appears, as do both stories of bacon being given to dogs, and the wild boar who joins Brigit's herd of pigs.[67] A few stories can be found in *Vita I* that are not in Cogitosus, one of which involves a fisherman who struggles to land a 'bull of the sea', that is a seal, and whose boat is dragged across the Irish sea. Eventually losing the seal, he nonetheless later finds it beached, a gift from God and Saint Brigit. Others are more familiar provisioning miracles or replacements of livestock.[68] It is noteworthy, however, that *Vita I* contains three miracles involving the control over or taming of horses, none of which is represented in Cogitosus.[69]

The most glaring absence in Cogitosus is, however, the tale of Brigit as a child in the house of the 'magus', where she is unable to eat and vomits daily. According to the account in *Bethu Brigte*:

> When it was time to wean her the druid was anxious about her; anything he gave her [to eat] she vomited at once, but her appearance was none the worse. 'I know', said

65 *Vita I S. Brigidae*, no. 104, p. 134.

66 Ibid. no. 98, p. 133. Laurence of Durham's *Vita* of Saint Brigit subtly alters the story, having a calf appear in the morning 'similar' to the previous one: *Vita V*, no. 89, p. 185. It does seem part of Laurence's agenda to conventionalise aspects of Brigit's legend; for example, he removes the reference to a white cow from a story early in the *Vita*, removing the magical symbolism from the animal: no. 15, p. 173. Compare Laurence's version with that of *Vita I*, no. 8, p. 119. Also, Laurence's version of the tale of the untamed fox, while it does not alter the plot, heavily embroiders it rhetorically, in order to emphasise the themes of compassion and mercy, thereby obscuring the original story's mischievousness: *Vita V*, nos. 60–3, p. 180.

67 *Vita I S. Brigidae*, no. 98, p. 133, adds the detail that there were three bishops who visited Brigit; for the dogs see, no. 11, p. 119, no. 101, p. 133, and for the wild boar, no. 102, p. 133.

68 *Vita I*, no. 73, p. 129; no. 40, p. 123; no. 81, p. 130; no. 100, p. 133. The story of the 'bull of the sea' is also to be found in *Vita IV*, where the animal is explicitly named as a seal: no. 42, p. 166.

69 *Vita I*, no. 29, p. 122; no. 48, p. 124; and no. 71, p. 128. Cogitosus, ch. 17, no. 18, parallels no. 48 in *Vita I* somewhat, but does not involve miraculous control over a horse as such. Horses were, of course, a sacred animal in Irish paganism.

the druid, 'what ails the girl, [it is] because I am impure.' Then a white red-eared cow was assigned to sustain her and she became well as a result.[70]

If this version was known to Cogitosus, it is perhaps unsurprising that he chose to avoid it, given that his concern was to reconcile the legend of Brigit with patristic tradition. Animals marked red and white in this way are associated with the underworld in secular stories.[71] The rather bald account of the *Bethu Brigte* contrasts somewhat with the more developed account in *Vita I*, where the cow is, however, described only as white. Additionally, in *Vita I*, Brigit is assigned a Christian woman, named Christiana in fact, to milk the cow to feed Brigit. *Bethu Brigte* is the latest account of the three, of course, but may represent at least part of the original story.

Both Cogitosus and the author of *Vita I* may have been concerned with the folkloric aspects of Brigit's story, the former consigning it to oblivion, and the latter embroidering the account to lessen the folkloric element. *Vita I* is much more willing than Cogitosus to engage with vernacular elements in the legend of Brigit, and indeed it has been noted that the opening line is remarkably close to the opening formula of vernacular saga, and the account of Brigit's conception, birth and youth matches the structure of secular stories.[72] Of course, the structure of hagiography in general and some opening lines are not entirely dissimilar to that found in *Vita I*. It is possible that *Vita I* created the story of the white cow, and that *Bethu Brigte*, while compressing it, 'folklorised' it further. This seems less likely than if *Bethu Brigte* was more faithful to an original version or versions, which were found by the earlier hagiographers to be somewhat eccentric from a patristic point of view. In either case, it is clear that while the genre of animal stories in seventh-century Irish hagiography borrowed much from patristic tradition, which it was able to adapt to Irish conditions and concerns, non-patristic elements from vernacular tradition are just visible at this opening of the Irish tradition. The influence of vernacular stories becomes more apparent in those eighth-century *vitae* which are thought to have survived essentially intact in the *Codex Salmanticensis*.

These *vitae* are very various and not all of them are particularly marked by animal stories, while some lay enormous emphasis on the saint's powers over nature, those of Saint Ailbe in particular. The hagiographic agenda to a great degree remains similar to that of seventh-century *vitae*, and thus it is easy to find many miracles that could have been modelled on, or are consistent with, the patristic tradition. Saint Luguid has the honour of defeating a sea monster while still a boy. Whilst swimming across a pond with two other boys, a monster the size of a ship rises from the water. The boys swim quickly to the shore, with the monster following, but unfortunately once on shore one of the boys looks behind him and, seeing the terrible beast, dies. Luguid raises him from death and blesses the beast, and from that day it harms noth-

[70] *Bethu Brigte*, no. 5, p. 21.

[71] Karen Gail Borst, 'A Reconsideration of the *Vita Sancti Cadoci*', in Ford, *Celtic Folklore and Christianity*, pp. 1–15, at p. 11.

[72] McCone, 'Introduction to Early Irish Saints' *Lives*', p. 36.

ing.[73] At the other end of the natural scale, Saint Cainnech is quite ruthless when it comes to the irritations of nature. He banishes mice from an island for damaging food, and on the saint's word they gather together and throw themselves into the sea. Another time noisy birds bother the saint on another island, so he commands them to be silent, and they obediently keep quiet.[74]

Nature serves Cainnech more picturesquely also. The saint is alone in the forest when a stag comes to him and allows him to use its antlers as a rest for his reading. One day the stag wanders off with the book, but the next day the book is found resting in the antlers of the animal, which, as if it were a repentent monk returning to his abbot, came back to the saint.[75] The patristic theme of taming wild animals for the saint's use can also be found in Cainnech's *Vita*. The saint had no breeding cattle to produce milk, so one day a doe with her calf came out of the nearby forest and allowed itself to be milked.[76] Thus too Saint Fintan used wolves as sheepdogs to guard his father's flocks when he was a boy, a miracle which convinced his father to allow him to pursue a religious life.[77] The saint later encountered a man with some wild oxen, but when Fintan hitched one to his cart, it immediately became gentle and tame.[78]

Another standard patristic theme is the colonisation of nature by saints; in a type of story familiar from western European hagiography Saint Ailbe sent two stags to a nun to till her fields, and on the saint's command the animals returned every year to carry out the same labour.[79]

One of the leading patristic morals of the saint and animal story was the pessimistic observation that while beasts were always willing to obey God and his saints, mankind was more likely to disobey or shun the Christian saint. This moral finds an echo in a succession of miracles of Saint Finanus (Fínán Cam). Some horses of his are kept across the lake from the saint, who lives on an island, and one day one of the horses leads the herd across the lake to the saint's house. Upon seeing the horses, apparently yearning for him, the saint gives them a blessing and returns them to their side of the lake.[80] On its own this story could be taken as an idyllic evocation of the earthly paradise in the presence of the saint, but it is accompanied by a cluster of nature miracles, followed by a long story involving the obdurate and violent King Nechtan.[81] In context, the miracle of the horses seeking blessing functions as a contrast to the king who will not acknowledge the saint, highlighting the turpitude of men. Part of the point of nature miracles is to emphasise how men should obey the Church in the same way that creation obeys the saints. In the face of a king like

73 Heist, *Vita S. Luguidi*, ch. 26, p. 136.
74 Heist, *Vita S. Cainnechi*, chs. 29–30, pp. 189–90.
75 Ibid. ch. 43, p. 193.
76 Ibid. ch. 36, p. 191.
77 Heist, *Vita Prior S. Fintani seu Munnu abbatis de Tech Munnu*, pp. 198–209, at ch. 3, pp. 198–9.
78 Ibid. ch. 14, p. 202.
79 Heist, *Vita S. Albei Episcopi in Imlech*, pp. 118–31, at ch. 38, p. 127.
80 Heist, *Vita S. Finani Abbatis de Cenn Etigh*, pp. 153–60, at ch. 19, p. 156.
81 Ibid. ch. 21, pp. 156–7.

Nechtan, who refuses obedience, the saint has no option but to curse, or rather to prophesy the destruction of the king's power, which naturally comes to pass. The great number of nature miracles in early Irish hagiography may thus reflect the difficulties the Church faced in Ireland in this early period.

Very many of the miracles in eighth-century *vitae* parallel the types of miracles found in seventh-century *vitae*. Thus there is a considerable emphasis on livestock and the marvellous fruitfulness of the saint's power. Confronted with a barren orchard, Saint Ailbe summons a rain of apples.[82] Fínán Cam is sent out to care for the calves, who run to mix with their mothers. To solve this problem, the saint pulls his staff after himself through the earth, and not one of the calves dares to cross the mark left by his staff. The cows are, however, allowed to lick their calves over the saint's boundary.[83] Another time, when the saint is taking hospitality with a holy man known as the son of Garbe, his host kills a calf for him, which happens to be the only cow he has. On the next day, the saint prays to God and a beautiful calf comes to replace the other.[84] Saint Fintan, while on the road, meets a rich man named Enan Mac Nisse, whose cattle are diseased. So Fintan blesses a river, and the cattle are healed when they drink from it. Until the end of his life, the water from that river heals men and cattle. In return, the rich man gives Fintan some fields where he establishes a monastery.[85] Saint Aed Mac Bricc, like others, is able to control rain to save his household's harvest. Later he helps a man whose herd of animals has fled into the forest. The saint's prayer brings them back again.[86]

While these miracles are marked by Irish economic concerns, there is innovation of another kind in a remarkable type of miracle which, while reconcilable to patristic themes, uses a uniquely Irish motif. Saint Cainnech one day receives a complaint from his man, who has responsibility for the milk cows, that a wolf has eaten two of the calves. The concern here is that the cows would cease to give milk without their calves. Cainnech instructs the man to go back to the cows and to clap his hands. When he does this, the wolf emerges 'with humility and penitence', and assumes the calves' position with the cows. The cows interpret the wolf as their own calf, licking and mothering the wild beast, who himself comes daily, morning and evening, 'in payment'. In that place for ever more there is peace between wolves and cows.[87]

In one sense this can be read straightforwardly as an obedience story, where nature acts for the saint's convenience. Yet despite the possible resonance with Isaiah 11:6, it is not really an Edenic story along normal patristic lines.[88] The closing miracle, where the peace between cow and wolf is made 'eternal', might well be

[82] Heist, *Vita S. Albei*, ch. 12, p. 121.

[83] Heist, *Vita S. Finani*, ch. 3, p. 153.

[84] Ibid. ch. 13, p. 155.

[85] Heist, *Vita S. Fintani*, ch. 9, p. 200.

[86] Heist, *Vita S. Aidi Episcopi Killariensis*, pp. 167–81, at chs. 10 and 13, pp. 170–3.

[87] Heist, *Vita S. Cainnechi*, ch. 59, pp. 197–8.

[88] Isaiah 11:6, 'the wolf also shall dwell with the lamb . . . and the calf and the young lion and the fatling together'. There is no direct allusion in the vocabulary of the *Vita Cainnechi* to Isaiah.

intended to carry that Edenic reference, but this is an addition to the central motif, of the wolf as calf. The wolf is not so much transformed in nature, as it is acting in payment of a debt, or making restitution. It is acting according to the rules of a human society. The saint is not here transforming or taming wild nature, so much as extending the rules of society to include wild animals as if they were responsible actors like human beings. The story may thus carry other metaphorical resonances: the saint as guarantor of social equity when the predatory and powerful among men harm others. The wolf as such a symbol is not of course alien to biblical imagery, but this could be a case of a hagiographer finding in Irish tradition a motif which could be reconciled to present Christian themes and ideas.[89]

A similar analysis can be made in another case of the same motif, in the *Vita* of Saint Fínán. Here the saint is visiting a 'devout' man named Mokelloc, who is concerned about his one remaining calf, the other having been devoured by a wolf. One of the saint's household assures the man that his calf will not be in any danger while the saint is there. Unfortunately, it seems that this is not the case, as a wolf does come in the night and devoures the calf. This incident begs to be read metaphorically as a case where the promised peace of the Church as mediator in conflict has been broken by some powerful and violent figure, personified by a wolf. Just as the Church would have to reassert its weight in a genuine event, the saint must redeem the promise made in his name. For the fictional saint, the outcome is certain and miraculous: the wolf comes in 'humility and penitence' to stand with the cows and allows itself to be licked as if it were a calf.[90]

However, from here the story diverges from the Cainnech version. The saint declares that it is not enough for the wolf to be humiliated by standing in for the calf, but demands that the wolf find a replacement for the calf. The wolf duly comes back with a 'white calf with red ears'. The wolf from then on guards the cows as if it were a 'humble dog', emphasising the wolf's humiliation from his noble wildness to his status as a socialised servant. The patristic theme of the reversal of wild nature is employed here, but in addition to the mysterious, and clearly supernatural, calf. The calf's function appears to be to attend the cows when giving birth, and then

89 For a convincing case that Irish writers of this period were concerned to use Irish traditions to reconcile the Irish past with Christian literature and theology, see McCone, *Pagan Past and Christian Present*. On the role of wolves see particularly p. 129, where in one secular saga the fruitfulness of a king's reign is measured, among other things, by the seven wolves held hostage in the king's house, to ensure that only a limited number of cows are taken each year. The wolf hostages even have a man to speak for them in the king's court. This story is pregnant with a metaphorical interpretation of the wolves as human predators. On the fine line between the human and the lupine, see ibid. pp. 212–13.

90 Heist, *Vita S. Finani*, ch. 32, p. 159. The description, both here and in the Cainnech story, of the wolf as 'humble and penitent', is the only coincidence of vocabulary between them, so probably does not represent any direct dependence of one story upon the other. The description is in any case crucial to the motif of the wolf's adoption of human social rules, so the coincidence is not a surprising one.

to leave, with the wolf then guarding the resultant calves.[91] This white calf with red ears is clearly a fertility figure from Irish folklore, but one which the hagiographer felt was either compatible with his meaning or essential to the story in some other way.[92] More than in seventh-century *vitae*, these eighth-century saints' legends are prone to influence from non-Christian sources. The seventh-century writers were aware of those elements in the legends of their saints, but were more punctilious in excluding them or adapting them more closely to Christian models.

A very rare story in Christian hagiography before the eighth century is the 'hermit and hunter' legend, which appears once in Gregory of Tours, and in Sulpicius Severus' account of Saint Martin.[93] The story turns up in the eighth-century Irish *vitae* twice, once each in the *Vitae* of Saint Ailbe and Saint Cainnech. A stag chased by a hunter and dogs crosses to the island where Saint Cainnech is staying, and stands before him. The saint prevents the dogs from stirring, enraging the hunter, who threatens the saint. This unwise reaction meets with a seemingly very severe punishment: he is bound to refrain from appearing in public until his death.[94] Once again, this story appears to be symbolic of a Church claim to restrain the powerful, to protect the socially hunted against the socially predatory. The saint only releases the man when he is mortally ill. The passage could be taken to imply that the hermit has banned the man from hunting again, or in the much more debilitating legal sense of a ban from public affairs – an excommunication perhaps. Either way, the story in its punishment of the hunter goes beyond the cursory narratives that appear in Sulpicius Severus and Gregory of Tours. Even if the hagiographer has been influenced by patristic examples to include the story, it appears that there was a native tradition of the 'hermit and hunter' tale in Ireland that was the source for the story.

The influence of folklore appears even more likely in the same story type as it appears in the *Vita* of Saint Ailbe of Emly. St Ailbe saves a wolf and cubs from hunters: the Araid people (of north-eastern Limerick) are hunting 'as one' in order to drive the wolves from their territory. The she-wolf takes refuge with the saint, placing her head beneath his cowl. Ailbe explicitly makes his aid a *quid pro quo*: 'Do not be afraid. It is fitting that you should flee to me and that I should defend you from your persecutors. Indeed, I, in the days of my infancy, when men had spurned me, was gently nourished by your kind.'[95] The wolves are made safe at Ailbe's table, where they eat bread along with the brothers. For a saint to be protecting *wolves* is unprecedented in the hagiographic tradition, and this in itself would hint at a non-Christian source for the story.

[91] 'Et fuit vitulus iste albus vitulo albo cum vaccis usquequo effete errant. Dixit Finanus . . . Cum effete fuerint tue vacce, non erit tecum vitulus iste albus. Lupus vero iste, quasi canis modestus, erit custos vitulorum tuorum usque ad mortem suam.'

[92] White animals with red ears are fairy animals, as appearing, for example, in later Welsh literature, with the white hounds with red ears of a king of the Otherworld: *Mabinogion*, p. 3.

[93] See above, Chapter 1, p. 16, and below, Chapter 6.

[94] Heist, *Vita S. Cainnechi*, ch. 49, p. 195: 'Et comminatus est ei Kannechus et iuramento vinxit eum ne se proderet nisi ante horam mortis sue.'

[95] Heist, *Vita S. Albei*, ch. 52, p. 130.

However, this is by no means the only element in Ailbe's *Vita* which implies a folkloric background to his legend. Indeed, it has been suggested that Ailbe is really the Christianisation of a pagan guardian hound of the Otherworld, probably used by a major Munster church to counter Armagh's claims to primacy on the basis of Saint Patrick.[96] Ailbe is the illegitimate son of a man and a bondmaid in King Crónán of Araid Cliach's household. His father flees at the pregnancy, afraid of punishment, and the king will not have the baby reared with his own sons, so Ailbe is abandoned in the wilderness under 'a certain rock'. This rock turns out to be the den of a she-wolf, who loves the baby Ailbe and raises him with her own cubs.[97] That Ailbe later saves a she-wolf from the people of Araid indicates that the 'hermit and hunter' element to Ailbe's legend is probably an integral part of the story, and not an addition from elsewhere. The motif of the hero raised by wolves, or other animals, is of course well-known, but it is so ubiquitous in folklore that it should not automatically be assumed that such a story is based upon classical precedent.[98] Ailbe is later found by a good man called Lochan, who takes him away while the she-wolf is absent. Distraught, the mother wolf comes to find Ailbe, but is turned away by the man. She leaves 'crying and howling'. In one sense this sequence can be read as the liminal journey of the hero, expelled from society, to be re-socialised in a different status, and with a changed nature. In this saint's case the clear consequence of this episode is his miraculous powers. However, it is worth pausing to question the more concrete meanings in this liminal progress. The unspecified rock under which Ailbe is laid could represent death, or even the underworld, a supernatural place to which the loving and grieving wolf-mother can be easily assimilated as an Otherworldly character in her own right. Ailbe then derives his miraculous power, in a folkloric sense, from his journey to the land of the dead. This is what liminality is all about: symbolic death and rebirth.

It is not only in saving the she-wolf from hunters that the folkloric elements of Ailbe's story are revealed. While on a journey through the continent, Ailbe resurrects a king's two beloved horses, which have been eaten by lions. The lions react to Ailbe in a suitably affectionate manner, in keeping with patristic models: they 'rub their manes over his feet as if they were linen'.[99] However, the principle of *quid pro quo* is re-introduced. Unlike the rescued she-wolf, who dines on Saint Ailbe's bread, the lions require more wild food, quite unlike the lion in the passage from Isaiah 11:7, who 'shall eat straw like the ox'. Ailbe's story might involve control over nature, but not in the Edenic sense of patristic imagery. Rather, Ailbe demands of the king, in return for the resurrection of his horses, a tribute of one hundred horses as a due payment for his lions. While the king complains that he does not

96 McCone, 'Introduction to Early Irish Saints' Lives', p. 50, notes the identity of Ailbe's name with Mac Da Thó's hound in saga. Such hounds were guardians of the Otherworld hospitaller god's possessions, and were symbols of martial values.

97 Heist, *Vita S. Albei*, chs. 1–2, p. 118.

98 McCone, *Pagan Past and Christian Present*, pp. 191–2, notes the appearances of the motif in Irish secular saga and compares those instances with Ailbe.

99 Heist, *Vita S. Albei*, ch. 8, p. 120.

have a hundred horses to give, Ailbe promises to solve the problem. He ascends a mountain and prays, so that out of a great cloud the required horses appear, and Ailbe gives them to the lions to eat. Ailbe's stupendous powers may here be linked to heaven, but unlike in patristic tradition, the animals are rewarded on their own account, as if the basic rules have not been superseded in the saint's presence. The logic of Ailbe's power as a saint is rooted in his liminal experience as a baby, in the wilderness or the Underworld, and is based on the principle that something given must be rewarded. This is not the logic of the patristic tradition in relation to animals, but it would be the commonsense logic of a peasant economy when dealing with the natural world.

If the legend of Ailbe associates the saint with supernatural motifs of a non-Christian origin, the same may be true of others of the eighth-century saints. The motif of the white animal with red ears appears with some persistence in these *vitae*, as it also appeared in the *Bethu Brigte*. The motif appears casually in Saint Luguid's *Vita*, where a man named Bledne received a dream that a cleric with 'five white cows with red ears' would be arriving shortly, and that Bledne should become his monk and give him his lands. Luguid is that cleric, and his supernatural cows arrive at Bledne's place before him.[100] Fínán Cam, as noted above, has a wolf fetch a white calf with red ears as replacement for another calf. On another occasion, his horse dies, and Jesus sends him in replacement, from out of Lake Lein, a splendidly harnessed horse with a white head.[101] Despite the hagiographer's pointed reference to Christ, the emergence of an animal from a lake carries obvious Otherworld associations. That the motif of the animal with the white head, and sometimes red ears, is an ambiguous one in an otherwise Christian context is made clear by the story of Colmán Élo and the raven.[102] This story is fashioned as a miracle of the saint's foreknowledge, as he knows before being told that a raven has polluted some milk. The story ends with a boy sent to the scene, seeing the raven apparently standing there with 'a shining milky head'. The rather smug-seeming raven is here a demonic figure: it is the fairy that soured the milk, underlining the general character of the white-headed animal as an Otherworld creature, only superficially absorbed by the Christian hagiographers.

It is in the context of the folkloric associations of the seventh- and eighth-century Irish saints that a prominent class of miracle should be considered. These are the miracles of the healing, and more often resurrection, of animals. There are very few, and tenuous, precedents for these miracles in the patristic tradition. Simeon Stylites is well known for having healed a dragon. However, here the saint was exacting repentance from a clearly symbolic creature.[103] As a precedent for the resurrection miracles, there is a story in Gregory the Great's *Dialogues*, which has been suggested as a model.[104] Boniface of Ferentia as a boy observes a fox taking away one

[100] Heist, *Vita S. Luguidi*, ch. 32, p. 137.

[101] Heist, *Vita S. Finani*, ch 14, p. 155: 'veniens de stagno Lein'.

[102] Heist, *Vita S. Colmani Abbatis de land Elo*, pp. 209–24, at ch. 28, p. 218.

[103] See above, Chapter 1, p. 4.

[104] Felim Ó Briain, 'Saga Themes in Irish Hagiography', p. 39, argues that resurrection of animals was

of his mother's hens. The boy prays, and the fox returns with the hen in its mouth, leaves it, and falls dead before the saint. This is not, however, a resurrection miracle, unlike those found in Muirchú's *Vita* of Saint Patrick, for example: the hen is not restored to life, and it is returned simply at the boy's request of God that the animal be restored. The story is not therefore a convincing source for what is clearly a well-developed Irish topos, even by the seventh century.

A second example is from the *Acta* of Saint George the Martyr, which may possibly have been available to seventh-century Irish writers, although it may, as it stands, be a later composition. While in prison, the saint heals a number of sick people and resurrects the bull of a rich man, which leads the man to convert to Christ and declare His greatness in public.[105] Although this is a true resurrection miracle, the context is quite different, and it lacks some of the key details found in many of the Irish miracles. Moreover, one miracle story of a relatively minor saint would not be enough on its own to encourage the growth of a major class of miracles in Irish hagiography. In themselves, resurrection miracles are, of course, central to the Christian message of redemption and a new life in Christ. Thus, resurrections of people can easily be found in the patristic tradition, where saints naturally reproduce one of Christ's own best-known miracles. This precedent may have justified the animal resurrections in Christian terms, but the motif itself must have derived from pre-Christian folklore.

Some of these Irish miracles look utilitarian on the part of the saint, as when Saint Fínán heals his horse's foot with the sign of the cross so that it can carry on its journey.[106] There are large numbers of miracles where a saint resurrects horses and cows, and in a number of these instances the context is one where a saint has been taking hospitality. Such a miracle can be diluted into a simple replacement miracle, as when the son of Garbe kills his only calf for Saint Fínán. On the next day, the saint asks God for a replacement and so a beautiful calf miraculously appears.[107] The same story structure appears in a restoration story in the *Vita* of Aed Mac Bricc, where the saint is given roast mutton to eat in a nunnery guest house.[108] Noticing the nuns' lack of provisions, the saint orders the bones of the consumed sheep to be collected

not invented by Irish writers, citing Gregory, *Dialogii*, bk 1, ch. 9, pp. 90–3, and a miracle of Saint George the Martyr. Another possible, but not very plausible, source for resurrection stories comes from a fragment of Coptic apocrypha, dating perhaps from the fifth or sixth century, where Christ resurrects a cock that had been cooked for the apostles' dinner: *New Testament Apocrypha*, ed. Elliott, p. 672. The basic level of similarity between this story and Irish resurrection stories is more likely to point towards the wide geographical spread of the fundamental motif in folklore than to any literary connection.

105 *Acta Sancti Georgii*, p. 121. Another resurrection story appears in an early Coptic text, where an Abba Aaron restores a donkey essential to the working of a man's mill: Paphnutius, *Histories*, p. 130. It is most unlikely that this story would have been available to Irish hagiographers, and it, like the Saint George story, follows a quite different pattern compared to the Irish resurrection stories.

106 Heist, *Vita S. Finani*, ch. 28, pp. 158–9.

107 Ibid. ch. 13, p. 155.

108 Heist, *Vita S. Aidi*, ch. 20, pp. 173–4.

up and placed in their original place, along with the empty vessel of wine. This done, everything is found 'restored and intact, as if nothing of it had been eaten'. This is not clearly a resurrection miracle, but it is a marvel of restoration which follows an interesting form. In order to restore a consumed animal, the animal's bones and skin must be brought together again.

The same formula appears when Saint Cainnech stays with some nuns, but this time it is a lamb that is killed for the saint's dinner.[109] Cainnech is saddened by this when he learns of the lovable nature of the animal, and has the skin of the lamb stretched out before him. The saint calls to the animal and the lamb is restored to life whole. Unlike other stories, this one does not simply indicate the miraculous fruitfulness of the saint, but also a concern for animal life apparently for its own sake, which is unusual for the eighth century, even in Irish hagiography. It is possible that the emotional aspect of the story was an interpolation by the hagiographer into the well-known story type, on the same logic as the story of Saint Patrick and the sacrificial fawn. The hagiographer was contrasting the pacific motives of the Christian saint with the bloodier context of past pagan heroes, who were able to accomplish similar feats. Resurrection miracles, having been established in seventh- and eighth-century *vitae*, remain a common topos in Irish hagiography, and all the variations found in the early stories can be found in one or another of the later ones. The Irish *Vita* of Colum Cille, for example, adds a story of the resurrection of an ox to the legend of Columba, where the saint cooks an entire ox for the benefit of one Mael Uma. The hero consumes the entire ox at one sitting and the saint has the bones gathered in one place: 'Thus it was done. Columb blest the bones, and their own flesh was around them.'[110]

In a possibly late development, the topos of the resurrection of animals from their remains, and Saint Ailbe's protection and feeding of animals, appear in combined form in the thirteenth-century *Vita* of Saint Abban.[111] As a child, Abban is worshipping while the other boys are playing, when a poor she-wolf comes out of the forest with her cubs and stands before the calves, which the boys are meant to be watching. The boy, showing his piety, pities the wolves and commands them to eat one of the calves: 'Is it not a great miracle that the wolves hungry for their food, and not touching it, came to the saint, and the calves, seeing their fellows devoured, came to him, and did not flee from the servant of God?' The hagiographer goes on to note that God has done this so that the saint will love Him further and be freed from mundane duties to serve Him, thus framing the story in standard patristic terms, but the core of the story is by no means a traditional one. The wolf thanks the saint for its meal, but the other boys are less than impressed, and the shepherds distraught at their loss. Thus, Abban begins to pray over the consumed calf: before all eyes 'the flesh

[109] Heist, *Vita S. Cainnechi*, ch. 58, p. 197.

[110] *Life of Columb Cille*, in *The Book of Lismore*, lines 1055–63, p. 179. For a guide to the other examples, see the immensely useful motif list by Dorothy Ann Bray, *A List of Motifs in the Lives of the Early Irish Saints* (Helsinki 1992), pp. 88–90.

[111] Plummer, *Vitae Sanctorum Hiberniae*, I, *Vita Sancti Abbani*, pp. 3–34, at ch. 7, pp. 6–7: 'misera luppa'.

and skin covered the bare bones'. The calf, restored to its previous colour and size, rises from the ground and runs to the other calves. Hearing of this the king finally gives Abban full freedom to follow the religious life. It is impossible to know when this story first appeared, since the extant version of the *Vita* is a thirteenth-century redaction of a probably older text.

That the story may have an earlier origin is suggested by its presence in other late texts. A late vernacular *Vita* of Saint Maedoc includes a number of miracles where the saint feeds wolves. In one incident the young Maedoc allows eight starving wolves to eat a sheep apiece. His foster-mother is naturally furious, but eight sheep appear as replacements. The sheep are of the exact colour and form of the original sheep, making the story look like a watered-down resurrection motif.[112] Later on while the saint is praying in a cell, some wolves come and fawn about until the saint takes compassion upon them and gives them a calf to eat. This creates a problem with the mother cow, so in order for her to carry on giving milk, Maedoc blesses the top of a brother's head, and the mother licks that instead and so gives up her milk. Once again, a she-wolf comes, starving, gentle and fawning, and is given fish and bread miraculously transformed from leaves.[113] The story recalls somewhat Christ's miraculous loaves and fishes, but that such a parallel should emerge in a story where a wolf is being fed, indicates more than patristic or biblical influences at the root of the story.

The resurrection of animals does not simply have to do with the saint's ability to produce abundance but, in these wolf stories, is connected to the saint's relations with the wilderness's top predator in medieval Ireland. At the heart of this relationship is an ambiguity about the saint and his powers, and their origins, as well as a sense that the world functions through a careful application of the principle of *quid pro quo*. This is a popular apprehension of the spiritual and miraculous, rather than an ecclesiastical one. The case of Saint Ailbe demonstrates most clearly a strong folkloric influence upon the legends of the early saints. This saint is indebted to another world, which is not exactly the Christian heavenly one; however much the hagiographer has carefully Christianised his material, the whiff of the Otherworld remains. A host of other stories, involving white animals with red ears, Brigit's fox, and perhaps even oddities like Columba's crane, indicate that the legend of Ailbe is not alone in feeling this influence. The hagiographers themselves were serious Christians, and were certainly up to the task of Christianising their material. In some cases, they may have deliberately borrowed motifs from pagan Irish culture to demonstrate the superiority of Christian heroes, or at least their ability to compete on equal terms with past heroes. Other hagiographers, most particularly those of the seventh century, seem more circumspect, and anxious to repress those non-Christian inspired elements which had crept into the legends of Patrick, Brigit and Columba. Those same motifs and topoi appear more strongly in the eighth-century *vitae*, perhaps simply through the pressure of the continuing popularity of such stories in Irish culture.

112 Plummer, *Lives of Irish Saints*, II, *Life of Maedoc II*, pp. 184–281, at ch. 9, nos. 20–1, p. 189.

113 Ibid. ch. 31, no. 77, p. 206, and ch. 34, no. 94, p. 209.

The question remains why the animal resurrection motif should be so particularly popular in the Irish hagiographic tradition, when it had been effectively unknown in the patristic tradition up to that point. One answer may lie in the nature of the saint as perceived by early Irish society. Above all the stories of resurrection recall widespread and ancient motifs of the rejuvenation of divine and legendary figures from dismembered remains, from Lemminkäinen in the Finnish *Kalevala* back to the Egyptian Osiris. These stories are rooted in the liminality of the shamanistic initiation ceremony, the death and rebirth into a new status, as in Saint Ailbe's story. Folklore stemming from shamanistic traditions could have suggested the resurrection of animals as a motif for the new Christian cultural heroes. It has been argued in another context that the Irish saints owed something of their nature to shamanistic motifs.[114]

The Irish tradition shows the adaptation of the Christian hagiographic tradition to a society quite different from those developed class societies where the tradition was born. The patristic tradition remained highly relevant to Ireland, and in very many of the Irish stories, despite local colouring, the essential emphasis of that tradition remained intact. Nonetheless, Irish society exacted its own influence on patristic tradition, and did in the end produce a hybrid tradition, where folk motifs alien to the main Christian tradition were adapted into the literature. It is perhaps precisely because Irish society had not yet produced a fully articulated and dominant ruling elite by the seventh century that these folkloric elements could make their presence felt on the tradition. Ecclesiastics in Gaul or England did not have to pay much attention to rustic stories in the seventh and eighth centuries, any more than members of the elite there would engage in agricultural labour as the Irish saints did. It is not necessarily the case that the folk motifs that appear in Irish hagiography were specific to Ireland. Rather, that layer of folktale was excluded from other European hagiography; the apparent uniqueness of Irish legendary material may be more an artefact of the different social constructions of hagiography than a reality of underlying story traditions. However, in one respect the Irish tradition does have some resonance with hagiography of a later period beyond Ireland. Ireland was the earliest but not the only place where stories of the resurrection of animals appeared. Before the question of the animal resurrection motif is fully resolved, those cases need to be considered.

[114] See Daniel Melia, 'Law and the Shaman Saint', in *Celtic Folklore and Christianity*, pp. 113–28, particularly pp. 21–2.

CHAPTER 5

Sainted Princesses and the Resurrection of Geese

OUTSIDE Irish hagiography, the resurrection of animals is a marginal type of miracle, yet it does appear in a distinctive form in the *vitae* of six western saints, all of which are relatively minor works of hagiography. At first sight, the six miracles follow an almost identical narrative. The story typically begins with the news that geese are devastating the fields belonging to the saint. The saint then orders a servant of some description to drive the geese into an enclosure. This being done, the servant decides to take one of the geese for supper. On the following day the saint comes to the geese to give them permission to leave, but the geese appeal for their missing fellow. The saint, understanding the cause of the birds' distress, resurrects the stolen goose, explicitly from the remaining bones and feathers in most cases. Thus satisfied, the geese depart, sometimes with the saint's order never to return to her fields again. It is immediately apparent that this story is not dependent upon the Irish resurrection miracles, although there are some occasional motifs in common. The Irish miracles invariably involve livestock rather than wild animals, and are largely concerned with the miraculous ability of the saint to provide all provisions at need. The story of the geese is of an altogether different kind, involving a clear relationship, even a kind of reciprocal deal, between the saint and the animals, where the geese exchange obedience for protection. This in itself departs from the standard logic of the hagiographic tradition, which generally emphasises the dominion of the saint over nature, rather than mutual obligation. This deviation from usual narrative logic is one indication that this type of miracle story does not arise simply from a clerical or monastic context.

These resurrection miracles are even more distinctive within the normal standards of hagiographic tradition as four out of the six saints involved were women: Saint Wereburga of Chester in an eleventh-century *Vita* and a twelfth-century chronicle, Saint Pharailde of Ghent, Saint Amelberga of Tamise and Saint Opportuna of Sées, all from late eleventh- or twelfth-century *vitae*. Saint Vigor of Bayeux's goose miracle is a later addition to the eleventh-century redaction of his *Vita*, and itself exists in two distinct redactions. The earliest of all the miracles appears in the tenth-century *Vita* of Saint Waldebert of Luxeuil. The relationship between these miracles, if there are indeed direct connections between them, is clearly crucial to establish. Saint Wereburga is almost certainly the earliest of the eleventh- and twelfth-century versions of the legend, but before comparing her legend to that of Saint Waldebert, it is necessary to establish the origin of her own *Vita* and its relationship to the chronicle version of the goose miracle in William of Malmesbury's *De Gestis Pontificum*.

Wereburga was a seventh-century abbess, reputedly of many houses, whose remains rested in a monastery at Chester by the eleventh century.[1] The late-eleventh-century *Vita* is the earliest surviving account of this saint of any length, and its attribution to an author or a monastery is not a settled issue. One candidate often favoured as author is Goscelin of St Bertin, who would have written probably between 1078 and 1084, and probably for the abbey of Ely.[2] More recently the attribution of many similarly obscure *vitae* to Goscelin has been doubted, and another view has the *Vita Wereburgae* written at Chester, on the basis of a putative earlier Anglo-Saxon life written at Hanbury in Staffordshire, where her relics rested for some time.[3] It is natural to assume that the monastery holding the relics of a saint would wish to have a *vita* for its saint. Thus Chester looks like a logical home for the work. However, there is no positive evidence that it originated from Chester, and indeed Chester does not produce any other hagiographic material in this period.[4] As

[1] For a discussion of the monastery of Chester and the records and legends of Wereburga, see *The Chartulary or Register of the Abbey of St. Wereburga, Chester*, ed. J. Tait, Chetham Society 79 and 82 (1920, 1923). The abbey was reformed in 1092–3, with Benedictine monks replacing the canons. The two earliest accounts of Wereburga, of any length, are the *Vita* and a brief account in Florence of Worcester, *Chronicon ex Chronicis*, ed. Benjamin Thorpe, English Historical Society 10 (1848–9), 2 vols, at I, p. 32. Tait, *Chartulary of Chester*, vol. 1, pp. viii–ix, notes that although there is no fact in Florence that is not in the *Vita*, there is no reason to suppose the former based his account on the latter. Both writers may well have been working from the same apparently sparse sources. Florence does not mention Chester, or any tradition of Wereburga's miracles, except that her body was uncorrupted until the 'time of the Danes'.

[2] Goscelin of St Bertin was a prolific hagiographer: see Charles H. Talbot, 'The *Liber Confortatorius* of Goscelin of St Bertin', *Studia Anselmiana* 37 (Rome 1955), pp. 1–118; see pp. 7–11 for his dating of Goscelin's *vitae*, including the *Vita Wereburgae*. The lower limit for the *Vita Wereburgae* is based on a reconstruction of Goscelin's career; the upper dating limit of 1084 is based on the *Vita*'s note that Saint Eadburga was still buried at Lyminge in Kent: *Vita Sanctae Wereburgae Virginis*, *AASS* 3 February, pp. 384–90 at p. 386. This dating is complicated by the controversy between St Augustine's, Canterbury, and the Priory of St Gregory, outside Canterbury, over the possession of Saint Mildrith's relics, which St Gregory's began to claim from about 1087, along with the body of Eadburga: see David Rollason, *The Mildrith Legend: A Study in Early Medieval Hagiography in England* (Leicester 1982), pp. 21–3. St Gregory's claims may have been controversial, but the writer of the *Vita Wereburgae* would not have claimed that Eadburga was buried at Lyminge after 1087, which should be taken as the upper limit for the *Vita*. Goscelin's involvement in this controversy on the side of Canterbury does not preclude him having been the author of the *Vita Wereburgae*, which would have been written before he came to Canterbury. A more recent discussion of Goscelin's career is in *Three Anglo-Latin Saints' Lives*, ed. and trans. Rosalind C. Love (Oxford 1996), pp. xxxix–xlviii. A brief discussion of Goscelin and his presentation of Wereburga, in the context of hagiographical writing, is in Sharon K. Elkins, *Holy Women of Twelfth Century England* (London 1988), pp. 8–9.

[3] This view is offered in Rollason, *The Mildrith Legend*, pp. 26–7; the interpretation is expanded in Susan J. Ridyard, *The Royal Saints of Anglo-Saxon England* (Cambridge 1988), pp. 60, 179, 181, 185–6n. The *Vita*, if written at Chester, would have been produced after 963. For the context of the translations to Hanbury and Chester see David Rollason, *Saints and Relics in Anglo-Saxon England* (Oxford 1989), pp. 117–18, at p. 154.

[4] Some of the material in Henry Bradshaw's *Life of Saint Werburge of Chester*, ed. Carl Horstmann,

far as the extant *Vita* itself is concerned, Chester has a remarkably dim presence: the opening line states that Wereburga's relics lie in Chester, but thereafter there is no mention of the city or any cult there. This is a strange silence for a *Vita* supposedly written for the community there.[5] The *Vita* is not similarly silent in regard to Ely, making as much as possible of her conversion there and the traditions of Ely's saints in general. In marked contrast, William of Malmesbury's account states that Wereburga took her vows in Chester.[6] The former account is more plausible historically, yet the latter account is more plausible as a tradition native to Chester.

There is another element in the *Vita* which looks unlikely to have been the product of a Chester tradition. This is the legend of Wereburga's incorruptible body dissolving so that it would not be mishandled by the Vikings.[7] It is more likely that such a story would emerge in a place that had no physical remains of the saint, and perhaps no extensive written tradition either, and yet which valued the saint. The legend, and its rhetorical elaboration, minimises the need for the physical presence of the saint. The *Vita* emphasises the hope for eternal rather than corporeal life that is given through God's demonstration of his power to dissolve the body of a saint if necessary. An eminently suitable site for this tradition would be Ely, which had no connection in the present or the past with the body of the saint, and yet for whom Wereburga was one of a host of interrelated Anglo-Saxon female royal saints associated with the monastery.

Direct evidence for the cult of Wereburga in the eleventh century at either Ely or Chester is largely lacking. Ridyard notes that there is no indication that Wereburga was much venerated at Ely before 1100, and suggests that her inclusion in saints' calendars could thus be the result of her promotion by the clerks of Chester. Moreover, while Wereburga is described as a nun of Ely in the *Vita*, she is an abbess in

Early English Text Society os 88 (London, 1887), may date back to the eleventh or twelfth century: see particularly bk 2, chs. 5–7, pp. 154–8. If so, this underlines how unlikely it is that the *Vita Wereburgae* was written for Chester, since the latter contains no reference to those of Bradshaw's stories located in the eleventh century.

5 It seems the fourteenth-century summariser of English *vitae*, John of Tynemouth, felt Chester received too little acknowledgment; he ends his version halfway through the translation section and then adds a repetition of Wereburga's connection with Chester: *Nova Legenda Anglie*, II, p. 424.

6 *Vita Wereburgae*, ch. 2, pp. 387–8. The account of her translations and the dissolving of her incorruptible body, nos. 17–18, pp. 389–90, while mentioning her residence at Hanbury, fails to mention Chester at all. William of Malmesbury's main account of Wereburga is in his *De Gestis Pontificum*, bk 4, ch. 172, pp. 308–9. His account is clearly based on Chester tradition, opening with Wereburga's conversion at Chester. William also mentions Wereburga in his *De Gestis Regum Anglorum*, ed. William Stubbs, Rolls Series 90 (1887–9), 2 vols, at I, ch. 76, p. 78, and ch. 214, p. 267.

7 *Vita Wereburgae*, ch. 4, no. 18, pp. 389–90. Rollason, *Mildrith Legend*, pp. 25–6, notes this and infers from it that the putative source *Vita* must therefore have originally been written at Hanbury. However, it would not seem to be a legend any more appropriate to Hanbury than Chester. A posthumous miracle whereby her body is secured for the former is more plausibly part of a Hanbury tradition: *Vita Wereburgae*, ch. 4, no. 15, p. 389.

the twelfth-century *Liber Eliensis*.[8] However, this evidence could be interpreted in the light of Ely's gradual development of the cults of the various royal Anglo-Saxon women associated with its history. A previously peripheral character like Wereburga began to gain in importance as the saintly pantheon increased in scope and detail. From a minor character, she was gradually given more veneration at Ely, in association with her relatives, in the course of the eleventh century. Eventually a minor *vita* was required. After the *Vita* was written, it would be natural for her legend to increase in popularity at Ely. As the *Vita* itself states that she was the abbess of many midland monasteries in her time, it then became reasonable for the account in the *Liber Eliensis* to elevate her status to that of another abbess of Ely.[9]

This pattern would also make sense of the manuscript evidence for the *Vita*: two of the three twelfth-century recensions appear in collections of hagiographic material of the royal women associated with Ely.[10] Finally, there is another detail in the *Vita* which ought to preclude any association with Chester and encourage the association with Ely. While William of Malmesbury's version of the miracle of the resurrected goose is located clearly in Chester, the *Vita* places it in a Northamptonshire village called Wedon Bec. It seems beyond credibility that Chester would wish to locate the miracle in such a place, only emphasising the lack of historical association with its own saint. William's version in contrast is clearly the Chester version of the legend, stating that the saint owned land outside the walls of the city.[11] The placement of the miracle at Wedon Bec does not make sense for Chester, but might make ample sense for Ely. Wereburga's second miracle is also located at Wedon, which may be a genuine early cult centre for Wereburga. This does not mean that the goose resurrection miracle originated there; if the story originated at Chester, it would make sense for an Ely *vita* to relocate it to Wedon, writing Chester out of the picture. In developing the cult of Saint Wereburga, Ely would have been in competition with Chester, and would have every reason to minimise the latter's association with the saint.

The *Vita* then was written for Ely in the late eleventh century, using traditions probably from Ely, Hanbury, Wedon and Chester, but the authorship of the work by Goscelin of Saint Bertin is also disputed. Goscelin produced a large number of hagiographies for various monasteries in England, and is known to have travelled the country widely, so he remains a plausible candidate.[12] One ambiguous

[8] Ridyard, *Royal Saints*, pp. 185–6n, and p. 179; see also *Vita Wereburgae*, ch. 2, pp. 387–8. For the twelfth-century Ely account of Wereburga, written between 1131 and 1174, see *Liber Eliensis*, ed. Ernest O. Blake, Royal Historical Society 92 (1962), bk 1, ch. 15, p. 32; ch. 17, p. 35; ch. 24, p. 42; chs. 36–7, p. 52.

[9] For Wereburga's legendary role as abbess of Ely see *Liber Eliensis*, bk 1, chs. 36–7, p. 52. The saint is abbess of Ely after already being abbess of the houses mentioned in the *Vita*: see *Liber Eliensis*, bk 1, ch. 24, p. 42.

[10] Ridyard, *Royal Saints*, p. 60n. See T. D. Hardy, *Descriptive Catalogue of Materials Relating to the History of Great Britain and Ireland*, Rolls Series 26 (1862–71), 3 vols, Wereburga, nos. 948–53.

[11] William of Malmesbury, *De Gestis Pontificum*, bk 4, ch. 172, pp. 308–9.

[12] Talbot, '*Liber Confortatorius*', pp. 16–17, saw the style as good evidence for Goscelin's authorship.

clue to authorship is the statement at the close of the goose miracle that 'a miracle of exactly this kind can be read in the Life of the most blessed Virgin Amelberga, which we have copied out with our own pen'.[13] This Amelberga has sometimes been assumed to be Saint Amelberga of Tamise in Flanders, who does indeed perform a very similar goose resurrection miracle, which is discussed below. This connection is almost certainly mistaken, for it is much more likely that the author was referring to the *Vita* of the English Saint Milburga, which is associated with the same group of *vitae* as Wereburga, and has also been attributed to Goscelin.[14] Perhaps neither *Vita* was written by Goscelin, but the circumstantial case for Goscelin's authorship is very strong.

More important is the miracle to which Wereburga's is compared. The Milburga miracle is simply one of control of geese who were ravaging some fields, and does not contain any of the subsequent resurrection story. It is much more plausible that Goscelin's reference is to the Milburga miracle rather than to Amelberga of Tamise. If it were the latter, it would need to be explained why, of all the miracles Goscelin could have borrowed to fill out the sparse information he had on Wereburga, he would choose a miracle so unprecedented within the western hagiographic tradition. Rather, by reference to Milburga, the hagiographer was justifying Wereburga's very strange miracle by comparison to a more conventional one. There is then a clear case for the goose resurrection miracle in Wereburga being a tradition Goscelin found among the far-flung sources for his saint, just as each other substantive story can be traced back to an existing cult site. Also, Chester would be the most probable location for the attachment of the miracle to the legend of Wereburga, and its transposition to Wedon explained by cultic rivalry.

The relationship between Goscelin's and William's versions of the story is crucial to determining its character and origin. Goscelin reports that 'many miracles were allowed to shine forth for this most worthy Virgin', implying he knew of other miracles associated with Wereburga. He also indicates the oral transmission of the story: 'this playful and celebrated miracle was proclaimed from generation to generation by the whole of her people'.[15] If Goscelin's reference to other miracles is not

Rhetoric in the *Vita*, concerning the royal bride of Christ, is eminently comparable to other associated *vitae*: see Ridyard, *Royal Saints*, pp. 82–92.

[13] *Vita Wereburgae*, no. 11, p. 388.

[14] For the supposed Flemish connection see A. Poncelet, 'Les biographies de Sainte Amelberge', *Analecta Bollandiana* 31 (1912), pp. 401–9, at p. 403, and for the connection to the English Saint Milburga see Talbot, '*Liber Confortatorius*', p. 8. Rollason, *The Mildrith Legend*, pp. 25–6, discusses Milburga, and objects to the attribution of her *Vita* to Goscelin on grounds of the differences of emphasis, style and wording compared to the hagiographer's account of Mildrith. However, the latter would have been written later in Goscelin's career in a different context, which is enough to explain these differences. A version of the Milburga *Vita* is in Horstmann, *Nova Legenda Anglie*, II, *De Sancta Milburga Virgine*, pp. 188–92; for the miracle which is compared to Wereburga's, see p. 191. On the presentation of the miracles of female saints in associated *vitae* see Susan Millinger, 'Humility and Power: Anglo-Saxon Nuns in Anglo-Norman Hagiography', in *Distant Echoes: Medieval Religious Women*, ed John A. Nichols and Lillian T. Shank (Kalamazoo 1984), pp. 115–29.

[15] *Vita Wereburgae*, ch. 9, p. 388: 'jocundum et celeberrimum a generatione in generationem hoc eius

dismissed entirely as a topos, it suggests that these would have been contemporary miracles from Chester. This is supported by William's statement at the end of his account that the saint responds to the prayers of all, but most particularly to those of women and boys, implying the existence of a miracle cult. William also implies that the miracle was transmitted orally, stating that 'it deserved to be remembered and repeated by the people'.[16] There is little sign in William's account of a clerical, literary tradition of Wereburga at Chester.

As noted, Goscelin's version of the miracle begins at Wedon in Northamptonshire, where there was 'a great number of wild birds, called geese' who were ravaging the fields.[17] Wereburga's 'rural servant' tells her of the problem, and she orders him to gather the geese and enclose them as if they were domestic herd animals. The servant is astonished by this order, which appeared to be mad or nonsense, as the wild birds would simply fly away at his approach. Wereburga repeats the order: 'Go as soon as possible, and by our order lead all of them into our custody'. Naturally, the birds obey the order, and go before the servant 'like captive sinners', and 'with submissive necks'. The next day they beg pardon and permission to leave from Wereburga. Thus far the miracle seems well within familiar patterns: wild animals are tamed and shamed by the virtue of the saint. Indeed there is some similarity to the miracle of Saint Cuthbert and the ravens, particularly in the penitential attitude of the birds.[18] The peculiarity of the story is that a peasant servant should deliver the miraculous order, rather than the saint herself.

The second half of the miracle departs entirely from hagiographic tradition, and differs importantly in William's and Goscelin's versions. In William's rendition, the peasant servant, seeing that the birds are so docile, decides to eat one for his supper. Goscelin merely says that the bird was stolen and hidden by one of the saint's servants. In Goscelin, Wereburga, after a night of prayer, gives the birds permission to depart, being 'most benign towards all creatures of God'. The birds refuse to leave, fluttering about the saint, asking 'as if with human voice, "Why when all of us relax in your clemency, is one of us captured? And can this iniquity rest in the house of your sanctity, and foul rapacity fare well under your innocence?"'.[19] A similar confrontation occurs in William's version, where the saint soon understands the cause of the birds' distress, and she makes 'a sign of healing and flesh and skin reappeared on the bones, while from the skin feathers began to sprout until the bird came back to life, and after first giving a little jump soon flew free up into the air'. In Goscelin's version, Wereburga merely identifies the culprit and restores the captive goose to its confederates. She then forbids the birds ever to return to her lands, and off they fly. Goscelin's second part, in lacking the resurrection motif, looks peculiar in the light of William's version. Clearly, Goscelin suppressed that motif of the story, perhaps finding it inappropriate and strange.

miraculum asseritur ab ipsa plebe tota'.

16 Ibid. 'ab incolis'.

17 Ibid. no. 10, p. 388.

18 *Vita Cuthberti*, ch. 20, pp. 222–5.

19 *Vita Wereburgae*, ch. 11, pp. 388–9.

Goscelin's emphasis at the end of the story is on the wonder of animal obedience to the Creator. However, it is the resurrection of the goose, in William's version, which demands attention here. The geese actually argue to the saint that they have a right to protection, and to make that right good, Wereburga resurrects a wild animal. In contrast, Goscelin's understanding of the importance of the story is revealed by his reference to Saint Milburga, whose miracle contains no resurrection or restoration motif. For Goscelin the restoration of the goose is not the significant part of Wereburga's miracle: it is the obedience of the animals that makes the two miracles comparable. If Goscelin was suppressing the resurrection of the goose, it was because that motif was outside his understanding of the patterns of hagiography. Indeed, the reference to the Milburga miracle is an indication of the hagiographer's discomfort with the story. The miracle was adaptable to the preconceptions of the literate hagiographic tradition, but underneath Goscelin's version lie substantially different assumptions.

The rarity of animal resurrection miracles outside Ireland puts the distinctiveness of Wereburga's miracle and Goscelin's dilemma into perspective. The Irish model of animal resurrection does not appear much outside Wales, where the earliest example seems to be a miracle of Saint Germanus, appearing in the ninth-century *Historia Brittonum*. Here the saint resurrects a calf provided for him and his followers by a poor servant of an obstinate king.[20] Rhigyfarch's eleventh-century *Vita* of Saint David includes a story where the saint resurrects some cattle, killed, it seems, by a saintly curse in the course of a property quarrel. The story is comparable to Muirchú's story of Saint Patrick and the resurrected horse.[21] Another story which may be considered as a candidate for Irish influence comes from the late-eleventh-century *Vita* of Saint Malo: here a swineherd kills a mother sow by accident, and the saint resurrects the pig in compassion for the boy's predicament in regard to his master.[22]

The picturesque imagery of the piglets continuing to try to suckle their dead mother recalls Irish hagiographic imagery of cows and their calves. An earlier story from Brittany does involve the restoration of a goose, but is otherwise a very different story from the main group of 'goose resurrections' considered here. The ninth-century *Vita* of Saint Winwaloe recounts how the saint's sister lost an eye in an attack by a domestic goose.[23] Directed by an angelic visitation, the saint gathers

[20] *The 'Historia Brittonum'*, ed. David N. Dumville (Cambridge 1985), ch. 32, p. 67. Following the marginal character of resurrection miracles, this story naturally does not appear in the original *Vita* of Saint Germanus: see Constantius, *Vita Sancti Germani Episcopi Autissiodorensis*, MGH SSRM 7 (1920), ed. B. Krusch and W. Levison, pp. 247–83.

[21] Rhigyfarch, *Vita Beati Davidis Archiepiscopi et Confessoris*, in *Rhigyfarch's Life of Saint David*, ed. and trans. J. W. James (Cardiff 1967), pp. 1–28, at p. 34. For Saint Patrick see above Chapter 4, p. 66.

[22] Sigebert of Gembloux, *Vita S. Maclovii sive Machutii*, PL 160, cols. 729–46, at ch. 14, cols. 738–9.

[23] Wrdisten, *Vita S. Winwaloei Abbatis*, *AASS* 3 March, pp. 245–54, at ch. 1, no. 6, p. 251. G. H. Doble, *Saint Paul (Paulinus) of Léon: Bishop and Confessor* (Lampeter 1941), p. 7, states that this story is the inspiration for a story of Saint Paul gathering some sea-birds into captivity, but there is no textual

the geese together, isolates the miscreant goose, eviscerates it, retrieves his sister's eye unharmed, and restores her to her former whole beauty. Somewhat as an afterthought, it is noted that the goose is returned to its flock, also whole and healthy. Despite the goose resurrection, this strange miracle cannot be the source of the other goose resurrection stories, lacking as it does all the key elements found in those apart from the resurrection itself. Its relationship to the other stories will, however, be discussed further below.

The few other resurrection stories from the eleventh and twelfth centuries tend neither to follow the Irish pattern, nor provide any parallel for Saint Wereburga. Saint Kentigern's boyhood master, Saint Servanus, had a pet gull, which obeyed him in all things and showed reason by the grace of God. However the old man's disciples were made jealous, which 'convicted them of disobedience'. The monks killed the bird and blamed Kentigern, who then resurrected the bird to prove his innocence to Servanus.[24] The welfare of the bird is a minor part of the story: its themes are monastic obedience and the persecution of the just holy man. Thus this story, despite the resurrection motif, serves a didactic purpose well within the patristic tradition. Conforming less comfortably with hagiographic tradition are the *joca* of Saints Faith and Thomas Becket, where the saints save various domesticated animals. Saint Faith, for example, resurrects a partly flayed donkey, though whether for the benefit of the animal or its owner is unclear.[25] These *joca* are all posthumous miracles included in large miracle collections and may therefore represent popular ideas of dead saints' miraculous behaviour. Certainly the author of the Saint Faith miracle collection referred to the *joca* and *ludi*, which had caused the saint to be mocked, as 'unheard of and new miracles'.[26] Equally, the author of the Becket miracle collection referred to one of the animal miracles as being among *sua ludicra*.[27] This sense of discomfort with the status of these miracles is matched by Goscelin's characterisation of the Wereburga miracle as being 'playful' and may in all these cases be a sign of the popular origin of the stories.[28]

It seems likely that William of Malmesbury's version of the Wereburga legend is closer to the original version of the story, although written about forty years after Goscelin's *Vita*, which in contrast seems to be a sanitised rendition. As noted, William states that she took her vows in the city of Chester, which is entirely at variance with the earlier accounts by Florence of Worcester and Goscelin, indicating

basis for a connection between these two stories, however many other correspondences there are between the two *Vitae*: see Wormonoc, *Vita Pauli*, ch. 4, pp. 217–20.

24 *Vita Kentigerni*, ch. 5, pp. 170–1; trans. pp. 42–3. This story is closely related to Gregory the Great's story of Florentius and the bear: see above, Chapter 3, p. 43.

25 For Becket see William of Canterbury, *Miracula Gloriosi Martyris Thomae Cantuariensis Archiepiscopi*, ed. James C. Robertson, Rolls Series 67 (1875), vol. 1, pp. 173–546, at bk 6, ch. 147, p. 528; ch. 157, p. 536; ch. 158, p. 537. For Saint Faith see *Liber Miraculorum Sancte Fides*, ed. Luca Robertini (Selestat 1994), pp. 91–2, and *The Book of Sainte Foy*, trans. Pamela Sheingorn (Philadelphia 1995), pp. 56–7.

26 Sheingorn, *Sainte Foy*, p. 24.

27 *Miraculorum Gloriosi Martyris Thomae*, ch. 147, p. 528.

28 *Vita Wereburgae*, ch. 9, p. 388, 'jocundum'.

that he was working directly from a Chester tradition.[29] While William's account of the miracle is, in general structure, almost identical to Goscelin's, there is no sign whatsoever of any quotation from the latter, and there are notable differences in the accounts which tell against any literary dependence of one upon the other. In William, wild geese were destroying the crops in the countryside of Chester, and a peasant man comes to Wereburga, and asks for help.[30] However, she only needs to tell the man once to lead the geese into a house, whereas Goscelin has Wereburga issue two speeches to the peasant. In William, the man thinks Wereburga is joking,[31] rather than stating 'nonsense or madness', but finding her serious, does as he is told. In William, the geese complain to the saint of their loss as soon as she arrives, whereas in Goscelin they are admonished by the saint and set free before they realise they are missing one of their number. These differences cannot be easily explained if William was working from a copy of Goscelin, whereas if both had separately recorded oral versions of the story, such differences would be a matter of course.

Further ruling out any direct literary transmission is the lack of coincidences of vocabulary in the two versions. The terms used to describe the saint are similar, William using *domina*, *virgo* and *herilis*. Goscelin refers to Wereburga as *domina*, but his preferred term is *virgo*, although he also once calls her *alma*, in reference to her lands. Yet the two writers contrive not to use the same terms at the same points in the story. In Goscelin, the word *domina* occurs where the peasant is talking to the saint, whereas *virgo* is used when Goscelin is narrating to his audience. This serves to emphasise her class role in relation to the peasant and her spiritual role for Goscelin's monastic audience. No such distinction is made by William. The only possible quotation is the *pietas virginis* to which the geese in both stories appeal, but this phrase is too conventional to sustain a case for literary dependence. William's vocabulary comes closest to Goscelin's when the obedient geese 'walking with bent necks after their enemy, were shut up under a roof'. However, while Goscelin makes much of the penitence of the geese throughout his account, this is the only trace of the theme in William.[32] Thus Goscelin embroiders a standard

[29] William of Malmesbury, *De Gestis Pontificum*, ch. 172, p. 308. William is in fact known to have quoted from Goscelin's other hagiographies elsewhere in his chronicles: see Talbot, '*Liber Confortatorius*', pp. 11–12. However, there is no reason to suppose therefore that he had read the *Vita Wereburgae*; indeed, his accounts of Wereburga elsewhere would seem to indicate his ignorance of the Ely tradition concerning the saint: see William of Malmesbury, *De Gestis Regum*, ch. 7, p. 78, and ch. 214, p. 267. In his *De Gestis Pontificum*, ch. 183, p. 323, Wereburga is mentioned in the context of the rule of Ely by her mother Eormenilda, but is not actually herself connected with Ely.

[30] William of Malmesbury terms him *villicus*, *agrestis*, and *rusticus*, as opposed to Goscelin's *domesticus ruricola*. The different terms are one indication of separate literary genesis. In contrast to William, Goscelin seems very keen to make the peasant unobtrusive by avoiding descriptive references to him.

[31] 'putabat ludere'

[32] The geese's bent necks are 'collis demissis' in William of Malmesbury rather than 'summissis collis' as in Goscelin. The submissive attitude of the geese is thus very likely a part of the oral story told at Chester, which each writer expresses slightly differently. The motif would have been familiar enough to both from Bede's description of the penitence of Cuthbert's birds: *Vita Cuthberti*, ch. 20, p.

hagiographic topos here, while William's account is more spare, approaching what might be expected from a popular story.

A further indication of the popular origin of William's version of the story lies in the presentation of the geese. Here, the geese show 'avian sense' and importune Wereburga until she understands the cause of their distress. In contrast, Goscelin's geese are more miraculous, acting as if they had human voices. Thus it seems that the wit of the geese is a part of the oral story, recorded differently by each writer. However, William's choice of words is significantly different: he does not imply the patristic miracle of the reversal of wild nature, but an animal sense of preservation. Goscelin was grafting patristic topoi onto a popular story in which the assumptions were significantly different. For Goscelin, the importance of the story lies in its repetition of hagiographic tradition: that saints perform the same miracles is an indication itself of their sanctity.[33] In contrast, it was perfectly natural in William's version of the story for the geese to demand their rights of the saint. Life and rights restored, all the geese fly off after giving thanks. Here is another glaring contrast to Goscelin's account, where the geese are commanded never to return to the saint's lands. There is no mention of this banishment in William, so that the story ends on the climax of Wereburga's resurrection of the goose, rather than on the miracle of obedience. Goscelin's narrative emphasises the traditional patristic theme, where William emphasises the popular wonder.

As William's version was likely closer to the original oral story, it may preserve the logic of popular understanding rather than patristic tradition. For the *plebs* of Chester, the power of a saint is not only bound up with her ability to control nature, but also involves a contract with the animals, who expect protection from predators, in this case the servant. Rather than being penitent or even coming to serve the saint, as in some of the patristic stories, the unchanged wild birds fly off again. The popular story is compatible with Edenic topoi, but does not insist on the submission and domestication of animals to a human hierarchy. William reports that this miracle had been long celebrated by the inhabitants of the area of Chester, and concludes by saying how Wereburga responds to the prayers of all, but most particularly to those of women and boys. This saint is the protector of the weaker in society, and perhaps her protection of small animals is symbolic of this role. The story hints at the popular sense of the shrine: the sanctity of the place is shown through the miracle, and the miracle is remembered through the shrine. This is the structure of oral memory, which fixes a narration on a place, in this case the site of Wereburga's holy remains.

It is perhaps necessary to explore why William might be relatively faithful towards a popular story, where Goscelin was determined to bring it within patristic tradition as far as possible. Partly, the framework of the twelfth-century chronicle allows

224, 'et summisso ad pedes eius capite'. Thus no case can be made here for borrowing from Goscelin to William of Malmesbury. It is more probable that Bede's image had entered the imagination of monks and secular people alike.

[33] Compare Wereburga's miracle to Goscelin's story of the animals of Saint Edith, discussed above, Chapter 3, p. 54, where much is made of patristic parallels: *Vita Edithae*, ch. 10, pp. 65–8.

for the straightforward recording of wonders and prodigies without judgement or interpretation on the writer's part. Whatever the chronicler's larger purpose, some such entertaining asides are acceptable.[34] Nonetheless, William does seem to signal to his audience that he is recording a diverting popular story. He uses derogatory terms for the peasant at every opportunity, whereas Goscelin keeps the servant out of the story as much as possible, perhaps to maintain some dignity for the miracle. William gives no commonplace moral for the story as does Goscelin; rather he introduces the story with the peasant telling of the problem of the geese to the saint, among other *fabulae* of the day. William's choice of words here is probably not innocent: while referring simply to daily business, he is also signalling to his readers that this is an amusing *fabula* featuring a *villicus*. Within these terms, William is very likely a good guide to the essence of the popular oral story.

It is, then, very likely that Goscelin's story was taken from an oral tradition of Chester that was later recorded in a version more faithful to the original by William of Malmesbury. However, a very similar story of a goose resurrection is recorded in the tenth-century *Vita* of Waldebert of Luxeuil, written by Adso, a monk of that house.[35] As this is the earliest of the goose resurrection stories, it might be expected to be the literary origin of the rest. There are immediate problems with this assumption, which would otherwise be natural in a hagiographic context. If the Wereburga story originated in Chester, then Waldebert is a very distant saint from whom to borrow a strange miracle for the local saint. Saint Waldebert himself would have been generally known through his presence in the corpus of hagiography attached to the *Vita* of Saint Columban, but this tenth-century account clearly had a narrower significance. Its context was the attempts to reform and re-establish the monastery of Luxeuil in the tenth century, a project which saw no lasting success until the twelfth-century revival in the monastery's fortunes.[36] Goscelin of Saint Bertin was only a little more likely to have come across the Waldebert story, but if he did, then he might have been expected to refer to that story as a justifying precedent. The first notable oddity of the Waldebert story is that it was a miracle performed while the subject was a layman, *before* he became a monk. The location of the miracle in the saint's birthplace of Nant, in the diocese of Meaux, possibly Nanteuil-lès-Meaux,[37]

[34] For a discussion of prodigies and other entertaining stories in contemporary British chroniclers, see Nancy F. Partner, *Serious Entertainments: The Writing of History in Twelfth-Century England* (Chicago 1977), pp. 114–40.

[35] Adso, *Vita S. Waldebertus Abbas Luxoviensis*, *AASS* 2 May, pp. 274–82, at ch. 1, no. 5, p. 278.

[36] See Gérard Moyse, 'Les origins du monachisme sans le diocèse de Besançon (Ve–Xe siécles)', *Bibliothèque de l'école de Chartres* 131 (1973), pp. 21–104, 369–485, at pp. 304–5 on Waldebert's hagiographic record and the issue of monastic reform, and pp. 440–1 on monastic reform in the region and Luxeuil itself in the tenth century. Involvements of Cluniac abbots with Luxeuil in the second half of the tenth century also provide a context for Waldebert's new *Vita*. See also René Locatelli, 'Luxeuil aux XIIe et XIIIe siècles', *Revue Mabillon* 60 (1981), pp. 77–102, for the history after the tenth century.

[37] See *Miracula SS. Waldeberti et Eustasii Auctore Adsono*, MGH SS 15 (2) (1887), ed. O. Holder-Egger, pp. 1170–6, at p. 1172. This edition of the *Vita Waldeberti* omits the goose miracle.

in itself hints at a popular origin for the miracle. It does not occur within the monastery, as does the earlier hagiography of Waldebert, or even within any kind of religious context, but emerges from a place which might be expected to have been a significant cult site for popular sensibilities.

Detailed comparisons between the Wereburga and Waldebert stories further reveal how unlikely this is as a case of literary transmission. The major difference between Goscelin and Adso is the presence of the full resurrection motif in the latter: 'feathers and other remains were gathered up' and after the saint's prayer the bird was 'restored'. On the surface the stories are substantially similar in structure, both beginning with geese ravaging the fields and a servant going to his lord for help. The birds are imprisoned and judged by the saint who forbids them to return. If Goscelin was working from the Waldebert miracle then he added his own extra bit of drama, with the servant's amazement at the saint's command to pen up the geese, and the repetition of that command. This moment is entirely absent from the Waldebert story, and the immediate penitence of the geese is only lightly echoed by reference to them as 'sorrowful birds' on their way to the enclosure. In Goscelin and William of Malmesbury, the birds are kept only overnight, whereas Waldebert subjects them to a three-day fast. This contrast is hard to explain if literary transmission is assumed, since it reveals two entirely different narrative solutions to the same moral problem raised by the story. Whatever the focus of meaning in a putative popular version, the hagiographic emphasis in both the Wereburga and Waldebert stories is on the penance for sin expiated by the geese, but while Goscelin describes in detail the penitence of the birds, Adso emphasises rather the punishment due to penance.

Now the two authors may well have chosen these two different narrative elaborations through their own moral-theological preoccupations, but it is difficult to see why Goscelin would alter the basic architecture of the story and then insert his own penitential imagery to make good the lack. If he were working from the Waldebert story, it would have been more natural for him to emphasise the penitence of the geese within the three-day fast, rather than inserting that imagery into the confrontation of geese and servant, and then geese and saint. The difference makes more sense if both Goscelin and Adso were faced with a similar story to which they added a penitential meaning using two independently conceived narrative embellishments. It is notable that the penitential theme is almost entirely absent within William's version of the story, with the 'bowed necks' of the geese, as they go into captivity, needing to signify submission to power only, and not necessarily having a penitential implication.[38]

There is another difference in the fundamental architecture of the story which is difficult to explain by assuming literary transmission. In Goscelin the saint arrives in the morning and, sternly ordering the geese never to return to her lands, allows

[38] A similar image of wild animals, submissive without implying penitence, can be found in the Welsh romance, *The Lady of the Fountain*, where a monstrous wild man commands a host of creatures: 'And he looked on them and bade them go graze. And they bowed their heads and did him obeisance, even as humble subjects would do to their lord': *The Mabinogion*, p. 159.

them to fly off. Only then is there an avian head-count before the geese ask the saint for the return of their missing companion, having to make a great fuss to bring the saint out of her house again – 'their forces spread out everywhere and completely covered the sky' – and appealing as if with human voice. The different account of William follows this structural pattern, although differing in detail, with the saint merely scolding the geese for damage to property, and the appeal to the saint following, only slightly less dramatically, but without pause to tally numbers. The Waldebert story reverses this sequence. The arrival of the holy man is followed immediately by the appeal of the birds for their companion and they fly around the roof, rather than outside, making much noise to communicate with the saint. The full resurrection motif follows, and only subsequently is the banishment motif introduced, with the comment that the geese never again dared to trouble the saint's fields. The saintly command to the geese is only present by implication. The only narrative significance to this reversal is perhaps a slightly greater emphasis on the resurrection motif in Adso, but as Goscelin had suppressed that anyway, it is puzzling why he would need to further alter a literary source.

These differences in narrative structure and elements amount to considerable changes in a short story that is otherwise immediately recognisable. It is difficult to see why there should be so many if this were a genuine case of literary transmission.[39] Moreover, if Goscelin were working from Adso's version of the story, some similarities in phrasing and vocabulary might be expected. There are in fact even fewer coincidences here than could be found between Goscelin and William, nor are there any clear borrowings between William and Adso. The coincidences that do occur would be entirely natural to a story the authors received orally. Thus Goscelin, while referring to wild geese, *auca indomita*, notes that they are also called *ganta*, while Adso more specifically says the wild ganders, *anseres agrestes* are called *ganta* by rustic custom due to the sound of their cries. The slight coincidence here, within otherwise different phrasing and vocabulary, is simply explained if both were introducing what they knew to be a popular story. Similarly, the saint's command is *Vade* followed by entirely different phrases in William, Goscelin and Adso. While both Goscelin and Adso use the same two words, *causa* and *intellego*, to show the saint's understanding of the birds' complaint, the sentences containing these words have otherwise entirely different meanings.[40] These slight coincidences of vocabulary only underline how remarkably different the two stories are in composition, where some more substantial overlap should occur if a literary link is assumed. It might be argued that Goscelin, having once read the Waldebert story, then reproduced it for his *Vita* of Wereburga, without the text held in memory or in his hand. Yet this raises

[39] In contrast to the differences between Goscelin and Adso is the case of purely literary transmission between Goscelin and Henry Bradshaw's account of Wereburga. In the goose miracle he follows Goscelin exactly, changing none of the architecture of the narrative, and only adding the key differences from William of Malmesbury's account as a postscript: Bradshaw, *Saint Werburge*, pp. 97–8.

[40] Compare Goscelin, 'Egressa ergo divina Virgo ad murmur tantae plebes et quermoniam, *intellexit causam*, acsi preafatis verbis auditam', to Adso, 'Qui mox *causam intelligens*, depositum, inquirit, poenas jussisse debitas pro crimine profitetur, non necesse intulisse'.

the original question of why, of all the miraculous topoi with which he could have chosen to embellish the saint's story, Goscelin should have chosen this singularly strange wonder tale, and then proceed to suppress the central resurrection motif.

Just as Goscelin's and William's versions of the Wereburga legend seem certain to be independent of one another, so the Wereburga and Waldebert versions of the story also betray separate origins. Both Goscelin and Adso signal the peasant context of the stories, and the conclusion must be that the essential elements of the story arose from peasant folklore, evidently from a widespread tale. If this is a case of independent hagiographic adaptations of folklore then the appearance of other such stories in hagiography around the same period is to be expected. Thus the appearance of the story in the probably late-eleventh-century *Vita* of the eighth-century Saint Amelberga of Tamise may support an argument for popular, folkloric origins, as much as it might add to the impression of the spread of a literary topos.

Beneath the extant *Vita Amelbergae* lies a complexity of possible previous accounts and connections to other late-eleventh-century *vitae*, which makes attribution very difficult. Clearly the oldest substantial part of the *Vita* is the core romantic narrative of the saint's entanglement with a Frankish king, identified with Charlemagne by the late eleventh century, whose attentions she was able to escape.[41] Of a different character are a handful of miracles inserted into this text, most likely in a later redaction. The earliest possible date for the *Vita* is after 917, yet all the manuscripts are twelfth-century, with the exception of one possibly late-eleventh-century manuscript. A late-eleventh-century or early-twelfth-century context is most convincing as two other *vitae*, which rely on some of the same material as the *Vita Amelbergae*, were written at this time. One possible author is Abbot Thierry of Saint-Trond (d. 1107), who in writing the *vitae* of many saints spent time in the abbey of Saint-Pierre of Ghent, where Amelberga's relics were held after 1073, although there is good reason to doubt this attribution.[42]

Dating the *Vita* depends upon the connections to two other eleventh-century *vitae*. A late *Vita Sancti Willibrordi*, written before 1105, relates information concerning Amelberga that appears in similar form in the *Vita Amelbergae*.[43] The *Vita Sancti Bertulphi*, written between 1073 and 1088, records the story of the opening of the reliquary of Saint Amelberga, when she was found to have the veil in which she was consecrated by Saint Willibrord. The *Vita Amelbergae* contains a story of the saint's acquisition of the veil.[44] In the case of the veil there is nothing in the *Vita Bertulphi* that requires its information to be derived from the *Vita Amelbergae*. In the

[41] *Vita Sanctae Amelbergae Virginis*, *AASS* 10 July, pp. 89–103; see also Poncelet, 'Amelberge', p. 402.

[42] Poncelet, 'Amelberge', pp. 403–4. Poncelet doubts that Thierry could have written the *Vita* on the basis that in his *Vita* of Saint Landrade, he refers to the legend of Amelberga and the king, while noting that nothing is known for sure about the saint. The *Vita Amelbergae* makes much of the connection between Amelberga and Landrade, and shows none of the doubt expressed by Thierry.

[43] The better-known eighth-century *Vita* of Saint Willibrord by Alcuin does not contain this information, and the eleventh-century redaction has been attributed to Theofrid, abbot of Echternach, who died in 1100: Charles H. Talbot, *The Anglo-Saxon Missionaries in Germany* (London 1954), p. 2.

[44] Poncelet, 'Amelberge', pp. 406–7, and *Vita Amelbergae*, nos. 39–40, pp. 100–1.

first case, there does appear to be some quotation from the *Vita Amelbergae* to the late *Vita Willibrordi*, but that does not absolutely date the extant recension, since the quoted phrases would likely be part of any earlier account of the saint. The connections between the three *Vitae* do however give a good context for the assembly of Amelberga's *Vita* between the translation of 1073 and the early twelfth century, probably before 1105.

The assumption has been that Amelberga's *Vita* was written at Ghent as part of the cult there, but despite the translation of 1073, there is little that connects the hagiography with the town or with Blandin, the abbey of Saint Peter, there.[45] A key omission in the *Vita* is highlighted by the *Vita Bertulphi*'s account of the discovery of Amelberga's veil at the opening of her reliquary at the Blandin Abbey. The relics of Saint Bertulphe of Renty were also at Ghent, where his *Vita* was most likely written.[46] In contrast the *Vita Amelbergae* makes no connection to Ghent in the context of the veil, or indeed anywhere else.[47] This is also in considerable contrast to the twelfth-century account of another of Blandin's saints, Saint Gudwal, who had no connection to the abbey in life, but whose *Vita* makes up for that lack in a substantial translation section.[48] Just as it was notable that the *Vita Wereburgae* made no reference to Chester, so it is with Amelberga and Blandin, which leads to the suspicion that another monastery may have composed the *Vita Amelbergae* in response to Ghent's translation of 1073, as a way of making a competing claim for the saint. In addition the *Vita* tends to emphasise the seniority of Saint Landrade over Amelberga.[49] This would seem an unlikely emphasis if the *Vita* was written at Blandin, given that the latter had an intense rivalry in the eleventh century with Saint-Bavo, the resting place of Saint Landrade as well as other saints.[50]

Among various houses that may have had an interest in developing a cult of Saint Amelberga was Münsterbilsen, for whom she would have been a legendary second

45 The monastery would have had a viable claim to Amelberga's original resting place of Tamise in the eleventh century, on the basis of a traditional eighth-century donation: see the Bollandist comments, *Vita Amelbergae*, p. 81. The prominence in the *Vita* of Amelberga's first resting place at Tamise, or Temsche, is not therefore an argument against the *Vita* being written at Ghent. Nonetheless, it remains peculiar that there is no attempt to connect Tamise with Ghent.

46 Poncelet, 'Amelberge', p. 406.

47 *Vita Amelbergae*, nos. 39–40, pp. 100–1.

48 *Vita Sancti Gudwali*, *AASS* 6 June, pp. 728–48, at ch. 5, nos. 50–1, pp. 741–2; see also Gilbert H. Doble, *Saint Gudwal or Gurval: Bishop and Confessor* (Truro 1933), pp. 8, 19–20. The Blandin *Vita* also includes a story of the saint resurrecting a sheep which had been slaughtered by a wolf: *Vita Gudwal*, ch. 4, no. 36, p. 738. It is possible that this story could be an example of Irish influence, but unlike the story of Saint Malo and the sow discussed above, there is nothing in particular which links the story with Irish resurrection narratives. By this point in the twelfth century there are many possible hagiographic sources of inspiration.

49 *Vita Amelbergae*, particularly nos. 5–6, p. 92, no. 8, p. 93, and no. 11, p. 94, but note also Landrade's further role in the story at no. 12, p. 94, and no. 14, p. 94. It is possible that Landrade's role was expanded from an original narrative, most of which takes place in Tamise, well away from Landrade's monastery of Münsterbilsen.

50 For the cultic rivalry, see *Ysengrimus*, ed. Jill Mann (Leiden 1987), pp. 82–5.

abbess succeeding the foundress, Saint Landrade. Münsterbilsen, a wealthy and well-connected house of female canons in the diocese of Liège, had lost the relics of Saint Landrade to the abbey of Saint-Bavo at Ghent in the ninth century, and would plausibly have wished to rebuild lost cults by the late eleventh century. Münsterbilsen would have suffered a further insult by Thierry of Saint-Trond's production of a *vita* for the cult of Saint Landrade at Ghent.[51] Surviving records of the house, which are few for this period, show a reorientation around the cult of Saint Amour at the time, but this would not exclude an interest in Amelberga or the various sites associated with her.[52] There is not enough evidence to prove that Münsterbilsen did produce the *Vita Amelbergae*, but it remains a possibility, and it does seem unlikely for the work to have been produced at Ghent.

Thierry of Saint Trond's sceptical reference to the story of Amelberga and the king does suggest that an effort to assemble this legend of the saint was made after or around that point in the late eleventh century.[53] The extant *Vita Amelbergae* thus represents a redaction of the legend after 1073 and very probably another redaction later in the eleventh or early twelfth century, which added the unrelated miracle stories, including the goose miracle.[54] These miracles, concentrating on the saint's commanding position as an abbess and her thaumaturgic power, lie in stark contrast to the more conventional narrative of the religious woman's escape from overbearing male secular power. They are clearly an insertion into the existing legend of Amelberga. It is thus highly unlikely that the goose miracle was attached to the *Vita* before the late eleventh century, and the context of the development of her legend certainly rules out Goscelin of Saint Bertin as an author, as his movements in England throughout this period are relatively well known. Following the probable origins of the *Vita*, the goose miracle likely arose not in Ghent, but in another of the sites associated with the saint, possibly Tamise or Mater (*Materna*) in Flanders.

The question remains of the relationship of Amelberga's miracle to the other goose stories. Amelberga's miracle follows the structural pattern of Waldebert rather than Wereburga but, as in the latter, the resurrection motif is suppressed.[55] It seems very unlikely that the miracle was derived from the Wereburga story, but the general structural similarity to the Waldebert story makes that a possible depend-

51 Édouard Michel, *Abbayes et monastères de Belgique* (Brussels 1923), p. 214, notes that among other powerful patrons were the counts of Loos. See also Joseph Lemmens, *La mémoire des monastères: une histoire de la Belgique du VIIe au XVIIIe siècle* (Brussels 1999), pp. 117–18, 26–7, 67, 192. For the writing of the *Vita* of Saint Landrade, see Poncelet, 'Amelberge', p. 404.

52 *Vita Amelbergae*, nos. 5–6, p. 92. The eleventh- and twelfth-century records of the convent are printed in Mathais Joseph Wolters, *Notice historique sur l'ancien chapitre de chanoinesses nobles de Munsterbilsen dans la province actuel de Limbourg* (Ghent 1849), p. 39 for the first attested abbess after Landrade, in 1109, and pp. 43–7 for the eleventh-century donation charters.

53 Poncelet, 'Amelberge', pp. 404–5.

54 Most of the miracle stories appear in a block, apparently inserted into the narrative of the saint and the king, at the point of the account of her consecration: *Vita Amelbergae*, ch. 3, nos. 22–32, pp. 96–8.

55 *Vita Amelburgae*, ch. 3, nos. 31–2, p. 98.

ency. However, if it were so, it is remarkable once again how there is no echo of vocabulary or phrasing between the two miracles. The saint's command is expressed entirely differently: 'Ite, ait, atque eas in custodia publica recludite', as against the 'Vade, inquit' formulation of Adso.[56] Different terms are used to indicate the birds' devastation of the fields: the servant is a 'servant boy' (*puer familiaris*), as opposed to the *minister* of Waldebert or the *domesticus ruricola* of Wereburga; and the naming of the birds as geese occurs in the middle of the story, as opposed to the beginning in Waldebert, and without any coincidence of phrasing or vocabulary, apart from the word for geese itself.[57] This evidence then tells against a literary dependence of the Amelberga story on the *Vita Waldeberti* or indeed on the *Vita Wereburgae*.

The theme and purpose of the goose story within the *Vita Amelbergae* is also difficult to reconcile within a model of literary borrowing. The hagiographer develops the miracle in such a way that the theme of hierarchical obedience is dominant, thoroughly overshadowing the restoration of the goose. The command of the saint is given not to one servant but to the religious household in general, who regard the task as being 'impossible'. The hagiographer extends the moment of the servant's astonishment at the order into a drama for the household in general. One nun, called Genevefa, seeing that the others were at a loss, admonishes the rest that if the *Domina* has given an order then it must be possible to accomplish. Thus the geese are led into captivity, with the females preceding the males. This detail might perhaps seem appropriate for a house of canonesses like Münsterbilsen. In an unusual reference in such a context, the geese are compared to Balaam's ass, although 'there were no public words', yet the birds acted in an observably humanlike way as they proceeded 'heads bowed and wings lowered to the earth'. The emphasis here, together with the Balaam reference, is not on penitence, as in the Wereburga story, but rather on obedience within a female religious house, where the geese become symbols of correct behaviour under the influence of the saint. Thus even the restoration motif becomes part of this theme. The obedience of animals is contrasted to the inadequate behaviour of humans, first being dilatory in carrying out the saint's orders and then a boy secretly taking a goose. The geese correctly appeal to the saint for the return of their fellow, and this granted, the saint commands them never to return to the fields, which order the birds have obeyed ever since.

The miracle as developed here fits into the pattern of the other miracles in the *Vita*, some of which also relate to power over nature. Thus a thief who stole from Saint Amelberga is killed by a wolf, the saint is able to provide a miraculous supply of fish, and is able to prevent a storm from flooding her field.[58] The themes of these miracles are similar to the dominant theme of the goose miracle: in illuminating the virtues of the saint, they preach obedience to her authority as *domina*. Given that the hagiographer had a few such stories available to him, and had already demonstrated his saint's powers of healing, banishment of demons and power over nature,

[56] Ibid. no. 31, p. 98.

[57] Compare Waldebert, 'anseres agrestes, quas a candore vel sonitu vocis more rustico *gantas* vocant', to Amelberga, 'quos communi vocabulo *gances* appellari solet'.

[58] *Vita Amelbergae*, no. 22, p. 96, no. 27, p. 97, and no. 30, p. 98.

it remains problematic why the section on miracles closes with the goose restoration miracle. If the hagiographer had wished for one further miracle emphasising due obedience within the monastery and good social order, then it was a peculiar decision to extract the goose miracle from the *Vita* of Saint Waldebert, then to suppress the resurrection motif, while building up a theme alien to the original miracle. There were many more conventional miracles the hagiographer could have borrowed. The reference to Balaam's ass, extremely rare in animal miracles, is a sign of the hagiographer's discomfort with the story, and his wish to find secure justification for it. The dilemma would be removed, and the hagiographer's arrangement of the story explained, if the story was a popular legend that had become attached to the saint at one of her cult sites. Thus the new redactor, fleshing out the earlier narrative of saint and king, felt obliged to include the goose miracle, but like Goscelin, suppressed the resurrection motif.

There is, however, another goose miracle from Flanders, of Saint Pharailde of Ghent, which affects this analysis of the Amelberga story. The eighth-century Saint Pharailde was the mother of Saint Landrade, and, confusingly, the daughter of another Saint Amelberga, of Mauberg, according to some accounts. The *Vita* of Amelberga of Mauberg was produced at the monastery of Lobbes in the eleventh century, and makes the claim that Pharailde was her daughter, which the *Vita Pharaildae* does not.[59] This claim, however, cannot be used to date the latter, since if, as seems likely, Pharailde's legend was composed either for the collegiate church of Saint Pharailde in Ghent or the neighbouring monastery of Saint-Bavo, the claims of another powerful monastery to a connection to the cult of their saint might not be viewed with favour.[60] In this sense the *Vita Pharaildae* might have been written as a response to the elaboration of genealogical legend elsewhere, and the absence of the more complicated genealogy does not mean it must have been composed before the *Vita* of Amelberga of Mauberg. Pharailde's relics arrived in Ghent in 939 and the first extant *Vita* of Pharailde contains some citations from a probably tenth-century *Vita* in leonine verse. The second *Vita* was written most likely after 1073, when her canons translated her relics into a new shrine, but could have been written any time in the next century. Another *Vita* was written in the late thirteenth century, which borrowed extensively from the *Vita* of Saint Gudule to flesh out the sparse material of the first account.[61] The goose miracle occupies an unusual position within the *Vita*, being appended onto the end of the account of the saint's death.[62] The miracle

[59] See C.-J. Destombes, *Les Vies de saints de Cambrai et Aras* (Lille 1887), 4 vols, at I, pp. 30–6, and Leon J. van der Essen, *Étude critique et littéraire sur les vitae des saints merovingiens de l'ancienne Belgique* (Paris 1907), pp. 303–7.

[60] It has been normally assumed that the cult was entirely associated with the collegiate church, but it seems likely that Saint Bavo also held relics of the saint, and that house is therefore also a candidate for the *Vita*: Mann, *Ysengrimus*, pp. 90–1.

[61] Édouard Hautcœur, *Actes de Sainte Pharailde* (Lille 1882), pp. v, xvi, and xci–xcviii.

[62] *Acta Sanctae Pharaildis*, in ibid. pp. 1–17, at ch. 4, pp. 15–17. The thirteenth-century *Vita* is printed in ibid. pp. 18–24, and the goose miracle, reproduced without serious differences from the original, pp. 22–3. This is then another example of literary transmission where the basic elements and narrative

was thus clearly added to a probably post-1073 redaction of the *Vita* at some point in the twelfth century.[63] The context for Pharailde's goose miracle is therefore Ghent in the twelfth century, and it most likely post-dates the Amelberga miracle.

Given this temporal relationship between the two stories, the Pharailde story might be expected to be a borrowing from the *Vita Amelbergae*. However, if there was a literary dependence, this would not explain the nature of the miracle. Where the Amelberga miracle suppresses the resurrection the *Vita Pharaildae* has the saint gather the bones and feathers of the dead bird together, and closes with the resurrection as the climax of the story. The saint's command that the geese never return to her fields is entirely absent. The story most resembles William of Malmesbury's version of the Wereburga miracle in its simplicity, but it is even more primitive than the latter. The saint in person drives the geese 'like sheep' into the enclosure with a walking stick: the saint performs agricultural labour herself, unlike in the other stories, where a servant performs the duty. Once again there are no signs in the vocabulary or phrasing of any borrowing from the *Vitae* of Waldebert, Wereburga or Amelberga. What is most crucial is the simplified narrative, with the saint in the peasant role, and the presence of the complete resurrection miracle as the clear climax. It makes little sense for a hagiographer to have taken the Waldebert or Amelberga stories and stripped them of their more elaborate elements, and to sharpen the focus on the resurrection motif, which some of the other hagiographers evidently found embarrassing. It is more likely that the goose resurrection miracle was a popular story at Ghent, which had become attached to the saint, and was belatedly included by the canons of Saint Pharailde in the saint's written legend, in a manner paralleling the process at Chester.

None of the possible relationships of the Amelberga and Pharailde stories tell against the goose miracle being a popular legend at Ghent. If the account of Amelberga was written elsewhere than Ghent, then it would seem that the same popular story existed in more than one area in the region and attached itself independently to two saints. If Amelberga's *Vita* was written at Ghent, but before Pharailde's, then the latter's miracle represents the popular version which Amelberga's hagiographer developed for his own purpose. In this situation, perhaps the original version was recorded by Pharailde's hagiographer in an act of local cultic rivalry, using the popular version to point out the superior authenticity of his saint's miracle. Finally, if Pharailde's miracle was recorded before Amelberga's then the latter represents simply the further elaboration of a popular miracle story.

Thus far there appear to be at least three, if not four, instances, in Chester, Luxeuil and Flanders, where there are good reasons to suppose that hagiographers were adapting a popular story involving the resurrection of a goose for use in the cults of local saints. The story appears twice more in the same period, in Normandy in the

of the story are not altered.

[63] Hautcœur, *Pharailde*, p. 73, prints some *lectiones* for the saint which refer to the goose miracle and which were quoted by the thirteenth-century *Vita*, but this does not help to date the miracle more closely since the *lectiones* themselves survive only in a fourteenth-century manuscript, ibid. p. xvi, and are otherwise undatable.

cults of Saint Vigor of Bayeux and Saint Opportuna of Sées.[64] Vigor was an attested bishop of Bayeux in the sixth century, but a context for the extant *Vita* comes with restoration of the monastery of St-Vigor-le-Grand outside Bayeux under Bishop Odo perhaps around 1064–6.[65] It has been argued that a core of the *Vita* dates back to the eighth century, but apart from the key dragon legend, what predominantly remains belongs to the eleventh century.[66] The history of the priory is obscure at this stage, but it certainly went through a period of dissolution during Odo's imprisonment and was only restored once more after 1092.[67] Out of the seventeen manuscripts of the *Vita*, only two are eleventh-century, and the goose resurrection miracle is absent from a number of the recensions, including the earlier eleventh-century manuscript.[68] The goose miracle is then an interpolation into the first eleventh-century redaction of the *Vita*, made probably after the 1092 restoration of St-Vigor-le-Grand.

The *Vita* survives in two versions, the second of which appears to be a twelfth-century, largely stylistic, correction of the first, but the goose miracle undergoes a third more significant revision, evidently later in the twelfth century.[69] The core of the story is actually closest to the Pharailde version, as it lacks the saint's command that the geese should never return and also has the saint himself carry out the herding of the geese. Thus together with the lack of any clear textual borrowing from Waldebert or Wereburga in the first version of the Vigor miracle, it seems that this is

[64] There is in fact one other idiosyncratic appearance of the story written in Normandy in the late ninth or early tenth century, but which clearly cannot be the origin for any of the subsequent stories since it differs so greatly from the essential story in all the versions which have been discussed here. This is a miracle in the second *Vita* of Saint Samson of Dol, where a fox kills a bird. Wild birds were pestering Samson and his monastery, but they are not named as geese. The saint himself performs the task of enclosing the geese. The fox is miraculously prevented from eating the bird, having killed it, and is commanded to return its prey, before the bird is returned to life. This narrative echoes some Irish stories of command over animals: *Vita Antiqua Samsonis*, bk 2, ch. 12, pp. 133–4. It is likely that this miracle indicates the long persistence of the underlying folktale, but it is impossible to discern whether the replacement of a peasant with a fox is an innovation of the hagiographer or not. The intended social use of this story by the monks of Pental would differ greatly from that possible for the later miracles discussed in this chapter. In the Samson version, the story has been adapted to the point where the only visible theme is the protection of that which is controlled by the Church, making it a peculiar variant of the monastic resource miracle. A story of Saint Paul of Léon may be related. Here the saint drove some malevolent seagulls into the cloister to stop them damaging the crops: Wormonoc, *Vita S Pauli Leonensis*, ch. 4, pp. 217–20. This may represent another suppression, this time total, of the resurrection motif, since the avian complaints while in the cloister recall their distress in the other stories, while being attached to an entirely different motif. Alternatively it may be a borrowing from a possibly Welsh source of another story concerning the control of birds damaging the harvest: see G. H. Doble, *Lives of the Welsh Saints* (Cardiff 1971), pp. 95–7, 110.

[65] D. R. Bates, 'The Character and Career of Odo, Bishop of Bayeux', *Speculum* 50 (1975), pp. 1–20, at p. 6n.

[66] On the dating of Vigor's *Vita* see Chapter 1, note 27.

[67] Bates, 'Odo, Bishop of Bayeaux', pp. 18–19.

[68] Auborg, 'Saint Vigor', p. 319.

[69] *Vita Vigoris*, pp. 303–4.

also an independent appearance of the goose resurrection story. The clear climax of the story is the resurrection, which Vigor does from the bones alone, omitting mention of the feathers, unlike the Pharailde miracle. The Vigor and Pharailde miracles share the detail that the miracle happened in winter, while no other story specifies a time of year. The *Vita Pharaildae* notes that it was the time when the winter wheat, having been sown, was showing, where the Vigor version notes simply the planting of seeds by a peasant, before specifying not only that it was winter, but giving an extended description of the stormy weather of the day.[70] Thus while the two stories introduce similar details not found elsewhere, the difference between the stages of cultivation indicates that this is not a case of borrowing.

Equally, where the Pharailde story launches straight into the account of the saint driving the geese, the Vigor story recounts the peasant's appeal to the saint for aid, before telling how the saint, using his staff, drove the geese into a barn. Once again, the simplicity of the Pharailde story rules out a borrowing from the more elaborate Vigor narrative. In the unlikely case that the Pharailde story was the earlier, the differences in seasonal detail, as well as numerous changes in the order of the narrative of the stealing of the goose and the saint's actions, make it highly unlikely that the Vigor story was elaborated from Pharailde's story. Thus the Vigor story confirms the probability that in the popular version of the tale, it was the saint who performed the task of driving the geese. It would be natural for clerical hagiographers to take such a story and introduce a layer of narrative separating the saint from agricultural labour: from a peasant, the saint becomes a landlord, who does not labour but commands the labour of others.

The *Vita Sancti Vigoris* does show signs that the hagiographer felt a need to justify the miracle, but the manner in which this is done is unique. Vigor is given a full speech when praying to resurrect the goose, the point of which is to emphasise God as the creator and conserver of all life, for whom nothing is impossible.[71] The third version of the miracle alters the speech somewhat, keeping the sense of the first, but also asking God to show that he commands the living and dead for all eternity.[72] Thus this strange miracle is justified by its demonstration of God's dominion. The third version of the Vigor story makes a major change in the narrative by introducing the saint's command to his servant to pen the geese, removing the story another degree from the probable original popular version, and bringing it into line with the narratives found in Waldebert, Wereburga and Amelberga. It is possible that this change does represent a case of borrowing from one of those stories, since it occurs in the twelfth century, when they were all available. There are some very slight coincidences in vocabulary between the third version of the Vigor story and Goscelin's version of Wereburga, which may make the Wereburga story the most likely source for the change. This shift in the twelfth-century redaction of the Vigor story does, however, highlight the independence of the original version.

70 Compare Pharailde, 'Hyemali siquidem tempore, cum pigro et anili passu agrum, quo triticum seminaverat, viseret', to Vigor, 'contigit cuidam agricolae semina spargare campi'.

71 *Vita Vigoris*, ch. 10, p. 304.

72 Ibid. p. 303n.

There is one final detail in the third version of the Vigor story which is unique to this appearance of the goose miracle and that suggests the writer was influenced not only by literary versions of the story, but also by a continuing popular version. The servant, who takes and eats the goose, chooses the one goose that was lame.[73] This peculiar detail cannot be readily explained, except if the writer had heard a version of the story which included the lame goose. The significance of this motif cannot be explained through any hagiographic precedent, but does have a probable context in peasant culture.

The lame goose detail is echoed by a slightly different motif in the last of the goose resurrection stories to be considered here. The original ninth-century *Vita* of the eighth-century Saint Opportuna of Sées contained no miracles whatsoever, but two were added in the twelfth century, one of which is the goose story.[74] The abbey of Olmenèches-Argentan was restored about 1070, and nuns installed, but the insertion of the two miracles into the *Vita* was almost certainly twelfth-century.[75] The story is now extant only in the form of a thirteenth- or fourteenth-century vernacular poem on Opportuna, in which the two additional miracles play a prominent part.[76] Without the Latin text for comparison, the Opportuna miracle may be presumed to be dependent on or inspired by the Vigor story, and it does share the motif of the saint driving the geese herself, although it adds the saint's command not to return to her place. This motif could have been added to the story from any of the other versions, including the later Vigor recension. After the geese are released by the saint they come to the abbey complaining of their missing companion, the servant repents his folly of eating the bird, and the goose is resurrected. Here, however, the story adds something of its own: the goose is not fully restored since one bone remains broken.[77] This detail is similar to the lame goose in Vigor, but is clearly independent and once again cannot be explained by hagiographic precedent. It seems then that the writer of the Opportuna story, while probably making use of existing written versions of the miracle, was also influenced by an existing popular version of the story, which contained the motif of the unrestored bone.

This motif in the Opportuna story does echo very strongly another quite different story from Norse legend. The resurrection motif familiar from Irish hagiography appears here in independent form with the boar Sæhrímnir in Valhöll who

[73] Ibid. p. 303n: 'At ille minus curans de precepto sancti viri, unam, quam claudicantem intuitus est, presumpsit et comedit'.

[74] *Vita Sanctae Opportunae Abbatissae*, *AASS* 22 April, pp. 61–72, at p. 67, notes the existence of the two additional miracles but does not print the goose resurrection miracle. No edition of the *Vita* includes the miracle and it is not clear that it is any longer extant.

[75] See D. Guy Oury, 'Saint Opportune, sa vie et ses reliques', in *L'abbaye d'Olmenèches-Argentan et Saint Opportune: sa vie et son culte*, ed. Y. Chaussy (Paris 1970), pp. 221–36, at pp. 232–3, and Jean Fournée, 'Le culte populaire de l'iconographie de Sainte Opportune', in ibid. pp. 237–84, at pp. 267–9.

[76] L. de la Sicotière, *Légende de Sainte Opportune, abbesse d'Almeneshes au diocèse de Seez en Normandie* (Rouen 1966), pp. 3–9, and lines 145–92 for the miracle.

[77] Ibid. lines 178–84.

is boiled every day and comes alive again every evening.[78] In another story, Thor, on a journey with his goats, got lodgings with a farmer for the night, slaughtered and skinned the goats, and cooked them in a cauldron. Thor invited the farmer's family to eat also, instructing them to throw the bones upon the skins of the animals placed in front of the fire. However, the son of the farmer took one of the thigh-bones and split it to get at the marrow. On the following day when Thor attempted to resurrect the goats from the bones and skins, he found that one of his rejuvenated goats had remained lame, and knew that the farmer's family was at fault. In recompense, the children of the farmer became Thor's bondservants.[79] The coincidence between this story and Opportuna's resurrected goose with one broken bone is striking, but any sort of literary link between the two would be absurd.

The Thor story is in basic structure remarkably similar to the goose miracles, with an underling to a sacred character at fault, exposed by, or causing, the resurrection. In the context of Vigor's lame goose, who is chosen by the servant to kill and eat, the relationship between the stories is clarified. The Vigor story presupposes an awareness of the connection between lame animals and the rite of resurrection. The basic popular goose miracle from which the saints' legends are drawn is a story from deep within the substratum of peasant folklore. The motif of the resurrection of animals from bones and skin (or feathers) is not by any means restricted to western Europe but can be found in folktales across the world, including in native American cultures.[80] The Thor story is a particular development from this basic folktale of human societies, which is nonetheless clearly related at some distance to another particular development of the motif, the goose resurrection tale. In Irish hagiography it is the basic motif which appears in a number of forms, not entirely dissimilar to the Norse stories, but more generalised in variety.

The image of lameness may not have been restricted to the Vigor and Opportuna stories. There is a hint of it in William of Malmesbury's version of Wereburga, where the resurrected goose is described as giving a 'quick jump' before flying off into the air. It is certainly a folkloric element within the two Norman stories, but may have been common to the others before passing through clerical filters. The specific detail of lameness within the stories of Opportuna and Vigor is connected to a series of stories which help to locate further the origins and meaning of the original peasant goose resurrection story. The trope of the lame limb refers to journeys to the land of the dead and narratives of death and rebirth in an array of stories and ceremonies, often shamanistic, across a range of human culture almost as wide as the basic resurrection motif itself. The journey to the land of the dead marks the

[78] *The Prose Edda of Snorri Sturluson*, trans. Jean I. Young (Cambridge 1954), p. 63.

[79] Ibid. p. 69.

[80] See James George Frazer, *The Golden Bough: A Study in Magic and Religion* (London 1936), 12 vols, part 5, vol. II, pp. 256–9, and Carlo Ginzburg, *Ecstasies: Deciphering the Witches' Sabbath*, trans. Raymond Rosenthal (London 1990), pp. 243–50. Naturally the motif finds an echo in the Bible also: see Ezekiel 37:1–14, but far from being an independent basis for the resurrection miracles, it is noticeable that the hagiographers seem never to make use of it as a possible justification for their stories.

subject with an asymmetry, typically the leg, and the motif is found attached to animals as well as humans. In two Scottish versions of the Cinderella story, sacrificed animals are restored from their bones and skin, but limp thereafter.[81] Vigor's lame goose is not an ordinary animal: it is a magic goose, it has been to the land of the dead. The servant's decision to take the lame goose is a signal of the animal's role within a resurrection story that is not a mere curiosity, but is connected to crucial elements of peasant life and culture.

The non-Christian origins of the goose miracles may have been evident to the hagiographers, whose ambivalence about the stories is made clear by the suppression of the resurrection motif itself in Wereburga and Amelberga. Another clerical reaction underlines the point. A cleric of Ghent, either from Saint-Bavo or Saint Pharailde's church, in a mid-twelfth-century poem, identified his saint with the daughter of Herod, 'Herodias'. The context characterises her as the underworld goddess figure, Holda, who, he says, is followed by a third of humanity. Such figures, usually female, are particularly associated with the resurrections of animals in Eurasian cultures.[82] In the story an old peasant woman invokes Pharailde at the end of a series of pseudo-saints, to ensure that a wolf, once killed and dismembered, would not revive. The context, a story of dismemberment and the possibility of resurrection with the reference to Pharailde, suggests that there is a conscious allusion here to the goose resurrection story. Such an allusion would be clear enough to the Ghent audience, which is addressed by the poem. The identification between the Holda figure and Pharailde is not a direct product of popular folklore, but rather a reaction to the resurrection miracle itself.[83] The cleric is being humorous in this passage, but in doing so demonstrates his awareness of the associations of the resurrection miracle.

The meaning of the goose stories thus lies within a complex of notions and stories of death and rebirth that were part of a substratum of peasant culture that pre-dates Christianity. The peasants themselves would certainly not have viewed these conceptions and motifs as *un*christian by the eleventh century. Given that the motifs of resurrection and lameness appear very often not simply as stories, but as ceremonies of one kind or another, the goose miracles might also be viewed in this light. Most likely, the story would represent a harvest ritual carried out to ensure the return of the crops, or of the fruitfulness of the land, in the season to come. Two of the miracles, that of Saint Vigor and Saint Pharailde, occur at different times in the winter, and it is possible that the other miracles occurred at similar times, alongside the southern migration of geese.

[81] See Ginzburg, *Ecstasies*, pp. 226–67; p. 247 for the Scottish Cinderella stories. The stories are found across Eurasia and in America, and the motif was first noted by Claude Levi-Strauss: see ibid. p. 267, n 1. Frazer, *Golden Bough*, part 5, vol. II, pp. 256–9, notes the widespread prohibition against breaking the bones of consumed animals.

[82] Ginzburg, *Ecstasies*, p. 148, n. 80, and Mann, *Ysengrimus*, lines 60–94, pp. 266–7, and pp. 89–97.

[83] Mann, *Ysengrimus*, pp. 32–6, for the importance of the body's powers of revivification in the poem generally. It might also be noted that the reference to Pharailde here strengthens the popular associations of the resurrection story, particularly if the allusion is accepted.

As the differences between the Vigor and Pharailde stories demonstrate, however, there is no reason to suppose the timing of any agricultural ritual remained constant across the whole geographical range of the stories. Such traditions in an oral setting would naturally be open to considerable change and adaptation. The general outlines of the ceremony seem to arise fairly clearly from the stories themselves. It is surely significant that four out of six of the miracles are performed by female saints, when thaumaturgic acts by female saints are so rare in western hagiography. At the centre of the ceremony then would be a woman, probably originally identified with a version of the usually female divinity associated with the generation and restoration of animals in Eurasian cultures.[84] As Christianity extended its purchase on the countryside, such customs could quite easily become attached to any available saint, with a preference towards female ones.

The goose might appear to be an odd element in a harvest ritual and the persistence of this particular animal is hard to explain. Yet it seems that it was essential to the meaning of the story, and in fact geese did once have serious sacral associations. The goose was sacred to the cult of Juno Moneta in Rome. While the reason for this sacredness lies in Livy's story of the warning to Rome of a Gallic attack, it seems most likely that this explanation was invented because the original had been forgotten. The goose was also sacred to Hera in Greece, where temples also sometimes contained sacred geese.[85] In the first century BC, a detail was added to the fifth labour of Heracles, which was to kill the 'Stymphalian' birds, identified with geese or swans. Diodorus wrote in this story that an 'innumerable flock of birds were ruining the crops in the surrounding countryside'.[86] Thus the opening element of the goose story appears in another mythological context, perhaps indicating that parts of the story had existed for some time. The crystallisation of the goose miracle as it appears in western Europe may have happened relatively recently before it first appeared in written form, or it may have been much older. Nonetheless, it is clear that it is not problematic to suppose an association of geese with sacral affairs.

Geese, among other birds, in more recent western European folklore have been found sometimes to symbolise the 'corn spirit', in Frazer's words, and are associated with a range of practices connected with the harvest. In nineteenth-century Shropshire, where the 'gander's neck' was the last handful of ears to be left standing, the harvester who won the neck was supposed to keep it in the house for good luck. Elsewhere there are numerous practices and beliefs associated with the harvest goose, which was often due to the labourer.[87] There is a sixteenth-century

[84] Ginzburg, *Ecstasies*, p. 135.

[85] See Gertrude Jobes, *Dictionary of Mythology, Folklore and Symbols* (New York 1962), 2 vols, at I, p. 676, and *Dictionary of Folklore, Mythology and Legend*, ed. Maria Leach (London 1975), s.v. 'goose', both of which note the widespread sacral associations of geese in Eurasian culture.

[86] John Pollard, *Birds in Greek Life and Thought* (Plymouth 1977), p. 98.

[87] Frazer, *The Golden Bough*, part 5, vol. I, pp. 268–78, 295–6; *Shropshire Folk-Lore*, ed. Charlotte Sophia Burne (London 1883), pp. 371–5; and Steve Round, *The Penguin Guide to the Superstitions of Britain and Ireland* (London 2003), pp. 213–14. It is not necessary to accept Frazer's conceptualisation of the folklore here to recognise the crucial connection between geese and harvest practices, stories

reference to the breastbone of a goose eaten at Martinmas Eve being said to predict the severity of the winter, while there are many other references to the use of geese for prognosticating weather.[88] Folklore is of course unstable by nature, and none of this can be used to make assumptions about practices in previous centuries, but it is all indicative that geese were not out of place in local agricultural ceremonies of the medieval period.

The goose resurrection miracles, if they are to be imagined as ceremonies, would probably be of the nature of a harvest celebration, perhaps with a feast, and a symbolic resurrection of an animal. This would presumably have been carried out normally by a village woman, ceremonially identified with an Otherworld spirit. If the driving of the geese was in any way enacted, it is easy to see how the peasant story could shift, in some cases the symbolic actor carrying out the task, in others it being delegated to other villagers. Thus the presence of the delegation element in the recorded stories could either represent hagiographic amendment to the story, to reflect the role of the saint as landlord, or it could reflect variations in the original story itself. It is finally worth noting that in none of the recorded stories does any punishment fall upon the servant who took the goose. The closest to an exception to this rule occurs in a somewhat courtly image of apology in the Opportuna poem.[89] This may reflect the role of the harvest and resurrection in the original ceremony, where the taking of the goose was not conceived as a transgression. It may be that it was the role of the Church in the adaptation of these practices which transformed the action into a transgression. Once the geese, and indeed the land, come to be seen as the property of the saint, or the property of the Church, then the eating of the harvest goose comes to be a theft, rather than an enactment of death and rejuvenation.

This discussion may also shed light on the peculiar ninth-century story of Saint Winwaloe's sister and the goose. In this story, the saint's sister loses her eye in an attack by a domestic goose while she was playing a 'girlish chasing game' with companions.[90] The sister is otherwise referred to as a 'virgin' as if she was not a girl so much as an unmarried woman, which, together with the unexplained violent intervention of the goose into the girls' play, raises some questions about the significance of the game. Although the story as it stands is clearly not related to the other goose resurrections, if the latter do represent a peasant ritual, then this may be another appearance of the story in hagiography. The girls' game may represent the goose ceremony itself, here being denigrated as a childish activity, rather than being absorbed into the *virtus* of a saint, as in the later stories.

However, the hagiographer is not simply dismissing the peasant ritual as childish, but is also symbolically linking it to death and disfigurement, which can be

and beliefs.

[88] From Skelton's *Garland of Laurel* (1523), cited in J. Brand, *Faiths and Folklore: A Dictionary*, ed. W. Carew Hazlitt (London 1905), 2 vols, at I, p. 284, and more generally see Charles Swainson, *The Folk Lore and Provincial Names of British Birds* (London 1886), pp. 147–8.

[89] L. de la Sicotière, *Légende de Sainte Opportune*, lines 169–72.

[90] Wrdisten, *Vita Winwaloei*, ch. 1, no. 6, p. 251, and see above note 23.

interpreted in a spiritual sense. By participating in a non-Christian practice, the young woman is exposing herself to grave spiritual danger, symbolised by the loss of her 'jewel-like eye'. Her parents are also reduced to extreme grief as they witness her slipping into death as a result of the injury. Fortunately for her, her brother is an *athleta Dei*, and is able to restore her to physical, or spiritual, health. The restoration of the goose, while presumably mirroring the popular story, also represents the saint's dominance over pre-Christian rites, and his restoration of earthly and spiritual harmony to the state before it was disrupted by the heathen rural 'game'. While the later stories attempt to absorb a rural practice into Christian miracle, the Winwaloe story represents an older strategy of denigration and suppression of pre-Christian beliefs and practices.

It is in the transformation of a peasant ceremony into a Christian miracle story that an explanation can be found for hagiographic interest in the goose-resurrection narrative appearing, first in the tenth century, and then almost all together in the late eleventh and the twelfth centuries. It is in precisely this period that the Church was truly beginning to spread throughout the countryside, at a greater or lesser pace in different regions. This was the period of the spread of parish churches, with the widespread imposition of Church time on labour, disrupting rhythms of peasant agriculture that dated back a thousand years or more.[91] In this context, the localisation of many of these miracles becomes significant. Goscelin locates the story in a village of Wedon, while William of Malmesbury specifically refers to Wereburga owning a strip of field outside the walls of Chester. Amelberga's miracle is located in the village of Mater, and Waldebert's in Nant, his birthplace. All these are very specific, as if to emphasise the control of the saint over the land and labour of those particular places. This reflects the social relations which gave birth to the story, if not literally where the story was first transformed from village ritual to Church miracle.[92]

The occasional appearance of the command that the geese never return to the land is thus not only the addition of a standard hagiographic motif of the domination of nature. It is also an encoding of the abolition of independent peasant social relations and associated elements of old belief. If the goose resurrection miracles represent in some form the appearance of popular culture in hagiographic literature, they do not do so as the accidents of hagiographic whim. Neither are they 'pure' relics of a popular culture. Rather, the narrative and motifs of the story reflect the real social relations of the countryside, and a real step change in the power of the ecclesiastical

[91] For the parish system and peasant labour see Moore, *First European Revolution*, particularly pp. 52–60.

[92] There are later appearances of the goose miracle in other saints' legends, which may either reflect the stories' transformation into a new literary topos, or a similar social process happening elsewhere, and perhaps some combination of these two factors. In England there is a goose miracle in the apparently fourteenth-century *Vita* of Saint Eanswide. This is another example of the saint conducting the geese herself, so cannot easily be seen as simply a copy of Saint Wereburga's story: *De Sancta Eanswida Virgine et Abbatissa*, in Horstmann, *Nova Legenda Anglie*, pp. 296–300, at pp. 298–9. For other late examples see Fournée, 'Le culte populaire', p. 271.

elite over the peasantry. In another sense, the 'meaning' of the story had changed in its transition from oral ceremony to written legend, as it encodes beneath a story of saintly fruitfulness and mercy the Church's dominion over all aspects of nature, and human labour within it. Thus the most exceptional story within the hagiographic tradition of the animal miracle reveals the social role of the dominant theme in the genre.

CHAPTER 6

The Hermit and the Hunter

THE goose resurrection miracles are an example of the absorption of an aspect of peasant culture into elite hagiography, not through a superstitious lapse on the part of hagiographers, but through the social relations in which ecclesiastical institutions were embedded. If that process happened in the case of the goose stories, then it might be expected to have occurred in other cases as well. The difficulty in assessing many miracle stories, particularly from the eleventh and twelfth centuries, lies in the large numbers of literary sources already in existence, while the same stories would have been circulating independently in popular and oral form. It was observed above, for example, that the 'Elijah and the raven' topos plausibly circulated at both levels by the eleventh century.[1] Determining how far a particular example of a topos may have been broadly popular or literary in origin depends upon contextual and internal judgements on each, which often cannot be definitive. Many traditional topoi to do with the control of animals may be expected to have appealed to the concerns of the peasantry, but a literary adaptation of a popular story along these lines might be indistinguishable from a story emanating entirely from a monastic context. One group of stories which is open to analysis is the 'hermit and hunter' topos, where the saint protects hunted animals.

However, before considering that topos there are a few idiosyncratic stories, also concerning saints and the wilderness, that hint at the widespread importance of folklore in the formation of miracles. There are a few stories of interactions between saints and wolves which go beyond the exercise of holy domination over these feared predators, and can even include a degree of reciprocity between animal and holy man. As a rule, the hagiographic role of wolves is overwhelmingly negative. They appear sometimes as demonic agents, and at others as symbols of human villains, heretics or bandits, as in the story of Saint Francis and the wolf of Gubbio.[2] Saint Columban was once surrounded in the forest by twelve wolves, apparently in their diabolical role, but his faith in God protected him. Similarly the twelfth-century English holy man, Godric of Finchale, reduced a wolf set on devouring him to

[1] See above Chapter 2, p. 28.

[2] Klingender, *Animals*, p. 456, for the wolf of Gubbio, and *passim* for wolves in medieval art and literature. The story of the wolf of Gubbio appears in the fourteenth-century *The Little Flowers of Saint Francis*, in *St. Francis of Assissi: Writings and Early Biographies*, ed. Marion A. Habig (Chicago 1972) (hereafter Habig, *Omnibus*), pp. 1295–1506, at ch. 21, pp. 1348–51. The story anthropomorphises the wolf to such an extent that it may well be an example of a late reconciliation miracle where a powerful human figure is represented by the wolf.

submissive humility.[3] In Italian hagiography, Elisa Anti found that into the eleventh and twelfth centuries saints increasingly acted as protectors against wolves. Anti plausibly links the growth in popularity of this type of story to widening cultivation and the confinement of wolves to ever smaller habitats, causing an increase in human contact with them.[4]

The subject of wolves is an area where both hagiographic interest in the exploration of a saint's *virtus* and peasant concerns with a significant threat could have interacted in some circumstances to allow the creation, propagation and recording of idiosyncratic miracles. During the twelfth century, Blandin Abbey in Ghent developed the cult of the bishop Saint Gudwal. The saint's original career lay in Brittany, as the successor of Saint Malo, but his relics now rested in Ghent. The *Vita* contains not only an animal resurrection miracle already noted above, but also two miracles concerning wolves.[5] In the first, the saint resurrected a sheep with a touch of his pastoral staff, and then tamed the wolf who had killed the animal.[6] Later, during a storm, Gudwal saw a wolf walking as if lame. The animal bowed its head to the saint upon being called over, and exhibited a thorn in its paw. The saint cured it with the same staff used to resurrect the sheep, but commanded the wolf to be vegetarian thereafter.[7]

There are multiple possible sources behind this cluster of animal miracles. It is possible to argue that the *Vita* was based upon an earlier presumably Breton account, which in turn was influenced by Irish hagiography, explaining both the resurrection story and the healing of the wolf.[8] However, the latter miracle does not have a match in early Irish hagiography, and the resurrection story is not obviously drawn from any particular early Irish model. It is more likely that the Blandin *Vita* was composed out of a minimum of existing knowledge, with miracles and other elements added through borrowing, as was the case for so many *vitae* of this period.[9] If a Breton exemplar for the miracles is not assumed, and given the presence of the Pharailde story in twelfth-century Ghent, it appears as if the animal resurrection motif was generally current in the area. The story of Gudwal's lame wolf recalls, of course, the tale of Androcles' lion, which had entered into Christian hagiography as a minor topos by this time.[10] Yet, some further explanation is required for the appearance of this rare motif attached to the usually villainous figure of the wolf.[11]

3 Jonas, *Vitae sanctorum*, bk 1, ch. 8, pp. 166–7, and *Vita Godrici*, ch. 18, no. 51, pp. 63–4.

4 Elisa Anti, *Santa e animali nell' Italia padana secoli IV–XII* (Bologna 1998), pp. 162–9. Anti notes that any earlier 'Celto-Germanic' culturally positive associations of wolves were increasingly lost in the Christian era.

5 See Chapter 5, note 48.

6 *Vita Gudwali*, ch. 4, nos. 35–6, p. 738.

7 Ibid. ch. 4, nos. 37–8, p. 739.

8 As suggested by Doble, *Saint Gudwal*, p. 19.

9 For an exploration of this model of hagiographic production see Head, *Hagiography and the Cult of the Saints*, particularly pp. 64–70, 202–7.

10 See above, Chapter 2, p. 21.

11 Another positive appearance for a wolf is found in the account of the martyrdom of the English

Here a consideration of Irish parallels, rather than direct influences, may be useful. Both Saint Ailbe's wolf-mother and Saint Fínán's wolf were figures clearly identified with the Otherworld.[12] In addition the motif of the lame animal has been encountered functioning as a signal of a narrative of death and rebirth, the key Otherworld theme, in the context of the goose resurrections of Saint Vigor and Saint Opportuna.[13] The same resonances might be at work here. Saint Gudwal's wolf may be a fairy figure, which would explain the saint's unusual dealings with the creature. A story of the gratitude of a non-Christian power in the shape of a wolf could have been a popular story in circulation around Blandin. In this model, the monks borrowed and adapted the story for their saint in order to promote the cult, thus attaching stories to him which would have had local resonance. This seems a more likely explanation for the unusual resurrection miracle and the atypical wolf story both appearing in the same *Vita*, than an otherwise unexplained literary borrowing of the rare Androcles motif, on top of an attenuated Irish influence.

Thus Gudwal's miracle would function on different levels. For the monks the story would have emphasised the saint's transformative and dominating power over the ambiguous supernatural forces, which would normally have been treated as simply demonic in nature. The appearance of the Otherworld in the shape of a wolf serves to reinforce its essentially malevolent character. However, in order to appeal to popular belief, the relationship between the saint and creature is ambiguous, allowing for a different understanding of the story in the popular sphere. In either case the superiority of the Christian saint over other supernatural forces would be clear. The story is a more subtle way of dealing with popular belief in possibly helpful fairy forces than the usual blunt insistence on their diabolical character.

Another tamed wolf of a clearly Otherworld nature appears in the probably twelfth-century Welsh *Vita* of Saint Tatheus. Among this saint's miracles are two animal restoration stories, one of horses revived after the saint's curse, and another of a pet pigeon returned unharmed after being taken by a kite. Both of these follow reasonably accessible hagiographic precedent by this time. Another story is somewhat more unusual, as a miraculously tamed stag offers itself voluntarily, through God's will, to be slaughtered for dinner.[14] Following this is a story whose opening is familiar from earlier Irish miracles. A she-wolf, having taken seven baby swine for its whelps, is required to deliver one of the cubs to the swineherd and to return tamely to the forest. From this point the story begins to diverge from

Saint Edmund, whose head is kept safe from other animals by a wolf: see Catherine Cubitt, 'Sites and Sanctity: Revisiting the Cult of Murdered and Martyred Anglo-Saxon Royal Saints', *Early Medieval Europe* 9 (2000), pp. 53–83, at pp. 63–4. Cubitt convincingly argues that much of the story of Saint Edmund arises from popular devotion and folkloric motifs, and notes also the importance of wolves in pagan cosmology. See also the story of Saint Kenelm where animals feature in a story largely constructed from folkloric motifs: ibid. pp. 69–70.

12 See above, Chapter 4, pp. 79 and 77 respectively.

13 See above, Chapter 5, p. 106.

14 *Vita S. Tathei*, in A. W. Wade-Evans, *Vitae Sanctorum Hiberniae* (Cardiff 1944), pp. 270–87, at chs. 5, 8–9 and 15, pp. 272–4, 276–8 and 282 respectively.

previous Irish models, as the wolf cub grows up tame and guards the flock: 'for the space of three years no wild beast injured the flock, nor robber'. The house wolf visited the saint every day for three years until one day it was hit on the side by an angry serving man: 'Being struck and offended, and turning itself three times, it went back to the wood, not returning to the flock again for anger and indignation'.[15]

Here, in enacting the three-fold movement for breaking a spell, ubiquitous in folklore, the wolf is clearly revealed as a fairy figure.[16] The wolf was a hostage and servant to the saint in payment for damage to the saint's property, but in a relationship that could be broken if the saint's side transgressed some unspoken aspect of the deal. The gifts of the Otherworld must not be abused. Nonetheless, in return, the she-wolf restored the young swine to the saint, apparently being just as capable as the saint of resurrecting the dead. The relationship between the saint and the wolf in this story is essentially one of equals, with the saint's power over nature somewhat overshadowed by the lupine fairies. Some may consider this Welsh story to be an exception to the general western hagiographic tradition, as an example of 'Celtic' folklore. However, Wales was well within the sphere of influence of dominant Church tradition by this point, so the appearance of such a story remains notable. Taken in parallel with Saint Gudwal, it remains evidence of a general western European folkloric pattern.

Firmly outside any question of 'Celtic' origins are the wolf stories in the *Vita* of Saint Norbert of Xanten. Here wolves are treated equitably by the saint. On one occasion, Norbert's monks came across a wolf devouring a roebuck, and chased it away, taking the prey back with them to the monastery. The wolf followed after and made a complaint outside the door, while sitting 'tamely'. Upon hearing this, Norbert inquired about events, and commanded that the monks 'return to him what is his, you have done an injustice taking what is not yours'. Having received his property, the wolf went away peacefully.[17] In one sense this story fits into the broad theme of the predator behaving tamely in the presence of the saint, but this is not at all a typical demonstration of holy prelapsarian power. It could be seen within the prism of twelfth-century reformers' concerns that Church institutions should not become acquisitive property owners, inflicting injustice upon others. No doubt this is part of the resonance of the story, but that alone would not explain why such a theme would take the form of a saint's kindness to a wolf.

On another occasion, one of the brothers was aided in guarding his flock by a wolf, who patiently minded the animals all day. As the monk returned to the house, the wolf followed after, but was locked outside the door, and made complaint by knocking on the door with his paw. Norbert, having discovered the matter, again

15 Ibid. ch. 16, pp. 282–5.

16 On this and related folkloric motifs see Stith Thompson, *Motif-Index of Folk Literature* (Copenhagen 1957), 6 vols; see for examples motifs D563, D1791, E501.14.3, R112.2. Also see T. Gwynn-Jones, *Welsh Folklore and Folk-Custom* (Cambridge 1930), pp. 61–2, for some striking parallel examples involving fairy relationships with mortals.

17 *Vita Sancti Norberti*, MGH SS 12 (1856), ed. Roger Williams, pp. 663–706, at ch. 17, p. 692

castigated his monk for not giving due recompense to the wolf: 'the labourer is worthy of his food', he declares, quoting Luke 10:7.[18] This story can be read on a number of levels. Firstly it is tempting to take it literally and to see the wolf as a feral sheepdog, which would not have been an unknown phenomenon at this time. Equally, it can be seen as an allegory of Saint Norbert's virtue in welcoming all kinds into his orbit.[19] Both these readings may be relevant to this story, but neither explains the genesis of the two wolf stories in this *Vita*. However, if the wolves had some supernatural connotation, as in the wolves of Saint Gudwal and Saint Tatheus, then a reason for the creation and remembrance of the two miracles is provided. The anthropocentric presentation of the second wolf while standing outside the door, knocking with its foot, might be one clue to a submerged reference to Otherworld powers. Once again, for the monks the story would signify the extension of monastic hierarchies into the natural world, but popularly it would illustrate the connections between Christian and Otherworld powers. In any case, all the wolf stories discussed here involve a recognition of rights or the exchange of favours between the saint and an animal. This pattern of *quid pro quo* was also found in the goose resurrection stories, and may in itself represent a characteristically popular logic in miracle stories, different from, but not incompatible with, standard hagiographic themes.

However these stories are interpreted, the saints occupy ambiguous positions, being at least as close to the wild as to the social. This holy ambiguity is recognised in the mainstream hagiographic 'companionship of animals' theme, where the saint prefers the Edenic company of obedient animals to sinful humanity. It is the holy man's liminality, his self-alienation from family and secular society, and consequent residence on the threshold of the civilised and the wild, or between the mortal and metaphysical worlds, that produces his miraculous power.[20] The saint's ambiguous position can align the saint more directly with the beastly, and for popular mentalities, this relationship between the saint and the wild was likely the context of wonders and miracles. If there is a submerged Otherworld theme in the wolf and saint stories, then this is an example of the liminal character of saintly power in popular understanding. The power of the saint enables him or her to deal safely with the forces of the Otherworld. This pattern was most clearly followed in the Irish *Vita* of Saint Ailbe, left under a rock as a baby, raised by a wolf mother, and manifesting his miraculous power after being returned to human society.[21] It is within these patterns and resonances of miracle stories that the topos of the 'hermit and hunter' miracle should be approached.

[18] Ibid. ch. 17, p. 692

[19] On this virtue of the saint, see Constable, *Reformation of the Twelfth Century*, pp. 70–1, 97–8.

[20] On the concept of liminality see Victor Turner, *The Ritual Process* (London 1974), and for its application to holy men and women see Christopher Holdsworth, 'Hermits and the Power of the Frontier', in *Saints and Saints' Lives*, ed. Keith Bate *et al.*, Reading Medieval Studies 16 (1990), pp. 55–76. See also Christopher Holdsworth, 'Christina of Markyate', in *Medieval Women: Studies in Church History: Subsidia 1*, ed. Derek Baker (Oxford 1978), pp. 185–204.

[21] See Chapter 4, p. 79.

The earliest example of this topos comes in Sulpicius Severus' Saint Martin, where a hare was saved from huntsmen's dogs: 'The blessed man through his pious judgement took compassion on it in its danger and ordered the dogs to leave off following it and let the fugitive get away. They pulled up at once, at the first words of the order . . . And so, with its pursuers pinned down, the little hare got safely away.'[22] The notable aspect of this story is that while it does demonstrate saintly control over nature, nothing is transformed by the miracle, which is wholly for the benefit of an animal. The hare remains untamed and does not come to serve the saint. It is thus unusual for a patristic animal miracle. As discussed above, the story appears centuries later in almost identical form in the case of Saint Anselm of Canterbury, where, in more homely fashion, the saint is moved to tears by the plight of the small animal pursued by the boys and dogs of his own household.[23] Certainly, Eadmer was conscious of the example of Saint Martin and wished to associate his contemporary figure with one of the greatest of the Fathers. Nonetheless, it remains a point in question why, at such a pivotal moment in the *Vita*, Eadmer should have chosen this one particular story to act as an affirmation of Anselm's place in the saintly tradition. A full consideration of the 'hermit and hunter' topos will provide a context for the medieval resonances of the story.

The most common version of the topos involves a large beast such as a stag or a boar. Possibly the earliest example is Gregory of Tours's miracle of the hermit Saint Aemilianus. He lived in a 'solitude' in the forest cultivating a small field: 'there were no other inhabitants there except the beasts and birds, who gathered around him every day as around a servant of God'.[24] A young man named Brachio, in the service of a powerful man, was hunting a boar through the forest. The boar came within the boundary around the saint's cell and the hounds were unable to go further. The boar was then allowed to escape into the forest while the saint endeavoured to convert the young man, who later became an abbot.[25] For Gregory, the point of this story is the conversion effected by a holy man, who thus creates another saintly father in his wake. Normally, the story leads more modestly to the moral regeneration of a king or great nobleman, and often his donation of land to the Church.

The tenth-century story of the hunted doe and Saint Giles is probably the most widely known example of the topos. Saint Giles, a hermit and abbot of the seventh and early eighth centuries, at one time was fed by the milk of a wild doe in the deep forest near Nîmes. Hunters chased this doe into the hermit's cave, but the dogs were unable to pass the saint, who was on guard. The king, anachronistically named variously as a Visigothic King Flavius, or Wamba, learning of the strange events, accompanied the hunt on its third attempt to capture the doe. On this occasion one of the hunters shot at the doe, but the arrow hit Giles instead.[26] Thus the king

[22] Sulpicius Severus, *Dialogi*, Dialogue 2, ch. 9, col. 208; trans. Hoare, *Western Fathers*, p. 115.

[23] Eadmer, *Vita Anselmi*, bk 2, ch. 18, pp. 89–91; see also above, p. 1.

[24] Gregory of Tours, *Liber Vitae Patrum*, ch. 12, no. 1, p. 712; trans. James, *Life of the Fathers*, pp. 81–2.

[25] Gregory of Tours, *Liber Vitae Patrum*, ch. 12, no. 2, pp. 712–13.

[26] *Vita Sancti Aegidii*, *AASS* 1 September, pp. 284–304, at ch. 2, nos. 11–17, p. 301.

discovered the saintly inhabitant of the wilderness, who rejected the king's offers of medical help, trusting to God instead. The king then frequently came to the hermit to talk of spiritual matters, and eventually the saint was convinced to become the abbot of a monastery, newly endowed for the purpose by the king.

The meeting between the sylvan saint and the king through the intervention of a hunted animal is the key ambiguous element of the topos. In the Giles version, the purity and miraculous power of the saint is linked to his mode of life unsupported by any social activity, to the point that he is fed by the milk of a wild animal. There is in fact a contradiction lurking at the heart of the story between the wild virtue of the saint and the institutional Church into which the king coaxes the holy man. From a story of the conversion of the king, it becomes a story of the conversion of the hermit to civilisation. The topos of the saint's reluctance to accept a position of authority does not entirely hide this structural shift at the heart of the story. Such a shift is absent from Gregory of Tours's version simply because the nobleman is recruited as a disciple of the saint, but this is a very unusual denouement in the genre. The Giles story is thus not a clear case of Christian virtue overcoming secular sin, since it is the fallible king who, in a sense, redeems the holy man by bringing him back within the realm of society. The story's structure thus reveals the ambiguity of the saint and his connection to magical wild forces.[27]

Other versions of the topos do not betray the same ambiguity to be found in the Giles legend. The Breton Saint Guenalius is celebrated in a late-ninth-century *Vita* for offering refuge while on the road rather than in a hermitage. A stag chased by hunters and dogs took refuge under his evidently voluminous cloak, and the dogs did not dare to hunt it further. The astonished hunters returned to their king to tell the story. In parallel with Saint Giles, the king sought out the saint in humility, and eventually gave him two villas.[28] In a probably eleventh-century *Vita*, another Breton saint, Brioc, encountered a hunter-king on the road, and rescued a stag by making the sign of the cross at the hunting dogs. Unlike the case of Saint Guenalius, this miracle does not lead to any royal relationship.[29] Both these stories avoid characterising the saint as a wilderness wonder in his own right, thus avoiding the contradiction found in the story of Saint Giles, but rather present the story in terms of the power of the Church over secular lords.

While many examples of the genre are pretexts for the beginning of a patronage relationship between hunter and saint, the path could sometimes be a fraught one. A Welsh king, Meirchion the 'Wild', is chasing a stag, which flees into the cell of Saint Illtud, according to his twelfth-century *Vita*. The animal kneels in fear and

[27] It is worth noting that the doe could have been seen as a sacred animal in popular belief. Certainly in Merovingian France there were repeated prohibitions on people dressing up as stags during the Kalends of January: see Yitzhak Hen, *Culture and Religion in Merovingian Gaul* (New York 1995), pp. 169–71.

[28] *Vita Sancti Guenaili*, *AASS* 3 November, pp. 669–79, at ch. 15, p. 677; see also F. Morvannou, 'Guénolé et Guénaël', *Annales de Bretagne* 81 (1974), pp. 25–42, at p. 29.

[29] *Vita Sancti Brioci*, ed. R. P. Plaine, in *Analecta Bollandiana* 2 (1883), pp. 161–90, at ch. 33, p. 176. This king is a *tyrnanus*.

exhaustion at the saint's feet, and the dogs outside cease to bark. The king is furious that the saint should presume to be living on his hunting land, but accepts the saint's hospitality. The king proceeds to behave boorishly despite the miraculous provision of fish, bread, salt and wine in successive acts of saintly wonders.[30] It takes a stern lecture from a heavenly vision that night for the king to acquire enough humility to grant the land to the saint.[31] The mark of wildness seems here to have been transferred from hermit to king. Another Welsh pair, King Maelgwn and Saint Cybi, have a dispute over a she-goat which has fled for protection to the saint's cottage. The angry king finds the saint unwilling to let the animal go unless the king agrees to give up all the land that the goat is able to run around in the course of the chase, which is itself a variant of a folktale type.[32] The king, not being a folklorist, agrees, and in the event, must give up the land as well as the goat, which has successfully run the circuit back to the saint's protection.[33] In both these cases the saint appears rather in the form of the cunning and magically aided hero of a folk-tale. The ambiguous saint associated with the liminal wonders of the wilderness is once again visible.

The crucial mediating role of the hunted beast is particularly prominent in the story of the sixth-century Saint Carileff, or Calais, the founder of the monastery of Anisole in Maine. The first account of the saint is probably ninth-century.[34] Carileff is living as a hermit in a place of horror, full of briars, thorns and serpents, but exercises control over the greatest manifestation of this desert, a wild bull of 'wondrous size and wondrous ferocity'. It is accustomed to come to the holy man and act as if it wanted a blessing, with its head bowed. The saint would draw the animal's head towards himself, and stroke it, claiming to his companions that this was a sign of the power of God: it came to them in anger but showed gentleness, prefiguring the actions of the king to follow.[35] The king, named unreliably as Childebert, hearing of the wonder beast and the saint's power, wishes to see for himself, as the beast is able to evade hunters, and even mere sightings, flying 'like a bird in flight from any seeing eyes'. This bull does not appear as a simple wild animal, but as a magic beast. Nonetheless, the cunning king tracks it to the hermit's dwelling, where it takes

30 *Vita Sancti Iltuti*, in Wade-Evans, *Vitae Sanctorum Hiberniae*, pp. 194–233, at ch. 8, p. 204.

31 Ibid. chs. 9–10, pp. 206–8.

32 See Tom Peete Cross, *Motif-Index of Early Irish Literature* (New York 1968), motifs H1584.2, K185.7, and Thompson, *Motif-Index*, motifs H1584.2, K185.1–185.8, particularly K185.5 and K185.7. As well as many Irish examples of the motif, there are also Indian and Russian variants. A modern variant appears in the history of the Catholic Church in St John's, Newfoundland: see Paul O'Neill, *Upon This Rock: The Story of the Roman Catholic Church in Newfoundland and Labrador* (St John's 1984), pp. 110–11.

33 *Vita Sancti Cybi*, in Wade-Evans, *Vitae Sanctorum Hiberniae*, pp. 234–51, at pp. 246–9. Another story which contains the motif of a gift of land secured by the hunted beast's circumambulation can be found in a twelfth-century story of Saint Oudoceus: *Liber Landavensis*, *Vita Beati Oudocei*, pp. 123–32, at pp. 129–30.

34 *Vita Sancti Carileffi Sacerdotis et Abbatis*, MGH SSRM 3 (1896), ed. Bruno Krusch, pp. 386–94, at pp. 387–9. See A. Poncelet, 'Les saints de Micy', *Analecta Bollandiana* 24 (1905), pp. 5–104, at pp. 31–44, and Head, *Hagiography and Cult of Saints*, p. 108.

35 *Vita Carileffi*, chs. 5–6, pp. 390–1.

refuge behind the holy man. The king is outraged that the saint should interfere with his hunt, and commands the monks to depart the place, but then finds himself unable to leave. Eventually he is forced to apologise to Carileff. Having been given an apparently substantial amount of wine, the king becomes 'merry', and promises to build a monastery in the place for the saint.[36]

The relationship between the king and the saint becomes a foundation story claiming royal grants for the saint's monastery. However, other miracles, such as those of Guenalius or Illtud, show that such a story does not require a marvellous creature to engineer this resolution. The wonder beast, which magically escapes from all sight yet which comes gently to the hermit, is best seen as a fairy beast, and the saint's virtue is here once again connected to ambiguous wilderness powers. Far from the saint destroying such demonic forces, he appears to be somewhat akin to the Otherworld, even protecting it from threats.

This reading of the story seems to be confirmed by the second *Vita* of Carileff, written perhaps relatively shortly after the first, but treating the story very differently. The imagery used to set the scene is entirely distinct, presenting the wilderness not so much as a place of horror, as a sylvan idyll of fruitfulness with gentle wildlife abundant.[37] The place of horror has been colonised through the process of hagiographic redaction. The bull's wondrous ferocity and capabilities are entirely downplayed, while the encounter between king and saint is greatly extended.[38] The emphasis of the story thus falls much more firmly on the relationship of the king and the saint, with the saint's control over nature a straightforward topos leading to the establishment of religious rule in the wilderness. If the first version of the story absorbed or adapted a folkloric motif in the wonder beast, then it seems the second redaction found this aspect inappropriate and suppressed it, restricting the story to a monastic foundation legend.

Certainly one major function of the 'hermit and hunter' topos within hagiography was to engineer a foundation story linking monasteries and saints to rulers, generally in the distant past. However, folkloric motifs appear to be embedded in a number of stories, which implies they were part of another dynamic, one between ecclesiastical institutions and popular culture. A second function would then probably involve the promotion of a cult to the surrounding population in general. It may be that many legends were adapted from popular stories rather than originating in a purely literary hagiographic context. If this is correct it would indicate the increasing permeability of hagiography by popular belief from the tenth century onwards. It might be argued, as an alternative, that the 'hermit and hunter' topos was a largely 'Celtic' influence upon the hagiography of western Europe. Certainly, with the exception of Gregory of Tours, the examples of the core genre appear earliest in Ireland in the eighth century, with Saint Ailbe and Saint Cainnech. The latter is a relatively standard story, with a stag rescued from a hunter. But here the hunter is not a king, and he is punished severely rather than being brought within

36 Ibid. chs. 7–10, pp. 391–3.

37 *Vita Sancti Carileffi Presbyteri*, *AASS* 1 July, pp. 85–99, at chs. 11–13, p. 93.

38 Ibid. chs. 14–18, pp. 93–4.

the saint's orbit.[39] Saint Ailbe's story is stranger, it being a wolf that is saved from hunters, eventually sharing bread at the saint's table.[40]

Neither of the early Irish stories is a clear model for the mainstream tradition, which can more easily be seen as proceeding from Gregory of Tours. The Welsh stories are, of course, later than many examples, and Wales cannot be assumed to be the point of origin for the Breton stories. Moreover, there are, including Saint Giles, many other examples of this type of story from around the same period, which cannot be automatically ascribed to 'Celtic' influence. The sixth-century Saint Avitus of Micy, near Orléans, also saved a doe from hunting dogs in a *Vita* probably of the ninth century.[41] The fourth-century Italian Bishop Bassiano of Lodi, whose *Vita* was written between the ninth and eleventh centuries, saved a doe and her two fawns from hunters.[42] The examples proliferate later, including that of another fifth-century saint, Mamertin or Marian, who saved a wild bull from hunting dogs, in a *Vita* written before 1214.[43] Thus while there does appear to be a concentration of the topos in Brittany, this should not be ascribed too easily to 'Celtic' culture as such, particularly as the early Irish examples appear to differ significantly from the more standard pattern found in the Breton and French versions of the genre.

Indeed, if Gaelic-speaking cultures are advanced as the impulse behind the spread of saint and animal stories, particularly of the 'hermit and hunter' variety, then it has to be explained why they appear only in certain areas at certain times. The Belgian region is one area where an Irish influence has sometimes been claimed to account for animal miracles, on the basis that Irish missionaries were present in the eighth and ninth centuries.[44] Yet the hagiography that contains possible parallels to Irish hagiography is much later, tenth-century at the earliest and largely twelfth-century. Conversely, these kinds of stories do not make a significant mark on English hagiography in the seventh and eighth centuries, where it reasonably might be expected if 'Celtic' influence was so pervasive. The 'hermit and hunter' topos in particular does not seem to appear in England until the twelfth century. It seems likely that parallels between Irish and Welsh hagiography and the continental hagiographic tradition owe more to a prior shared stock of stories than to the spread of a specific 'Celtic' pattern of saints' tales.

If there is a systematic variation in the regional appearance of the stories, it might be noted that in both the Irish and Welsh stories violent conflict between the saint and the hunter or king appears more consistently. The secular figure tends to be portrayed pejoratively rather than automatically being impressed by the saint's virtue, although such a portrayal can be found in magnificent form also in the story

39 Heist, *Vita Cainnechi*, ch. 49, p. 195.

40 Heist, *Vita Albei*, ch. 52, p. 130, and see above, Chapter 4, p. 78.

41 *Vita Sancti Aviti Eremitae*, *AASS* 17 June, pp. 360–4, at no. 17, p. 364. On the hagiography see Poncelet, 'Les saints de Micy', pp. 15–17.

42 *Vita Sancti Bassiani, Episcopi Laudensis*, *AASS* 19 January, pp. 221–6; ch. 2, no. 9, p. 223.

43 *Vita Sancti Mariani*, *AASS* 20 April, pp. 758–61; ch. 3, p. 760.

44 See Irène Snieders, 'L'influence de l'hagiographie irlandais sur les *vitae* des saints irlandais de Belgique', *Revue d'histoire ecclésiastique* 24 (1928), pp. 596–627, 828–67, particularly pp. 833–9.

of Saint Carileff. Nonetheless, different states of development of the Church and lordly power in Wales and Ireland compared to the rest of western Europe could explain the difference in frequency. Hagiography in western Europe was using the 'hermit and hunter' story at least in part as a parable for the benefit of secular lords, who should recognise the importance of the Church, co-operate with its leaders and endow its institutions with lands. The institutional power of both Church and secular lords, to different degrees, was far less stable in either Wales or Ireland than elsewhere even up to the twelfth century.

Whether or not the topos bears some imprint of 'Celtic' cultural influence, it became increasingly popular in western hagiography from around the tenth century, marking a notable divergence from the standard patristic tradition, where the saint is placed in domination over the wild, rather than in protection of it.

The 'hermit and hunter' genre may be connected to and influenced by another strand of popular belief involving the figure of the wild man. The connection can be explored through a story imported from Byzantium which became one of the most popular late versions of the 'hermit and hunter' topos. The legendary Saint Blaise of Sebaste was a fourth-century martyred bishop whose cult first appears in the ninth century, but which developed in western Europe between the tenth and twelfth centuries, and whose Latin legend appears to begin to spread in the tenth century, exploding in popularity in the eleventh and twelfth centuries.[45] The story of Saint Blaise is not strictly a 'hermit and hunter' miracle tale, since the saint himself is the wild prey of the hunters, rather than a protector of hunted animals. Blaise has retired to a cave in the mountains where wild animals flock to him and he cures them of their ills through blessing with his hands. On one level this can be read as an example of the 'companionship of animals' theme, where human society is so depraved that the saint must seek company in the wild. However, the story continues, unlike patristic examples of that theme. The hunters of the governor Agricola discover the extraordinary crowd of animals outside his cave, and investigating, find the holy man. When this is reported to Agricola, he orders them to return with soldiers to bring the holy man to him.[46] This being done, Blaise is, in due course, martyred, after performing a number of miracles. One of these involves a wolf returning a pig, apparently still alive, to a widow.[47]

The structural similarities between this story and the 'hermit and hunter' topos should be clear: the holy man's healing of wild animals replaces the protection of a hunted animal. Blaise's being brought to Agricola parallels the meeting of saint and king in the other stories, but the bloody denouement clearly departs from the standard narrative. This could be explained simply by the form of the martyr story, where the death of the saint brings redemption, rather than the saint's virtue precipitating the conversion of a king. In this view, the Blaise story would indeed be a variant of the 'hermit and hunter' topos simply adapted to the cult of a legendary

[45] Armand Tchouhadjian, *Saint Blaise: évêque de Sébaste* (Paris 2004), pp. 15–21, for the sources on Saint Blaise.

[46] *Prima Acta Sancti Blasii*, *AASS* 3 February, pp. 336–9; ch. 1, nos. 2–3, p. 337.

[47] Ibid. ch. 2, no. 5, p. 337.

martyr. However, this reading does not take into account the motif of the hunters' discovery of Blaise, which has another resonance altogether. In the character of Blaise, living in a cave surrounded by animals and serving them as a healer, the saint is almost fully absorbed into the world of the beasts.

The second *Acta* develops the legend further, placing the events in the time of the war between Emperors Constantine and Licinius, explaining that God sent the animals to him for consolation in his solitude.[48] Jacobus de Voragine followed a slightly different development of the legend, placing the story during the persecution of Diocletian, and added a different elaboration of the relationship between saint and animal, explaining that 'birds brought him food, and wild animals flocked to him and would not leave until he had laid hands on them in blessing. Moreover, if any of them were ailing, they came straight to him and went away cured.'[49] While these extensions on the basic legend are not in themselves remarkable within the hagiographic tradition, they do emphasise the saint's natural association with topoi of extreme anchoritic withdrawal. Blaise is a character of the deepest wilderness solitude, who is discovered by representatives of human society. The story recalls other early legends of extreme anchorites, where holy men virtually lose their human identity.

The minor theme of the naked or hairy hermit is present early in the hagiographic tradition, where the figure is sometimes angelic and sometimes bestial. Sulpicius Severus in the Postumianus dialogue recorded a story of a hermit of Sinai who, through the grace of God, was unaware of his nakedness and his hairy covering. This hermit ran from the sight of men, but was rumoured to talk with angels.[50] There are a few stories of naked or hairy anchorites in the *Vitae Patrum*, concentrated in the early sections of book six of the *Verba Seniorum*.[51] The stories themselves are various in detail and form, even though all concern the discovery of extreme anchorites by more familiar Egyptian holy men such as Saint Macarius. The essential form of these stories is thus akin to Jerome's story of Saint Anthony finding Paul the Hermit in the deepest desert. Macarius, however, finds two naked men on an island in the middle of an oasis. The two men live among the animals of the desert without fear, and by a dispensation from God, suffer neither from the cold nor the heat, and thus do not need clothes. Macarius states that he is not in fact a monk, as these two were more truly monks.[52] Another wild anchorite exists in a far less Edenic fashion. He is found by a 'solitary', himself dressed only in a linen bag, who had walked for three days in the desert, until standing on a rock, he saw a naked man browsing the grass just like

48 *Acta Sancti Blasii II, Auctore Anonymo*, *AASS* 3 February, pp. 339–44, ch. 1, nos. 1–3, pp. 339–40.

49 *Legenda Aurea*, ch. 38, pp. 167–9.

50 Sulpicius Severus, *Dialogi*, Dialogue 1, ch. 17, cols. 194–5; trans. Hoare, *Western Fathers*, pp. 88–9. Sulpicius provides a few legends of extreme anchorites in this dialogue, see chs. 15–16, cols. 193–4.

51 *Verba Seniorum*, cols. 1006–10. There are a few others elsewhere in the same work, see for example the hermit with a 'terrible and hairy appearance' who when asked if he is a 'spirit' answers that he is just a sinning man: *Verba Seniorum*, bk 7, ch. 12, col. 894.

52 *Verba Seniorum*, bk 3, ch. 4, cols. 1006–7.

the beasts. This is the wild anchorite, who then flees from the solitary, delivering the moral that if you wish to be saved you must flee from men and be silent. The wild anchorite is about as bestial as can be, yet the story appears to imply that his way is indeed the way to salvation.[53]

A third story tells of a hermit for whom the hair of his head serves as clothing: 'he thus had a terrible appearance'. This too is a bestial and monstrous hermit, but in this case the cause is a sin. The anchorite had been a bishop, but had avoided an opportunity for martyrdom, and was condemned to this way of life to expiate that sin.[54] A somewhat later story of Saint Macarius himself has the holy man naked and covered in hair, reduced to the status of a beast.[55] This is the earliest in a largely eastern tradition of the fallen holy man who must pass through a wild 'hairy' phase in expiation of sin, before returning to a superior holy state. The legend of Saint John Chrysostom as a naked hairy penitent, walking like a beast when captured and tamed, reached Italy in the fourteenth century and became popular in fifteenth-century Germany, although this and other similar stories evidently existed artistically in the east from about 1100.[56]

This legend appears earlier in the west in a thirteenth-century poem in the Picard dialect, where the hero saint is called 'Jehan Paulus'.[57] This hermit was destined to do such great penance that his great-grandmother would be released from hell through his sanctity. Along the way the holy man falls by raping the daughter of the king of Toulouse and throwing her into a crevasse. He then goes off to live like a beast in shame, but is eventually discovered by the king's hunters. The king tames the hermit and the daughter is found in the crevasse, having been entertained by angels and martyrs for all those years. The story ends happily, with the hermit as bishop of Toulouse. The poet says his story is from the *Vitae Patrum*, but the story long predates the arrival of the most nearly analogous stories (those of the hairy Chrysostom, Paphnutius or Onuphrius) from the east.[58] With the partial exception of the hairy Macarius, the remaining 'naked hermit' stories in the *Vitae Patrum* do not provide much of a basis for the Jehan Paulus story, and the poet's claim in this

53 Ibid. ch. 10, col. 1008.

54 Ibid. ch. 12, cols. 1010–11.

55 Charles Allyn Williams, 'Oriental Affinities of the Legend of the Hairy Anchorite', *University of Illinois Studies of Language and Literature* 10 (1925), pp. 9–56, and 11 (1926), pp. 57–119, at part 2, pp. 101–2.

56 Timothy Husband, *The Wild Man: Medieval Myth and Symbolism* (New York 1980), pp. 95–8.

57 Louis Karl, 'La légende de Saint Jehan Paulus', *Revue des langues romanes* 56 (1913), pp. 425–45.

58 This story is in structure very close to the Greek story of John Chrysostom, despite dating from some two centuries before the appearance of the Chrysostom story in the West. There are a few similar stories of 'hairy hermits' which are now included in the *Vitae Patrum*, but which appear not to have been added to the Latin corpus until the fifteenth or sixteenth century. For the late appearance of the Paphnutius and Onuphrius and other stories see Williams, 'Oriental Affinities', part 2, pp. 74–86. On the general problem of the *Vitae Patrum* texts, many parts of which arrived in the corpus in the later middle ages, see Dom Cuthbert Butler, *The Lausiac History of Palladius*, vol. 6 of Texts and Studies: Contributions to Biblical and Patristic Literature, ed. J. Armitage Robinson (Cambridge, 1904), pp. 58–77, and pp. 208–10.

regard is surely spurious.[59] Nonetheless, some combination of popular elements and literary models is likely to lie behind the development of this vernacular saint legend.

The core motif here, the encounter of a king and the bestial holy man, is a very ancient motif, appearing in the very earliest surviving work of literature, *Gilgamesh*.[60] The structural reversal of the Saint Giles story, where the saint is, in a sense, tamed by the king, is a clear parallel to the meeting of Gilgamesh and Enkidu. Naturally, this is not to suggest any *direct* relationship, but simply to note the shared echoes, which point towards a common stock of folkloric motifs. The 'hermit and the hunter' tale also appears in early *Vedas* of Hindu literature, where the saint and wild man figures are clearly one and the same. Thus the topos is connected to a corpus of ancient folklore spread throughout Eurasia. This series of connections is strengthened by a parallel series of connections between saints and the wild man figure in literature of the central Middle Ages.

In Geoffrey of Monmouth's *Vita* of Merlin, the hero in his madness was a *homo silvester*, living on 'herbs and the roots of herbs', while 'hidden like an animal'.[61] Jocelyn of Furness's version of the *Vita* of Saint Kentigern includes a reference to a *homo fatuus* named Laloecen (Lailoken), who disturbed the saint's prayers.[62] This man is in the keeping of the king and after Kentigern's death is distraught and prophesies the death of the king and one of his lords. A fifteenth-century version of the meeting of Kentigern and Lailoken shows the latter as 'naked and hairy', clearly a kind of wild man. Lailoken is a Christian exiled from society by his own sin and guilt. Like Geoffrey of Monmouth's Merlin, he takes upon himself the guilt for all those who died in a battle.[63] While this narrative is recorded very late, it may nevertheless indicate the existence of a twelfth-century version of the story, which Jocelyn largely suppressed in his version of Saint Kentigern, as he did other clearly existing popular elements in the cult of Saint Kentigern.[64]

Another meeting of a hermit and a wild man occurs in the *Vita* of the twelfth-century English hermit, Godric of Finchale. Here the hermit offers the magical

59 The poet's claim may reveal more concerning the status of the *Vitae Patrum* than his sources. Perhaps these patristic texts were often treated simply as an acceptable source for any strange story.

60 Williams, 'Oriental Affinities'; on Gilgamesh and Enkidu, see part 1, pp. 13–20, and on the 'hermit and hunter' story in the Hindu *Vedas*, see part 1, pp. 25–34.

61 Geoffrey of Monmouth, *Vita Merlini*, ed. John Jay Parry in *University of Illinois Studies in Language and Literature* 10 (1925), at no. 3, p. 34: 'utitur herbarum radicibus utitur herbis; utitur arboreo fructu'.

62 Jocelyn of Furness, *Vita Kentigerni*, ch. 45, p. 241.

63 H. L. D. Ward, 'Lailoken (or Merlin Silvester)', *Romania* 22 (1896), pp. 504–26, at p. 514. This extract is from the fifteenth-century *Scotichronicon*, and is likely to be an abridgement of an earlier existing version of the story. Similar sorts of folklore as that attached to Saint Kentigern appear in the thirteenth century involving Merlin. See A. O. H. Jarmon, 'The Welsh Myrddin Poems', pp. 20–30, at pp. 25–6, for Merlin and Lailoken, and Alexandre Micha, 'The Vulgate Merlin', pp. 319–24, at p. 319, for the similar conceptions in stories of Merlin and Kentigern, both in *Arthurian Literature in the Middle Ages*, ed. Roger S. Loomis (Oxford 1959).

64 See Chapter 1, pp. 12–13.

creature an apple, and perhaps by implication Christian redemption. The wild man apparently rejects the offer, turning back to the woods with a harsh approximation of human laughter, 'hach, hach, hach'.[65] Whatever patristic origins there are for the hermit as a wild figure, the non-Christian wild man was clearly an independent living cultural figure in the twelfth-century West. Audiences of the 'hermit and hunter' stories may well have naturally made the connection between the powers of the wilderness saint and the supernatural figure of the wild man.

Blaise himself resembles very closely the wild man figure who is a herder of forest animals and is sometimes met by heroes in romance stories of the twelfth century. Such a figure with clear supernatural associations appears in Chrétien de Troyes's *Yvain*.[66] In one of the Welsh stories associated with the *Mabinogion*, a monstrous wild man commands a host of creatures in a scene that is different in emphasis, but still structurally related to Saint Blaise's beasts: 'he looked on them and bade them go graze. And they bowed their heads and did him obeisance, even as humble subjects would do to their lord.'[67] While these wild men are quite distinct from patristic representations of hairy anchorites, the kinship between the two types is clear. The wilderness saints of the 'hermit and hunter' tradition are simply another variant of the liminal figure of the wild man, sometimes a Christian saint, and sometimes still a magical figure of popular folklore.

In most of the 'hermit and hunter' miracles, this layer of popular belief is absent or has been suppressed, but the nexus of motifs and tales provides an essential context for the type as a whole. The popularity of the Blaise story in the central medieval West may owe a good deal to its similarity to existing stories of the hermit as wild man, from which the 'hermit and hunter' story may have sprung. If the 'hermit and hunter' miracles were inspired by or adapted from existing popular tales of wilderness wonders and the encounter between the social and the wild, then the Otherworld connections of the saints in these stories are a natural function of their role in popular folklore.

There are then a series of relationships involved in the increasingly frequent appearance of the 'hermit and hunter' topos, with a few examples in the ninth century, and proliferating from the tenth century onwards. In general the stories mark an absorption of peasant lore into the cults of many saints for various reasons which often cannot be tracked on an individual basis. On one level the stories can be read in terms of ecclesiastical property claims, but this does not explain why this particular topos came to be so favoured for this purpose. The explanation is to be found in attempts on the part of Church institutions to demonstrate the power of a particular saint to people in a local setting. Adapting a powerfully resonant folkloric motif would have been a useful strategy for this purpose. The defence of

[65] *Vita Godrici*, ch. 135, no. 248, pp. 261–2.

[66] Chrétien de Troyes, *Yvain* in *Oeuvres complètes*, ed. Daniel Poiron (Paris 1994), pp. 339–503, lines 280–324, at pp. 346–7. For the various forms of the Wild Man in Chrétien de Troyes's *Yvain*, see Jacques Le Goff, 'Levi-Strauss in Broceliande: A Brief Analysis of a Courtly Romance', in *The Medieval Imagination*, trans A. Goldhammer (Chicago 1988), pp. 107–31.

[67] *The Lady of the Fountain* in *The Mabinogion*, p. 159.

animals against the aristocratic 'hunter' story would place the Church symbolically in a mediating position between commoners of various ranks and secular lords. The power of the saint would be guaranteed by his identification with a power of the wilderness, the wild man, or with the forces of the Otherworld, if these are not ultimately different expressions of the same extra-human power. The more important Church institutions became as local powers, as landlords or as the focus for social networks, the more important these kinds of relationships would have become. This development fits well into the various patterns of Church expansion, through monastic foundations and later the spread of parish churches from the tenth through to the twelfth centuries.[68]

In this scenario either party, peasant communities or the Church, could in individual cases have provided the impetus behind the creation of particular 'hermit and hunter' legends. The relative extent to which each account carries clearly folkloric motifs within the larger story may reflect the relative balance of cultural 'power' within any given moment during which the legend became entrusted to writing. That the topos already existed in the authoritative forms of Sulpicius Severus' Saint Martin and Gregory of Tours would have reassured clerical and monastic custodians of the cults, but it is not enough to explain the great expansion of this marginal early topos. As was the case with the goose miracles, the increasing depth and breadth of relationships between the Church and the peasantry provides the dynamic behind appearances of folkloric motifs in hagiography.[69] If the resonances of the 'hermit and hunter' miracle were widely understood, this would explain also the wish of hagiographers, like Eadmer in his account of Saint Anselm, to create such stories. The Anselm story does not simply demonstrate the saint's holy gentleness, but locates him in a nexus of associations with miraculous power exercised in conflict between Church and lords, and in Church protection of the weak. To the modern mind, Anselm's hare might appear curiously picturesque, but within medieval culture it had powerful associations, equal to the narrative of royal politics into which it was inserted.

Another hagiographic motif related to the topos, saintly kindness to animals, appears to become more common during the same period, and was likely born of hagiographic attempts to absorb popular motifs into an acceptable Christian framework. The type of motif to be found here is notably marginal in the patristic tradition. However, it becomes relatively common to find the gentleness of the saint exemplified by his feeding wild birds by hand. Saint Marian, Saint Aventin of Troyes, and Saint Galmier of Saint-Just provide examples from the early thirteenth century, the eleventh and early ninth centuries respectively.[70] The first two saints also performed 'hermit and hunter' type miracles. In the case of Saint Aventin these

68 See for example Moore, *First European Revolution*, pp. 11–12, 45–51, 75–9.

69 See above, Chapter 5, pp. 108–12.

70 *Vita Mariani*, ch. 3, p. 760; *Vita Aventini*, no. 10, p. 477, a sixth-century saint of Troyes, whose *Vita* is probably eleventh-century; *Vita Sancti Galmier*, *AASS* 27 February, pp. 683–4, at no. 5, p. 684. Galmier's *Vita* is probably from the late ninth century, whereas he is supposed to have lived around 660 in Lyon (he is also known as Baldomer).

wonders are accompanied by a late version of the Androcles myth, this time featuring a bear, and the saving of a doe from hunters.[71]

Saint Galmier's birds are more traditional, being actually angels from heaven come at an appointed time. Here the motif can be considered as a lyrical elaboration upon the Elijah topos. Another early version comes in the eighth-century English *Vita* of Saint Guthlac, where the saint suffers persecution from diabolical birds, only to feed both 'swimmers and flyers' from his hand, demonstrating his charity.[72] In a probably twelfth-century *Vita* of a ninth-century Bavarian priest, Saint Gamelbert took small birds away from the peasants who had caught them and made them free again.[73] In a variant motif, two hermits of the eleventh and twelfth centuries respectively, Saint Firmat and Godric of Finchale, were known to have cuddled small animals under their habits in the freezing cold of winter. Both are associated with animal miracles, in Firmat's case the taming and setting to penance of a wild boar, and in Godric the consistent prevention of hunting.[74]

Apart from the complex case of Saint Godric, probably few of these stories were popular in origin. While the Guthlac and Galmier stories may have been independent of the complex of motifs around the 'hermit and hunter' legends, it seems likely that later examples of these sentimental motifs were suggested to hagiographers by the topos, with which they are usually associated. If the purpose of the saint's action cannot gain meaning from ambiguous Otherworld and wilderness figures, then they must be explained by reference to Christian virtue. The virtue of gentleness is an obvious candidate to which hagiographers can thus refer. In addition it might be noted that in presenting the saint as a protector of the weak, to an extraordinary and impractical extent, the hagiographer would be reinforcing the ideological image of the social role which the Church wished to claim.

The relationship between folklore and hagiography should be seen as dynamic rather than static: it is not simply a case that at some points a Christian story may borrow from and supersede an unchanging stock of primal rural material. Indeed, peasant ideas and stories were surely likely to change under the impact of elite Christian narratives and structures, responding in turn with their own adaptations. Thus it is possible that the association of the saint, and the saint's cult sites, with special rules of miraculous non-violence, may have developed as an essentially popular idea in the course of the tenth to twelfth centuries. It might be presumed that ideas and practices concerning sanctuary would have some relation to this issue,

[71] *Vita Aventini*, no. 8, p. 487.

[72] Felix, *Vita Sancti Guthlaci*, in *Felix's Life of Saint Guthlac*, ed. and trans. Bertram Colgrave (Cambridge 1956); ch. 38, pp. 118–21.

[73] *Vita Sancti Gamelberti, sive Amelberti*, *AASS* 27 January, pp. 783–7. The earliest manuscript of the *Vita* is from the second half of the twelfth century.

[74] *Vita Sancti Guilielmi Firmati*, *AASS* 24 April, 334–42, at ch. 3, no. 25, p. 340; *Vita Godrici*, ch. 40, pp. 98–9. Both could of course be compared to the story of the animals which flocked around Saint Columban, and even climbed inside his clothing: Jonas, *Vitae Sanctorum*, bk 1, ch. 17, pp. 185–6. However, in the patristic story this reflects nature's delight in the holy man, not the holy man's concern for the animals' welfare, so the stories are not directly attributable to Jonas.

but it is not immediately visible in hagiography. However, this complex of beliefs, which will be explored through the next two chapters, would have developed at least partly in the context of the hermit and hunter topos, as well as through other instances of interaction between Church and popular belief.

In this context it is notable that 'hermit and hunter' type miracles start to appear apparently in the tenth century at the burial sites of saints. Saints begin to protect hunted animals not only in life but also in death, and no longer in the context of a living meeting with propertied aristocrats. Thus there is a story from tenth-century Namur of a stag who walked through a village, while neither dogs nor hunters dared molest it. At length, it reached an altar dedicated to Saint Eugenius of Toledo, and stayed there with a bowed head and rested as if in prayer.[75] This was reported to the hagiographer by a hermit named Robert who, being the custodian of this local church, saw the episode. This record has the hallmarks of a local cult which would be most likely to be open to the influence of rural stories. Another story involves a successor to Saint Martin of Tours in a late-tenth-century translation account. Here one Count Dording, hunting a stag with his dogs, comes to the resting place of Saint Arnulph, where the dogs cease to bark. The count asks a resident holy woman, Scariberga, what is happening, and being duly amazed by Saint Arnulph's power, gives what is necessary for the administration of the place.[76] Despite the standard donation motif, the involvement of a holy woman with this type of miracle does mark it out as highly unusual. The figure of Scariberga, supposedly the virgin wife of the saint, indicates the legendary nature of this material, and its possible popular origins, since female saints were so rarely associated with thaumaturgic miracles at this date.[77]

Similar extensions of the 'hermit and hunter' topos can be found elsewhere. In the cult of Saint Cuthbert in lowland Scotland in the twelfth century, there is an involved story, apparently emanating from the locality itself, of a stag who takes refuge from hunters in a churchyard dedicated to the saint. Because the animal is not ultimately spared, the guilty are punished very severely by the saint's power.[78] This is only one of many stories associated with the twelfth-century cult of Saint Cuthbert where it is forbidden for animals to be harmed in places associated with the saint. Unlike many of the stories discussed in this chapter, there is extensive documentation and comparative material for this cult. The cults of Saint Cuthbert and other

[75] *Translatio Sancti Eugenii*, ed. R. P. Morin, in *Analecta Bollandiana* 5 (1886), pp. 385–95, at ch. 39, p. 392.

[76] *Translatio Sancti Arnulphi*, in *Analecta Bollandiana* 8 (1889), pp. 97–8; also see the apparently very late *Vita Sanctae Scaribergae*, *AASS* 18 July, pp. 417–21.

[77] A very rare example of a female saint appearing at the centre of a 'hermit and hunter' miracle is the probably late-fifteenth-century Welsh *Vita* of Saint Melangell, who saved a hare from the aristocratic hunter, Brochwell, see Huw Price, '*Historia Divae Monacellae*', *Montgomeryshire Collections* 82 (1994), pp. 23–40, at pp. 37–8. The legend is however most likely much older than the *Vita*, ibid. p. 29.

[78] Reginald of Durham, *Libellus de Admirandis Beati Cuthberti Virtutibus quae Novellis Patratae sunt Temporibus*, ed. James Raine, Surtees Society 1 (1835) (hereafter Reginald, *Libellus*), chs. 86, 87, pp. 180–5.

northern English holy men of the twelfth century, which will be explored in the next two chapters, offer the opportunity to investigate the relationships between hagiography and popular belief in great detail.

CHAPTER 7

The Holy Wilderness: Farne Island and the Cult of Saint Cuthbert

In the encounters between saints and animals, the place of their meeting and the saint's miracle was very frequently the wilderness hermitage, and particularly in the 'hermit and hunter' stories it may be suspected that the place itself became identified with the miraculous. Indeed, in the *Dialogues*, Gregory the Great raises the issue of the posthumous miraculous powers of the saints, having his pupil ask why saints 'perform greater miracles in those places where they are not actually buried'.[1] The problem arose in a story of a mad woman who had stumbled unknowingly into the deserted cave of Subiaco where Saint Benedict had lived as a hermit. Gregory uses this story to teach the notion of the *virtus* of the saint, whose miraculous power was not tied to relics. The miracle itself was designed, according to Gregory, to prove to 'weak minds' that a saint need not be physically present to be 'listening'. Yet the story itself reads more easily as evidence of an underlying belief in the power of the holy place. It is likely that belief in the sanctity and power of Benedict's hermitage led to the creation of the story in the first place, and Gregory simply adapted the story to the message he wished to teach. Naturally, the miraculous literature left by the medieval Church emphasises relics and cult sites under the Church's own control. However, an exception is Saint Cuthbert's seventh-century hermitage of Farne Island, off the Northumbrian coast, where a number of his animal miracles were located. Here the relationship between popular belief, hagiography and the hermitage itself can be explored.

After Cuthbert's own time, his island hermitage retained some immediate significance, the saint being succeeded there by at least two followers, according to Bede.[2] Then there was a long hiatus until in the twelfth century a tradition of hermits reappeared and was recorded in three works of the late twelfth and early thirteenth century. The cathedral priory of Durham began to take an interest in its saint's old hermitage in the course of developing the cult of Saint Cuthbert at Durham itself. Reginald of Durham included nineteen miracles from Farne Island in his book of Cuthbert's contemporary miracles, written in the 1160s and 1170s.[3] Following that Geoffrey of Durham produced a work focused as much on Farne Island as its

[1] Gregory the Great, *Dialogi*, bk 2, ch. 38, pp. 246–9. This passage is also discussed above, Chapter 3, p. 41.

[2] *Vita Cuthberti*, ch. 46, pp. 300–6.

[3] Reginald, *Libellus*.

ostensible subject, the hermit Bartholomew of Farne, who died in 1193.[4] Finally around 1200 an anonymous author made a small collection of miracles of Farne, which purported to be stories told by Bartholomew himself.[5] This hermit, who came to the island in 1150, was the third of the known twelfth-century hermits on the island, and he occupied an unusual position as the custodian of a place which itself had considerable claims to sanctity.

Farne is marked by a number of remarkable animal stories, in particular those relating to the eiderducks who nested there and were said to be under the protection of Saint Cuthbert, and could not be hunted. Other stories involve the hermit Bartholomew's pet gull, and a story of a raven which the Durham writers use to recall the story of Cuthbert and the ravens.[6] Together with the abundant animal stories in Reginald of Durham's *Vita* of Godric of Finchale this amounts to a considerable interest in animal stories on the part of the monks of Durham in the late twelfth century. On the face of it, the animal stories of Farne, while often idiosyncratic, could be seen as variants upon various patristic themes. However, they need to be seen within the whole literary effort devoted to Farne Island for the popular impulses behind their creation to be clearly shown. It is the nexus of relationships between popular devotion, the hermits of Farne and the Durham writers out of which the miracles of Farne in general arise. The animal miracles were not created and did not function as an isolated group. The popular role in the formation of the animal miracles requires a broader context in the consideration of the other major strands of the cult on Farne: the sailors' miracles and the healing miracles. Before returning to the animal miracles of Farne and Finchale in Chapter 8, the popular and literary influences upon the Farne dossier as a whole need to be disentangled.

That popular belief and practices are a key factor in the development of the cult on Farne seems clear from the chronology of Durham's literary interest in the island. While Bede in particular provided material and precedent for a monastic cult of Farne, the early-twelfth-century historian of Durham, Symeon, made no effort to develop that material, only briefly describing Cuthbert's residence on Farne. Symeon's contemporary miraculous material about Cuthbert did not involve the island at all.[7] Even the date of Durham's repossession of the island is unknown. Reginald gives no date for the earliest twelfth-century hermit, Aelric of Farne, who we can only say inhabited the island some time before 1150. According to a story attributed to Bartholomew, a Lindisfarne monk called Edulf had tried to make the filthy island a fit place for monks, presumably before Aelric's tenure of the island.[8]

4 Geoffrey of Coldingham, *Vita Sancti Bartholomaei Farnensis*, in *Symeonis Monachi Opera Omnia*, ed. Thomas Arnold, Rolls Series 75 (1882–5), 2 vols, at I, pp. 295–325.

5 H. H. Craster, ed., 'The Miracles of St. Cuthbert at Farne', *Analecta Bollandiana* 70 (1952), pp. 5–19; trans. in H. H. Craster, 'The Miracles of Farne', *Archaeologia Aeliana* 29 (1951), pp. 93–107.

6 *Vita Cuthberti*, ch. 20, pp. 222–5; see also above, Chapter 3, p. 46.

7 See Symeon of Durham, *Libellus de Exordio atque Procursu istius hoc est Dunelmensis Ecclesie*, ed. and trans. David Rollason (Oxford 2000), at bk 1, ch. 7, pp. 38–41, and ch. 10, pp. 48–55, for Cuthbert's residences on Farne. The island makes no other appearance in Symeon.

8 *Vita Bartholomaei*, ch. 29, p. 319.

Geoffrey has Bartholomew, on his deathbed, stating that 'before my coming' laymen had visited the island and created the unsanctified mess which Edulf had to clean. The story underlines the old hermit's role as the living memory of the Lindisfarne cell, a possession of Durham Cathedral Priory, remembering the history of Farne through his miracle stories. Crucially, however, Bartholomew's narration indicates that lay people had an interest in the island before the monastic presence on Farne. The monks may have seen the unsupervised lay presence as a source of filth, but it is nevertheless likely that many of these lay people had come to the island for religious reasons.

Bartholomew's deathbed history of Farne is not the only evidence of the lay cult of Farne. While he was still a merchant, the hermit Godric of Finchale (d. 1170) visited Farne Island as part of the first of his many pilgrimages. Farne was the locus of his veneration of Saint Cuthbert, and Reginald describes him weeping and praying on the island.[9] Godric is described here as a *colonus*, emphasising his lowly class origins, at the time that his desire for a life of solitude began. It is remarkable that Durham Cathedral does not appear among the various regional and international shrines that Godric visited, as surely it would have if Reginald had had any choice. Apparently Farne had more significance for Godric than the presence of Saint Cuthbert's incorruptible body at Durham. Yet Godric's pilgrimage to Farne occurred around 1100, long before the priory showed any interest in the place. Lay devotion for Farne developed independently of any monastic encouragement.

Evidence for lay understandings of the nature of a holy hermitage is sparse, but worth brief consideration. The word 'hermitage' appears in place names, frequently so in France, where it has been assumed to mean simply a 'wilderness' or an 'uncultivated' place, without necessarily implying any religious habitation.[10] In one mid-thirteenth-century English record there appears to be an awareness that the popular and ecclesiastical definitions of a hermitage could be at variance. A hermitage 'near Chetwood' in Buckinghamshire, given to an Augustinian priory, was said to be 'popularly' called a hermitage by the 'lay people'. This was due to its 'solitude', as it was said that no hermit had ever lived there.[11] An uninhabited 'hermitage' may have been just a wilderness, yet the use of the term 'hermitage' does imply some special quality not given to all uncultivated land.

Godric's hermitage at Finchale was evidently a place that was once inhabited. Reginald reports that the 'old men' knew of remains of buildings and people there. Furthermore, these remains, evidently from a time beyond local memory, had acquired a legendary explanation, which in turn explained the name 'Finchale'. At one time this site had been occupied by a legendary British King Finc.[12] Reginald

[9] *Vita Godrici*, ch. 5, nos. 17–18, p. 32.

[10] Jean Leclercq, '*Eremus* et *eremita*: pour l'histoire du vocabulaire de la vie solitaire', *Collectanea Ordinis Cistercensium Reformatorum* 25 (1963), pp. 8–30, at pp. 21–3.

[11] William Dugdale, *Monasticon Anglicanum* (London 1817–30), 6 vols, at 6, p. 499, no. 2.

[12] *Vita Godrici*, ch. 22, no. 57, pp. 69–70. Archaeological work done at Finchale has not discovered remains dating before the priory; see C. R. Peers, 'Finchale Priory', *Archaeologia Aeliana* 4 (1927), pp. 193–220. As even Godric's original structures have been obscured by the later priory buildings, this

had hagiographic reasons to record this fragment of local folklore: Godric in taking over the place was transforming a kind of pre-Christian site into a holy place. The remains of King Finc could be seen as an echo of the remains of pagan structures which were part of the landscape for the Egyptian fathers. Thus Godric's adoption of Finchale could be seen to have mirrored the patristic practice of inhabiting pagan tombs to show the superiority of the Christian religion over its predecessors. Reginald includes the 'King Finc' story in order to compare Godric to Saint Anthony.[13] Clearly in Godric's case the site was not pagan in any genuine sense. For Reginald however, Godric's initial colonisation of the place looked forward to Durham's later control of the site, and the replacement of a local popular legend with the superior and civilised influence of Durham Priory.

As at Finchale, there may have been local explanations and stories concerning Farne Island, but the literary inheritance of Bede is likely to obscure any of these in the twelfth-century writings. Thus, Geoffrey's description of Saint Cuthbert as 'the first monarch of the place' could raise an echo of the kind of mentality that attributes a handful of remains to the presence of a mythical king.[14] However, this may be just a coincidence: Geoffrey was quoting Bede's description of Cuthbert's colonisation of Farne.[15] Nevertheless, those lay people who came to the island to be healed cannot be expected to have had the same understanding of the sanctity of the place as did literate monks. Their conceptions of the island, or the nature of a 'holy wilderness', would not appear, of course, in any direct form in Geoffrey's description of the island. That description, while deeply embedded in hagiographic tradition, is also ultimately contradictory, as a result of Geoffrey's attempt to reconcile monastic conceptions of the holy solitude with conceptions that probably arose from lay devotion. In order to make clear the role of lay conceptions in the miracles of Farne, it is necessary to consider the first side of the contradiction: the influence of hagiographic tradition upon Geoffrey's metaphysical picture of Farne.

Bede described Cuthbert banishing the devils from Farne, creating the natural spring, and otherwise making the island a holy outpost of humanity. This is the saintly colonisation of the place of horror.[16] The essence of these stories was repeated by Symeon. Before Cuthbert, Farne 'was absolutely wanting in water, produce and trees, and also frequented by evil spirits'. Cuthbert, however, 'made the place itself habitable' through his miracles.[17] There Symeon's interest in Farne ends: it is the saint's body at the cathedral church which is the real focus of attention. This is in contrast to Bede, who says of Cuthbert's resignation of the episcopacy that he was 'determined to return to the beloved strife of the hermit's life'. Symeon says simply that 'he returned to his island and monastery'.[18] Thus, Symeon downgraded the

is not surprising. There seems no reason to doubt Reginald's report in this matter.

13 *Vita Antonii*, ch. 7, col. 131.

14 *Vita Bartholomaei*, ch. 21, p. 313.

15 *Vita Cuthberti*, ch. 17, p. 216.

16 Ibid. chs. 17–18, pp. 214–20, and see above Chapter 3, p. 48.

17 Symeon, *Libellus de Exordio*, bk 1, ch. 7, pp. 39–41.

18 *Vita Cuthberti*, ch. 36, pp. 266–7; Symeon, *Libellus de Exordio*, bk 1, ch. 10, p. 49.

importance of Cuthbert's return to solitude on Farne, while not suppressing the fact itself. Of supreme importance to Symeon is the foundation of the long continuous possession of Cuthbert's body. Although the saint, for practical reasons, thought it better that his body remained on Farne, he gave the brethren the necessary 'permission and advice' to remove it. Thus for 'four hundred and eighteen years', monks had possessed the incorruptible body.

By the end of the twelfth century, Farne had become much more important to the monks of Durham. Geoffrey makes much of Bartholomew's desire to have his body rest on Farne. On his deathbed, with monks from Lindisfarne and Coldingham gathered about him, the twelfth-century hermit echoes Cuthbert's wish to be buried on Farne:

> He said 'I desire to rest my body here, where I hope my spirit will be raised up by its Founder, as I have soldiered a little for the Lord, and I have undergone many tribulations because of this, which in heaven is consolation. For truly I fear that if I were buried elsewhere, the books would be carried off, the vestments snatched away, the grace of the house of God would be vacated and transformed into the horror of its original solitude or turpitude. For this place is holy, which before my coming was not cultivated in the proper reverence. The celebration of divine offices was done rarely. Certainly, lay people lived in this place and there were many sinners . . . and if any came for grace in praying, they could neither bend their knees because of the filth, nor could they open their mouths because of the stench.'[19]

The miraculous colonisation of the island by the saint had been apparently obliterated by the attentions of laymen, and could be again if an institutional monastic presence were not maintained. Cuthbert's own concern, as described by Bede and Symeon, was that the monks of Lindisfarne should not be bothered by disreputable people fleeing to his shrine. If he were buried on Farne, Lindisfarne would be spared this influx. Yet even without Cuthbert's body, Farne had become a place where lay people would come with their sins and prayers. Where Geoffrey sees Farne as vulnerable to returning to its status as a place of horror without the institutional monastic presence, clearly for lay people it was a place of some significance and sanctity, by its very nature.

Bartholomew's concern for the institutional status of Farne reflects Geoffrey's wish to show that, despite the long hiatus in the religious occupation of the island between Bede's time and the twelfth century, he could outline a spiritual continuity in the nature of the place. This spiritual continuity depended upon the institutions of Benedictine monasticism in general and the traditions of Durham in particular. Thus the description of Farne follows Bartholomew's own four miracles which demonstrated his sanctity. Here Geoffrey explicitly showed the hermit to be the spiritual heir of Saints Benedict, Cuthbert and Godric of Finchale: 'he had their virtues, he was full of them in spirit'.[20] Bartholomew is the model of a Benedictine

[19] *Vita Bartholomaei*, ch. 29, p. 319. Reginald also refers to Cuthbert's wishes concerning his body, quoting from Bede; Reginald, *Libellus*, ch. 12, pp. 16–19.

[20] *Vita Bartholomaei*, ch. 19, p. 312.

hermit in following Benedict. He is the model of a hermit of Durham in following Cuthbert. Finally he is the model of a contemporary holy man in following Godric, whose cult belonged to Durham. A miracle is not just a miracle, but is a demonstration of spiritual continuity. Saints Benedict and Cuthbert stand at the centre of Durham's self-consciousness, and thus a holy man who emerged from Durham must encapsulate that consciousness through his miracles. While Godric obviously does not quite fit the pattern, his inclusion in the list is another indication of Durham's concern to respond to popular spiritual currents.

The spiritual continuity which Geoffrey pursues in describing Farne is strained by the issue of independent lay devotion, and hence the hagiographer lays great emphasis on the importance of Church institutions:

> For truly this was formerly a castle of demons, now it is a cloister and school of saints, a kind of earthly purgatory, wholesomely established for curing worthy bodies and souls. It always has men of virtues, or rather it makes them; because he who is led into its desert by the spirit, must be tempted by the devil, and either cultivates virtue or abandons the place of virtue.[21]

Farne makes the saints, but the saints have made the place, in a continual dialectic. Yet it is not enough to go out into the desert on your own without the benefit of an institution to guide you. Thus Farne is not simply a 'desert' but also a 'cloister'. The transformation from a castle of demons to a school of saints refers to Cuthbert's transformation of the island.[22] Geoffrey does, however, seem to admit that the island had some inherent quality of sanctity, apart from the spurious continuity of monastic institutions, by saying that the 'place of virtue' can itself make a holy man. On the other hand, Geoffrey had Bartholomew worry that the place would fall into turpitude once more if it were left to lay people. There is thus a contradiction in Geoffrey's conceptions of Farne. The idea of the inherent holiness of Farne simply does not fit with his emphasis on the importance of monastic institutions. The latter idea clearly mattered to the monastic community of Durham, for which a particular place of sanctity was less important than the historical continuity of a group of monks guarding the body of the saint.

The shadow of lay practices suggests that the idea of Farne as inherently holy came from outside the cloister. If Geoffrey were simply adumbrating a patristic conception of the desert as a place of horror and testing, he would not have developed the idea of Farne as a positive place. However, neither does Geoffrey develop the positive view of Farne in the other possible direction of hagiographic rhetoric, describing Farne as a kind of paradise due to Saint Cuthbert's former and continuing presence. Thus, somewhat remarkably, the continuity of saints on an inherently holy island does not make that island a new Eden. Admittedly, a cold inhospitable island such as Farne would be hard to sell as an earthly paradise. However, evil is present and Farne lies in the world. The positive view depends simply on the fact

21 Ibid. ch. 20, p. 312.

22 Cuthbert's sanctification of the island comes immediately after this chapter; ibid. ch. 21, p. 313.

that Farne is a place in the world where justice is actually served: 'Nothing is committed which goes unpunished there'.[23] Thus the reconciliation of the two views of Farne depends directly upon miracles in which wrongdoing is punished, and in these animals play a significant part.[24]

If Geoffrey was trying to reconcile popular and monastic views of Farne in the passages above, elsewhere he developed a more traditional picture of Farne as a place of spiritual warfare. The island is under constant siege by the demons Cuthbert had expelled from his *metropolis* to the 'suburb' islands. Black-cowled demons ride on goats, brandishing lances, and assaulting the monastic fortifications.[25] At Bartholomew's deathbed a group of monks from Lindisfarne were terrified by an apparition of a monstrous dog, among other horrors. The experienced holy man banished the devil with a few words.[26] Farne is not a place for novices of spiritual warfare. Here Geoffrey gives Bartholomew the allegorical status of an abbot, comforting and defending the young, even when close to death. The geography of Farne also adds to the picture of constant metaphysical struggle. Farne is composed of opposites: for example, the sea constantly assaults the land and the freezing inhabitants are reduced to 'terror and cold'.[27] Reginald's stories of Farne do not contain any sustained description of the place as a site of spiritual warfare, but the occasional phrase indicates a similar predisposition to see Farne in terms of metaphysical allegory. For example, the meeting of the overhanging cliffs and the sea made Reginald think of the 'gulfs of Hell'.[28]

Geoffrey's descriptions of spiritual warfare spring from a familiar biblical quotation:

> The contest there [Farne] is not between citizens concerning boundaries, nor against flesh and blood, but rather the mortal struggle concerning kingdom and ruler is perpetual against the princes and the powers of darkness.[29]

One prominent use of Ephesians 6:12 occurs in Athanasius' description of Anthony's struggles against demons during the colonisation of his final mountain hermitage.[30] In one respect, the use of this quotation simply associates the cult on Farne with the holiness of the desert fathers. However, the solitary struggle of Anthony

[23] Ibid. ch. 23, p. 314.

[24] See below, Chapter 8, p. 157–9.

[25] *Vita Bartholomaei,* ch. 22, p. 314.

[26] Ibid. ch. 30, p. 321. Note that Geoffrey's depiction of demonic visitations contradicts Symeon's assertion that after Cuthbert, 'no one who goes on to the island to serve Christ suffers any anxieties from the fantasies of demons'; Symeon, *Libellus de Exordio*, p. 41. Geoffrey was dealing with a living eremitical tradition where Symeon was not.

[27] Ibid. ch. 20, p. 312.

[28] Reginald, *Libellus*, ch. 33, p. 75.

[29] *Vita Bartholomaei*, ch. 20, p. 312; Ephesians 6:12: 'For we wrestle not against flesh and blood, but against principalities and powers, against the rulers of the darkness of this world, against spiritual wickedness in high places.'

[30] *Vita Antonii*, ch. 25, col. 149. It is discussed again in ch. 37, col. 155.

lies in contrast with the institutional hermitage that is Farne. While the passage from Ephesians could be seen to imply a rejection of secular authority in general, Geoffrey uses it to imagine a battle between two forces over who shall rule this microcosm of the world. The question is whether the monarch shall be a power of darkness, or a good monarch like Saint Cuthbert, and thus his institution, Durham Priory. Both the story of the warlike demons and the metaphysical description of Farne's geography appear as part of a series of allegories spun from the Ephesians passage.

Geoffrey's use of the quotation from Ephesians and his careful delineation of Farne's spiritual qualities implies a deliberate agenda: he may be implicitly contrasting Farne with other depictions of holy solitude. Another patristic use of the quotation, which was likely to be familiar to many monks, is made by Saint Jerome;[31] the saint emphasises the sheer agony of the temptations he encountered in his life of solitude. Possibly in conscious contrast to Jerome, Geoffrey has located the quotation within passages that emphasise instead the corporate nature of the holy island. The holy solitude is, then, a fortress or City of God. It is a *coenobium*, not a solitude.

The use of the Ephesians passage may have been meant to highlight a contrast between Durham's Farne and contemporary celebrations of the desert. The Cistercians, in particular, took the notions of solitude and of wilderness as the foundation of their new monasteries. The description of metaphysical struggle on Farne may have been a deliberate defence of Durham's traditions against other twelfth-century traditions, which were more normally associated with heroic asceticism. Indeed, the prodigious growth of the Cistercian order, among others, in the north of England and Scotland in the twelfth century would have made such a concern entirely plausible. There is nevertheless another notable effect of Geoffrey's description of Farne: he has almost completely obliterated the idea of the hermitage as a place in the wilderness, outside of society. It is this latter idea that would likely have dominated popular ideas about the place.

The complications of Geoffrey's picture of Farne would not be necessary if his only concern was to defend his own house's form of Benedictine monasticism. Clear models already existed, in Gregory the Great and Saint Benedict in particular, of a traditional Benedictine holy solitude. Rather, the contradictions in Geoffrey's picture of Farne must have another source: the social realities of devotion on Farne Island. Geoffrey needed to use the notions of the holy place and the particular miracles produced by popular belief and practice to build his picture of this holy island, and adapt them to the needs of the monastic priory of Durham. A defence of Durham's religious traditions could be made in terms of the cathedral itself in the early twelfth century, which is why Symeon of Durham paid so little attention to Farne Island. Only later in the century did Geoffrey, and Reginald also, see the pivotal importance of this popular cult. Geoffrey made the effort to incorporate the popular traditions of the island into Durham's own history, but the contradictions in

[31] Jerome, *Ad Eustochium*, *Epistola* 22, col. 396.

his picture of Farne are the marks of the adaptation of popular beliefs and practices into a monastic framework.

Thus, existing alongside the idea of Farne as a place of terror and strife is the idea of Farne as a place of innocent peace: 'there is no contest between citizens concerning boundaries there'. Neither is there a contest between animals and humans. The monks, we are told by all three writers on Farne, do not allow the eiderducks to be hunted. The ducks themselves have an aura of holy placidity in some images.[32] These little birds are central to the idea of the island as a place of peace, an element of the mythology of Farne which may owe most to popular belief. Nonetheless, a contrast between an island as a place of horror and of holy peace has precedent within hagiographic tradition. The original western island hermitage, Lérins, was alternately described as a place of trial and as a paradise.[33] Yet Geoffrey does not describe Farne as a paradise; rather Farne is 'a kind of earthly purgatory'.[34]

The history of the concepts of purgation and purgatory shows a complex interaction of doctrinal ideas and miraculous or visionary imagery.[35] Purgatory only gradually emerged as a singular place by the thirteenth century. Even the use of *purgatorium* as a singular noun was apparently absent before the 1170s; Bernard of Clairvaux still wrote of *loca purgatoria*, as a plurality of states of spiritual being. Nevertheless, ideas of actual purgatorial places on the earth were clearly current in the twelfth century.[36] In this sense, Geoffrey's description of Farne as a place of spiritual purgation for the monks is not unprecedented, though his use of the singular noun 'purgatory' is very early. Moreover, it does not appear to have been common to label a particular place as being one of these mysterious *loca purgatoria*.[37] Geoffrey seems to be fusing together various old and new conceptions of purgatory, at a time when they were not fully resolved, perhaps in order to make coherent the various strands of the cult on Farne. He does not seem to have been entirely successful in this effort. Farne may have been a place of continual solitary struggle and purgation for monks, but this was probably not the meaning it had for those lay people who so frequently visited the island. Certainly this is clear in Reginald's stories of those

[32] See below, Chapter 8, p. 156.

[33] Jacques Le Goff, 'The Wilderness in the Medieval West', in *The Medieval Imagination*, trans. Arthur Goldhammer (Chicago 1988), pp. 47–59; on Lérins see p. 50. However, the picture gained from Hilary of Arles, in his *Vita* of Saint Honoratus, is one of transformation of the dread wilderness into a kind of paradise, not of a constant oscillation between the two states: Hilary of Arles, *Vita Honorati*, ch. 3, no. 15, cols. 1256–7.

[34] *Vita Bartholomaei*, ch. 20, p. 312: 'quoddam in terris purgatorium'.

[35] Jacques Le Goff, *The Birth of Purgatory*, trans. Arthur Goldhammer (London 1984), for example pp. 199, 223 and 259. See pp. 61–85, for Saint Augustine's interpretation of tribulation and purgation, pp. 88–95, for Gregory the Great's handling of *loci poenales*, and pp. 135–52 for some twelfth-century interpretations of purgatory.

[36] Le Goff, *Purgatory*, pp. 135–46.

[37] One major exception is the legend of Saint Patrick's purgatory in Ireland. But this place is distant from the creators of its legends, not a familiar shrine like Farne. For Saint Patrick's purgatory see ibid. pp. 193–201.

sailors who came to Farne to recount their stories of terror upon the seas.[38] For them Farne must have been a peaceful haven, at the least.

For Reginald the main point of these stories is to show the effectiveness of Saint Cuthbert as a miracle worker. The saint is a 'counsellor of tribulations and reliever of sorrows' for whom any of the faithful may call, in 'whatever tribulation of sorrows'.[39] Among the miracle stories in Reginald's *Libellus* that relate to sea voyages, a high proportion involve laymen coming to Farne to report their experiences to the hermits there.[40] Perhaps this simply demonstrates that the hermits were a good source of information for Reginald concerning this kind of miracle. Many other sailors may have thought themselves saved by Saint Cuthbert, but their stories did not reach the monks of Durham. However, it might have been expected, in such a large miracle collection, that Reginald could have found one story of a sailor giving thanks to Cuthbert at the cathedral. There is no such story, which may be an indication that sailors specifically went to Farne rather than to the cathedral to deliver their gratitude.

The sailors were usually described as natives of the region. In one miracle, a number of the men were 'raised in his [Cuthbert's] land, and had frequently heard of his sanctity and miracles of virtue'.[41] During the storm, Cuthbert appeared to them, leading the vessel with his 'pastoral staff', and promised that he would not desert them until they were delivered to a 'port of safety'. This sort of vision is certainly evidence of the willingness of sailors to believe in the miraculous powers of their saint, particularly in desperate conditions. In itself this does not prove any particular devotion to Farne as the locus of the saint's power. It may be that Farne was simply a convenient place on the coast of Northumbria to escape from a storm, and Reginald does indicate that sometimes sailors took refuge from storms on Farne.[42] However, he does give the impression that Cuthbert himself chose the sailors' destination: 'pitying them, he led them to the island'.[43] The destination of Farne Island is thus integral to the miracle stories, and probably to the sailors' own perceptions of their experience. Stopping at Farne does not appear to have been an action of convenience or necessity in three out of the four Farne sailors' miracles.[44] In these cases the crisis had already passed, but the sailors put in at Farne itself. Choosing Farne was thus a deliberate decision, when the sailors could equally have gone straight to the nearby coast and delivered thanks at the church at Lindisfarne instead. The informants for these stories are never monks of Durham or, more surprisingly, monks of

[38] Reginald, *Libellus*, chs. 23, 30, 32 and 33; chs. 27, 31 and 34 also involve sailors detained at Farne through storms.

[39] Ibid. ch. 23, p. 50.

[40] Four out of six relate to Farne. Of the remaining two, one involves Ailred of Rievaulx himself on a journey to Clairvaux, and the other a knight who was bringing a valuable object to Durham Cathedral: ibid. chs. 83 and 75 respectively.

[41] Ibid. ch. 23, p. 52.

[42] Ibid. ch. 31, p. 70, and ch. 33, p. 74.

[43] Ibid. ch. 32, p. 74.

[44] Ibid. chs. 23, 30 and 32.

Lindisfarne. In stark contrast to Farne, the Lindisfarne cell provides Reginald with only one miracle story involving ordinary lay people.[45] Thus, Farne must have had some particular attraction to these sailors, independent of the specifically monastic cult of Cuthbert.

In one story, once Saint Cuthbert had led the sailors to the island, they told their story to Bartholomew with a 'sweet inundation of tears poured out in the presence of Blessed Cuthbert'.[46] In another, the sailors who escaped an attack by 'pagan' Frisians and are sped on their way by Cuthbert's control of the weather, sail to Farne Island. There Bartholomew treats them to a mass, while they give 'offerings', and report their story to the hermit, again amid inundations of tears.[47] Each of the stories is very different in most details, but certain elements turn up repeatedly, such as the mass and the offerings. The 'offerings' are not specified, and appear to be simply tears and personal devotion to Saint Cuthbert. Some of the repeated elements in these stories may partly be due to Reginald's rhetorical habits, however, it is unlikely that Reginald would have made up a series of rituals specifically for Farne. Such elements as the mass and the 'offerings' to Saint Cuthbert were details that probably came to Reginald from the hermits.

Thus the presence of the hermit appears central to the cult at Farne. Sailors may have given thanks to Cuthbert on Farne before the hermits were present, but there would have been no religious figure to structure the event as a devotional activity for the sailors, and then to remember their story. Thus no miracle could have been recorded, even if there had been a Reginald to write it. The presence of a holy man on the island would have encouraged the cult of Farne to crystallise: the hermit could 'certify' lay people's miraculous experiences. It may be that a hermit was the preferred witness to the sailors' devotion, in contrast to the monks at Lindisfarne for example. The latter, after all, could have given the sailors the same spiritual services. However Farne was chosen as the site of devotion, and this likely reflects an independent popular belief in the island as a holy place.

Could the sailors have regarded Farne in some way as a 'purgatory' as did Geoffrey? Reginald does present the sailors' stories as allegories of salvation. One story opens with a description of Cuthbert's power to save: 'Blessed Cuthbert plucked up souls into himself when they called to him from the frame of perdition'.[48] These sailors, who were to fall foul of the pagan Frisians, had themselves 'given their souls

[45] Ibid. ch. 105, pp. 234–6. Also see the anonymous early-twelfth-century collection, *De Miraculis de Translationibus Sancti Cuthberti*, in Symeon's *Opera Omnia*, I, pp. 333–62, which contains a number of stories relating to Lindisfarne. Some of these involve lay people but are of a quite different kind from the Farne stories. They are largely concerned with monastic property and rights, rather than miracles of benefit to lay people themselves. For another discussion of Lindisfarne's place in Reginald's collection, see Victoria Tudor, 'The Cult of St. Cuthbert in the Twelfth Century: The Evidence of Reginald of Durham', in *St Cuthbert, His Cult and His Community to A.D. 1200*, ed. Gerald Bonner, David Rollason and Clare Stancliffe (Woodbridge 1989), pp. 447–67, at pp. 461–2.

[46] Reginald, *Libellus*, ch. 23, p. 53.

[47] Ibid. ch. 30, pp. 67–9.

[48] Ibid. ch. 30, p. 67.

in the study of business, and they boiled greedily with the desire of gaining'. In each story, in common with others in the *Libellus*, trade is presented as inherently sinful.[49] It is better to suffer the 'misery of poverty' acquiring merit for 'the life of glory' rather than engage in trading in precious things which are 'mostly corrupt'.[50] The experience of maritime violence, and the sailors' suffering, does sometimes appear to be presented by Reginald as a spiritually cleansing experience. One man washed overboard in a storm is drawn underwater three times before being washed back on to the deck by Cuthbert's intervention.[51] Only through the protection of Saint Cuthbert was it that 'the sea could not swallow the small vessels of avarice or sink the sinning souls'.[52]

Through such miracles ordinary sinners are given a chance to repent, suffer and find a chance of salvation: 'the grace of protection in the rampart of favour preserves the souls of the feeble from desperation'.[53] Although their trading is inherently sinful, Reginald does not seem to expect the individuals concerned to give up such activities. The stories end only with the sailors' devotions on Farne. Evidently they resumed their normal lives thereafter, simply grateful for Cuthbert's protection against natural forces. It may be that Reginald himself put the 'purgatorial' spin on these narratives. It is nevertheless possible that a hermit like Bartholomew may have encouraged the sailors to see their experiences in terms of personal repentance and salvation. In either case, Reginald was certainly encouraging a 'purgatorial' view of secular life, in which suffering in this world can lead to salvation. The condemnations of trade probably were not meant as advice to traders to cease trading. On the contrary, Reginald's dramatic renditions and extreme language served to point out that even in a sinful life it is possible to ask for forgiveness and receive the protection and mercy of Saint Cuthbert. Salvation, he implies, is even possible for greedy merchants. Purgatorial imagery might well have appealed to the popular imagination, reducing the stark opposites of salvation and damnation to something more realistically obtainable in an ordinary life.[54]

The importance of salvation for the laity is also reflected in Farne's healing miracles. As in Reginald's sailors' miracles, these are written as allegories of salvation and damnation. Even men of good works or good life depend ultimately on Saint Cuthbert's clemency to heal their bodies. The miracle of healing comes about through their faith in Cuthbert's power and the grace Cuthbert thus offers them.[55]

49 See for example ibid. ch. 24, pp. 53–6.

50 Ibid. ch. 32, pp. 72–3.

51 Ibid. ch. 32, pp. 73–4.

52 Ibid. ch. 23, p. 52.

53 Ibid. ch. 32, p. 72.

54 In his preface, Reginald does claim that 'these untutored speeches can confer and produce remedies of some use to rude and rustic people'. This is not simply a case of a writer's humility topos; he goes on to say: 'We do not presume to teach the taught, but to instruct the poor; we assign [these speeches] to inform imbeciles towards good growth': Reginald, *Libellus*, ch. 1, pp. 3–4.

55 See particularly ibid., chs. 102 and 103, concerning a rich man of great charity, and a monk of Durham respectively.

One Northumbrian man 'very rich in might and power' became ill and then suffered from the 'solicitous industry of doctors'. However, with healthier advice, he went to Farne, made an offering and 'offered pious devotion of tears to the Lord'. Thus, without great fuss, he was cured.[56] For this same man's wife, however, purgatorial imagery is employed to describe the progress of her cure. Reginald describes her physical suffering in terms of alternating agonies of internal heat and cold. Eventually her entrails were so inflamed that nothing could cool her. Even 'with her whole body denuded' apart from underwear, nothing could reduce the 'asperity of burning cold'.[57] Finally taken to Farne, she gave some towels to cover the altar, and as she waited outside the chapel, she found herself cured as her gifts were laid on the altar. The sufferings this noblewoman felt might well be read as metaphor for the alternate heat and cold of purgatory, which cleanses the soul.

In the anonymous 'Miracles of Farne' collection, there is a similar healing miracle involving the local noblewoman, Emma de Grenville. Like Reginald's noblewoman, she suffered torments of heat and cold:

> In extremity of cold and of heat she laboured in the fourth degree, and while she was alive she had a foretaste of the alternate tortures of Hell. For we read of how the spirits of some, who are condemned to tortures among the shades, are carried from hot to cold and from cold to hot because of their changefulness and inconstancy.[58]

This story is thus once again written as an allegory of salvation and purgatorial suffering. Again, the noblewoman is reduced to humiliating nakedness, which nevertheless does not alleviate her suffering. Moreover 'humbled under the yoke, she went about bowed, leaning on two sticks which supported her'. Perhaps the writer meant all this humiliation to be seen as a significant spiritual advance for a noblewoman. Certainly the theme is in keeping with the rhetoric of Cuthbert's mortification of the body, announced in the collection's preface.[59]

It says something for the misogyny of Durham monks that it was two noblewomen, rather than two noblemen, who were chosen as the subject of miracles dealing with the humiliation of secular bodies. Unlike the poor sailors and traders, whose sin was external to their bodies, the two noblewomen suffered such torments apparently through the inherent sinfulness of their physical nature. Whereas rich or powerful men had access to Cuthbert's forgiving clemency, purgatorial suffering in this world seems to have been reserved for women and men of low status, the sailors. Nevertheless, the salvation of those people of lesser status seems to be the issue which prompts Durham's writers to search for purgatorial imagery. In

56 Ibid. ch. 118, pp. 263–4.

57 Ibid. ch. 119, pp. 264–5.

58 *Miracles of Farne*; ch. 4, pp. 12–13; trans. Craster, p. 99.

59 *Miracles of Farne*, pp. 9–10. The rhetoric of extremes of heat and cold in these stories may also be a borrowing from hagiographic tradition, where such suffering often occurs in visionary contexts. A conspicuous example comes from Bede's account of the vision of Dryhthelm: *Bede's Ecclesiastical History of the English People*, ed. and trans. Bertram Colgrave and R. A. B. Mynors (Oxford 1969), bk 5, ch. 12, pp. 488–99, esp. pp. 488–91.

this context, Geoffrey's unusual description of Farne as a 'purgatory' may reflect the monks' response to lay enthusiasm for Farne. Those lay people who came to Farne simply hoped for ease and help in a cruel world. The monks responded with sermons on the possibilities of salvation within the suffering of lay life. Although most monks themselves may have expected purgatory to be their own fate, in this context the idea of purgatory functioned as a middle ground between monastic religion and lay devotion, while Farne and its hermits provided the context for the two to mingle.

Both Reginald and the anonymous writer of 'The Miracles of Farne' recorded miracles according to their didactic purposes. The miracles recorded cannot be taken as a fair reflection of the proportions of people who sought one thing or another on this holy island, as the social status of a person could be highly relevant to the writer's purpose. Indeed, the wildly differing proportions of social groups who received cures in each collection are an indication of the subjective criteria by which each writer chose the stories to record. In Reginald's collection there are seven healing miracles relating to Farne, and none of the recipients of Cuthbert's clemency are ordinary lay people. Bartholomew himself, a monk and a monastic servant all receive cures.[60] There is a rich merchant and a regional nobleman.[61] The two women are both wives of nobles. One husband is a local knight, living in Embleton.[62]

This exclusive concentration upon people of high status is not typical of Reginald's healing miracles as a whole, and the cathedral itself attracted the poor and rich alike, even if Reginald probably had a bias in favour of high-status recipients of cures.[63] This could be taken as evidence that, despite the sailors' miracles, Farne was not popular with local people. However, the bias is clearly Reginald's. The anonymous collection shows the opposite spectrum of society, with only one cure of someone of clearly high status, Emma de Grenville, among ten healing miracles. Three miracles come from one peasant family who lived opposite Farne.[64] Other Farne miracles in Reginald and the anonymous collection involve poor lay people from the adjacent coast, which seems to indicate a strong local interest in Farne as a holy place. As none of the various named villages adjacent to Farne appears in lists of Durham's properties, these poor lay people and their cult on Farne appears to have been wholly independent of Durham Priory.[65]

60 Reginald, *Libellus*, chs. 120, 117 and 103 respectively.

61 Ibid. chs. 102 and 118.

62 Ibid. chs. 62 and 119.

63 For the numbers involved generally in the *Libellus*, see Tudor, 'Cult of St. Cuthbert', p. 465.

64 *Miracles of Farne*, chs. 6–8, pp. 14–17. For the two high-status people who appear in the collection, Emma de Grenville and Nicholas de Stuteville, see trans. Craster, pp. 95–6.

65 See for example the detailed confirmation of Durham properties offered by King John in 1204: *Victoria History of the County of Durham*, ed. William Page (London 1893–1940), 3 vols, at II, pp. 91–2. The lands directly opposite Farne, in Bamburgh, Embleton and Ellingham, appear to be held by secular lords; see Northumberland County History Committee, *History of Northumberland* (London 1895–1940), 15 vols, at II, pp. 10–14 and 224–32.

Apart from the monastic rhetoric of salvation, local people must have had their own reasons to believe in the possibility of healing miracles on Farne Island, as opposed to any other place. A saint's *virtus* was not necessarily restricted to any particular place, as the sailors' miracles show, but Farne was one place where people came hoping for a miracle. For the monastic writers, Farne was a place where metaphysical realities were tangible, but did ordinary lay people see the island in similar terms? The physically sanctified qualities of the island certainly appear to be crucial in a number of healing miracles. The household servant of the family of a monk was cured by drinking water poured over stones from the island.[66] A wealthy layman apparently suffering from something like migraine discusses his affliction with 'the brothers' on Farne, and places his head in a window of the guest house where Saint Cuthbert himself used to lay his head. The saint personally appears to advise the man to do this and so he was healed.[67] Reginald understood this miracle in terms of the incorruptible flesh of Saint Cuthbert, which itself echoes the cedar of Lebanon, which 'does not putrefy naturally'. Because Cuthbert had acquired all his virtue on Farne it 'had not lost its virtue of curing'. The anonymous author saw the origin of healing miracles in exactly the same terms as Reginald. The prologue explains the miracles in terms of Cuthbert's virtue, his mortifying of the flesh, and his consequent incorruptible flesh: 'it has come to pass that the good things which he did in the life of the flesh are testified afterwards by works of power'.[68]

Here Reginald and the anonymous author were not simply affirming the reality of the miraculous, but were also seeking an explanation for the phenomena on Farne. They found their explanation in the monastic intellectual tradition, where present events are explained and meaning developed through analogous relation to the sacred word. Today we would attempt different kinds of explanation of the miraculous. Analogies like 'holy radioactivity' or anthropological tools, as in the concept of liminality, can be illuminating, but in themselves offer no more than a modern intellectual rationalisation, in principle not dissimilar to Reginald's approach.[69] Yet miracles were a social phenomenon and emerged from the totality of social relationships in medieval society. Only thus could they have been so widely and persistently accepted. It is clear that ordinary lay people saw Farne as a holy place, and their beliefs and practices were the raw material out of which the monks built their descriptions of the miracles.

Miracles were thus the product of active social relationships, even once they had become written records. In this respect, the miraculous dialectic of Farne, between its holy men past and present and the isolated bleak geography itself, could be a visible yet extraordinary reality. Here what was impossible under ordinary social conditions could be expected to manifest. Problems insoluble within normal life can only be solved outside normal conditions: Farne and its holy men provided

[66] Reginald, *Libellus*, ch. 117, pp. 262–3.

[67] Ibid. ch. 102, pp. 226–9.

[68] *Miracles of Farne*; ch. 1, p. 10; trans. Craster, p. 97.

[69] For the analogy of 'holy radioactivity' see Ronald C. Finucane, *Miracles and Pilgrims: Popular Beliefs in Medieval England* (London 1977), pp. 25–30.

this for numerous local and more distant people. In this sense Geoffrey's expansive and contradictory descriptive approach to the nature of Farne goes deeper into the nature of the miraculous on Farne than Reginald's more rational scriptural approach.

Apart from the three healing miracles which conclude Bartholomew's *Vita*, the hermits of Farne were not themselves the source of such virtue.[70] This is in great contrast to Godric of Finchale, for whom healing miracles from his 'rustic belt', his bread and even a hair of his beard were prominent even before his death.[71] The hermits of Farne were simply overshadowed by the presence of Saint Cuthbert on the island. In one respect however, Bartholomew was able to fulfil the same role as Godric did at Finchale. Just as healing miracles arose socially from a wishful interpretation of events, so also visions could be created by the appropriate social context. Holy men could have a powerful comforting influence, encouraging 'spiritual' events of great personal importance, as when Godric cured a Cistercian monk of temptations.[72] Reginald reports that he wept when Godric told him of a vision in which the old hermit sang with Saint Nicholas and the angels.[73] There was a certain predisposition to believe in the reality of such things, and Reginald weeps that the heaviness of his sins prevented him from seeing the same things as Godric. However, Reginald is later rewarded with a vision, whose content had been predicted by Godric.[74]

Bartholomew had his visions too, and helped visiting monks through their apparitions of demons and angels.[75] However, lay people were also capable of seeing visions. One group, composed of men and women, was marooned on Farne during bad weather and was clearly in a state of some anxiety concerning provisions. Some of the group saw Cuthbert marching around the island and gesturing to them to reassure them of his protection. Some went to the hermit to report this, while others were adamant that they had not seen the saint at all. Bartholomew came and made the whole group pray all night until the morning when the storm abated, and all present agreed upon the saint's miraculous gift to them.[76] There is a prosaic undercurrent to this story, which perhaps says more concerning the social production of spiritual visions than many such stories. As some of a group of people were initially enthusiastic to see a vision, Bartholomew as a holy man could convince the group as a whole to accept the miraculous. The hermit here appears to be fostering the cult of Cuthbert through using and understanding lay people's own religious enthusiasm.

70 *Vita Bartholomaei*, chs. 34–6; one unidentified man was cured of a year-long fever, a woman was cured of madness, and a brother of Lindisfarne was cured of a swelling of the neck.

71 See Dominic Alexander, 'Hermits and Hairshirts: The Social Meanings of Saintly Clothing in the *Vitae* of Godric of Finchale and Wulfric of Haselbury', *Journal of Medieval History* 28 (2002), pp. 205–26, at p. 225.

72 *Vita Godrici*, ch. 141, no. 256, pp. 270–1.

73 Ibid. ch. 93, no. 192, pp. 202–3.

74 Ibid. ch. 107, nos. 211–12, pp. 223–4.

75 *Vita Bartholomaei*, chs. 26 and 27, pp. 316–18.

76 Reginald, *Libellus*, ch. 31, pp. 70–2.

Bartholomew was not just an organiser of lay people's hallucinations, he was a storyteller, and his stories may have done much to encourage the cult there. Bartholomew's predecessor on Farne, Aelric, seems to have been a foil for Bartholomew's narrative creativity. Aelric appears in three miracles in Reginald's collection and was remembered independently by the Durham community: Reginald reports that his nephew was a sacrist of the cathedral.[77] However, one of Aelric's Cuthbertine miracles, involving some wax stolen by a raven, was told in modified terms by Geoffrey as one of Bartholomew's miracles. In isolation this story might appear as a simple patristic literary miracle concerning the control of nature, but in context it can be seen embedded within a popular tradition of the island, abetted by its hermits.

Geoffrey writes that Bartholomew had told the story under Aelric's name out of humility, while the miracle truly happened through his own virtue.[78] Reginald gives no witness for his version of the story, which occurs on its own in the collection. The other two Aelric stories appear earlier and together in the *Libellus*, and Reginald gives Aelric and his servant Leving as witnesses to the first of these. It appears likely that the wax and raven story was indeed Bartholomew's own creation and that he was consciously adding to the miraculous memory of his predecessor. The two other miracles involving Aelric concern eiderducks and sailors, two dominant strands in the miraculous tradition of Farne in Bartholomew's own period. Bartholomew was not the creator of the miraculous traditions of Farne, but was a keen custodian of existing local belief.

Bartholomew appears as a mediator of conflicts and a mediator of culture. As a mediator of conflicts, his qualities are discussed in general terms by Geoffrey: Bartholomew censured the rich, 'the rumour of whose savagery had reached him'.[79] The rich were terrified when they came to see him, and were brought to rid themselves of 'unlawful gifts' ('munus illicitum'), to stop their injury of the poor, and to give alms. For the poor 'he brought forth pious bowels of compassion', and told them to be patient. However, Bartholomew's sympathies are probably best revealed by the miracle stories which are distinctive enough to be most clearly his own creations. The extra story the hermit created for Aelric involves a poor local couple, who come to Saint Cuthbert for help. Aelric received a gift of a small piece of wax from the poor couple, but through a misunderstanding this gift is left on a rock outside the hermit's cell. The hermit and the poor man emerge from the cell only to see a raven making off with the precious offering. Forthwith the hermit falls to his knees, imploring saintly intervention: 'Holy Cuthbert, where now are your merits of virtue and power?' The hermit demands Cuthbert's 'pious patronage' and tells the raven to return with the 'booty of his robbery'. Of course the raven does, so the mediation of the hermit, and Cuthbert's care for the least of his faithful, is vindicated.

The point of this story could not be so much to encourage tiny gifts to the monastery, as to assure the poor laity that their devotion was recognised and appreciated

[77] Ibid. ch. 27, p. 61. The three Aelric miracles are chs. 27, 28 and 78.

[78] Ibid. ch. 78, pp. 162–3; *Vita Bartholomaei*, ch. 17, pp. 309–10.

[79] *Vita Bartholomaei*, ch. 10, p. 303.

by the saint. Such rural people would have been accustomed to gift-economy relationships and so probably felt a need to give in return for spiritual services. Reginald presents the poor couple not as rustic *imbecilles*, as he calls their kind in his preface, but as dignified poor 'from the multitude'.[80] Geoffrey attributed a very different meaning to the story from Reginald, and changed the details significantly. The givers of the gift are indicated simply as 'sailors' and have no other role. The miracle is achieved simply because otherwise the little gift would be lost to the use of the church. Geoffrey reduces the story to a demonstration of Bartholomew's *virtus* in his saintly control of the raven. It seems likely that Reginald's version of the story was closer in intent at least to the story originally told by Bartholomew.

The original context of Bartholomew's story can only be imagined, and Reginald's purpose in recording the story would have differed from Bartholomew's purpose in telling it. Nevertheless, it is significant that this story, which out of all the Farne stories is most clearly the hermit's own, was concerned with the poor neighbours of Farne. In the original context of Bartholomew's stories, details and message would have had to appeal to and convince local people. Thus Bartholomew must have been at ease with the stories and beliefs of the local rural population, as equally he could talk to literate monks in their own cultural idiom. This is not to say that there was a cultural iron curtain between the two groups, simply that their respective stories and beliefs would have differed considerably, as much as they overlapped. The genre of the animal and saint story here again appears particularly flexible in its provision of stories which could move between the two poles of medieval culture.

The power of Farne as a holy place in the popular imagination is revealed in another story where Farne comes into contrast with the forces of the Otherworld. A young labourer, Richard of Sunderland, is bonded to a *paterfamilias* in Ellingham, both places being near to Farne.[81] Richard is sent on an errand by his master, and on the road is kidnapped by three young men dressed in green 'beautiful of stature and of countenance', on green-clothed horses: 'and they came to a valley which opened to them of its own accord. So Richard was led into the desert ('in desertum') by a spirit of fantasy, that he might be tempted.' Here he finds a 'diabolical convent', whose members are unquestionably fairies. They finally force him to drink a kind of ale from a green horn. But 'he remembered the sermons he had heard while he was among men, and what popular opinion handed down about things of this kind'. Protected by his simple faith, he is returned to the world, albeit dumb. Alongside his family, living opposite Farne, he gazes longingly towards the island, and is finally cured there, after Bartholomew gives him holy water.

There are two hermitages in this story: the evil desert of the fairies and the holy island of Farne. The explicit comparison of Farne and the fairy desert may have been a conceit of the author, or of Bartholomew himself, but the contrast is embedded in

80 Reginald, *Libellus*, ch. 78, p. 163.

81 *Miracles of Farne*, ch. 6, pp. 14–16; Richard is described as being 'humili genere progenitus, cuidam de Elingham marcennarii servicio fuerat mancipatus'. Perhaps Richard is a serf of some kind, but it is probably unwise to draw any precise legal conclusions from the story concerning the relative status of Richard and his master.

the story itself. The hermitage, whether evil or holy, was associated with the terrors and wonders of the spirit world. Perhaps both the complexities and conflicts of human communities and their wish for harmony are given expression in the opposites associated with the holy hermitage and the evil wilderness. Also it is possible that such a dichotomy encouraged the notion of Farne as a local 'purgatory'.

It is likely that demonic abduction was a general popular explanation for some other event, related to disease or violence. There is a similar abduction story in Reginald's book of miracles, of a child kidnapped by 'evil spirits', taken to 'foreign kingdoms', and losing his sense of reason. Eventually he is cured in Durham Cathedral.[82] The better-known 'green children' in William of Newburgh are another case where a 'fairy' story may be hiding violence against the young, or some other social disruption which was covered up by a wondrous tale.[83] William reports this story as an attested event for his own reasons, but again the story would have had a different meaning in its local context. Gerald of Wales tells a light-hearted story of a child who runs away to a land of little fairies because he has been too often beaten by his teacher.[84] These stories are all very different, but consequently they point to the mythology of fairies being a living part of popular culture, rather than being a stable topos of literate monks. One aspect which does connect the stories is that of mistreatment of the young.

It is thus possible to speculate about the original function of Bartholomew's story. When the young man disappeared his master went to look for him at the home of his parents, whose distress is given long treatment. Richard, when he reappeared, was evidently allowed to remain at home, and the master abruptly ceased to be a part of the story. The young man could not speak until he was taken to Farne where he told the hermit his story. Refusal to speak can be a form of protest. If 'fairy stories' were connected with violence against the young, perhaps the telling of such stories was a recognised form of social shaming directed against the perpetrator. In this case the story would also reflect social conflict between poor and rich peasants. It is possible in this story to see Bartholomew's practice of 'censuring the rich'.

It is unusual for the 'green' men in this story to be so richly described. It is likely that such mythological creatures were usually reduced to nondescript demons, a process which is demonstrable in the various versions of Godric's *Vita*. Reginald records one story in which a naked, hairy and dumb creature approaches Finchale.[85] The creature is clearly a typical wild man. The very same story appears in Geoffrey's

[82] Reginald, *Libellus*, ch. 122, pp. 268–9.

[83] William of Newburgh, *Historia Rerum Anglicarum*, in *Chronicles of the Reigns of Stephen, Henry II and Richard I*, ed. Richard Howlett, Rolls Series 82 (1964), vol. I, at bk 1, ch. 27, 'De viridibus pueris', pp. 82–4.

[84] Gerald of Wales, *Itinerarium Kambriae*, ed. James F. Dimock, Rolls Series 21 (1868), vol. VI, at bk 1, ch. 8, pp. 72–8; the fairy tale is from p. 75.

[85] *Vita Godrici*, ch. 135, no. 248, pp. 261–2. Reginald may have been embarrassed by this story, giving a clerical witness who only appears in one other story: ch. 138. Reginald does not normally give a witness to a story experienced by Godric alone. Also see above, Chapter 6, p. 126.

summary of the *Vita Godrici*, but the creature is simply a standard devil.[86] That the wild man appeared in Reginald's version is due to the hagiographer's particular agenda concerning the hermit. Godric was a purveyor of stories of all the weird and wonderful 'hairy' creatures which infest the wilderness.[87] For Reginald there was a contradiction between Godric's rusticity and his paradoxical and therefore miraculous sophistication. The hermit believed in all these marvellous creatures and was yet able to speak French and understand Latin.[88] Thus it is no accident that Reginald should embark upon a long description of monopods and hairy demons, large and small: they are needed for his characterisation of Godric. The appearance of elves in one of Bartholomew's stories may thus indicate a similar disjunction in culture between the hermit of Farne and the sophisticated hagiographers of Durham. Both hermits probably had a foot in both worlds. On the one hand, Bartholomew was a priest and a monk, yet he was enough a part of rural lay culture to create or connive in a story of elven abduction.

Although it is dangerous to assume any rigid distinction in culture and beliefs between the rural poor and the literate elite, Reginald for one clearly perceived a gulf of difference in mind and in culture. The hermits, as men separate from and adaptable to both sides of this medieval social divide, were just the figures likely to appeal to many different social groups, and to be able to talk to them in the language that appealed to each group. The hermits in this view were essential points through which belief and cultural forms, particularly in the form of miracle stories, could flow both ways between local communities and the monastery at Durham. The hagiographic picture of the cult of Saint Cuthbert at Farne is not, then, only the creation of monastic thinking any more than it is a simple record of a popular cult. Rather it is a product of the interactions of monastery and various sorts of lay people in the social relationships which created and maintained the cult at Farne. This interaction between monastic concerns and popular belief and practices likely lies behind the miracle stories of Saint Cuthbert's eiderducks. Moreover, the conception of Farne as a place of peace, and one where justice is served through the saint's miraculous power, appears to arise at least as much through popular belief as through the agendas of Durham's writers.

[86] Geoffrey of Coldingham, *Vita Sancti Godrici Eremitae, AASS* 5 May, pp. 68–85, at ch. 5, no. 58, pp. 81–2. The narrative of the story, which appears curiously incomplete in Reginald, is given a standard 'temptation' spin in Geoffrey.

[87] *Vita Godrici*, ch. 90, nos. 187–8, pp. 196–8.

[88] For Godric's miraculous sophistication and his facility with educated languages see ibid. ch. 79. no. 170, pp. 179–80, where he understands Latin, and ch. 94, nos. 193–4, pp. 203–4, and ch. 96, no. 196, pp. 206–7, where he understands French. Considering Godric's years of travel it should not have surprised Reginald that Godric could have picked up French and a good deal of Latin.

CHAPTER 8

Animal Sanctuaries of the Middle Ages?

THE cult of Saint Cuthbert on Farne is an illustration of the social context from which miracle stories could spring. Neither the sailors' miracles nor the healing miracles of Farne were in any way unusual within their genre of miracle, yet they can best be seen as the product of lay belief and practice on the island, in interaction with the hermits, the custodians of the cult of the island. The hermits cannot be seen simply as representatives of the monastic and literary milieu: Bartholomew was at least as much a representative of 'rustic' concerns and beliefs to the visiting monks, as was Godric at Finchale.

The story of the raven, who stole the poor couple's wax offering, was one indication of the hermit's mediating role in the creation of popular traditions. This would not be clear without the presence of multiple versions of the story and the surrounding miraculous context in each of the three writers of Farne stories. Geoffrey turned the story into an imitation miracle, linking Bartholomew to Cuthbert through comparison with the latter's chastisement of the ravens.[1] Reginald prefaced his version of the story with reference to the same miracle, and concluded that it was 'a wonderful and stupendous thing' that 'whilst brute animals sense the command of the virtue of Blessed Cuthbert, truly rational men of intelligence fear less his power'. Bede similarly felt that obedience was the key issue: 'men should seek after obedience and humility, seeing that even a proud bird hastened to atone for the wrong that it had done to the man of God'. It would seem that the key patristic theme of obedience is the main theme of the story for Geoffrey and Reginald. Indeed, Bede's story relates to the general colonisation of nature theme, with the implicit moral being a warning against the usurpation of monastic rights over resources.

Yet the twelfth-century story is not a standard obedience topos: it is the legitimate rights of the poor couple which have been usurped by the thieving raven, a character that would certainly have been familiar to a local rural audience. The underlying moral here was that on Farne Saint Cuthbert protects the weak against injury. The Church's property rights would almost certainly not have been the issue in Bartholomew's rendition of the story. The theme of animal obedience is secondary to the demonstration of the special nature of the island, where wrongs are righted by the power of the saint. The story should be compared to another of

1 *Vita Cuthberti*, ch. 20, pp. 222–5, and *Vita Bartholomaei*, ch. 17, pp. 309–10; also Reginald, *Libellus*, ch. 78, pp. 162–3.

injustice against the weak punished. A ship's boy, through innocent accident, endangered a skiff while fishing off the island. Bartholomew forbade the boy's master from punishing him, invoking the 'privilege of peace' of the island which forbade 'chastisement' to be carried out. The sailor disobeyed the hermit, but once out at sea was punished for this by his own death.[2] The special quality of the island as a holy place where the weak are protected or avenged is key to both stories.

This law of Farne also appears in relation to another small group of animal miracles concerning Bartholomew's pet gull. Reginald introduces his story noting that the island 'on account of being the ancient habitation of Saint Cuthbert, is greatly overflowing with virtue'.[3] Geoffrey notes about the little bird that 'every day in Lent in the first year [of the hermit's life on Farne] she brought along a sort of fish, which is commonly called a "lump-fish", to an appointed place for his sustenance'.[4] The pet gull is an idiosyncratic example of the Elijah topos, containing a strong hint of the bucolic, where a gull is sent to bring a rustic sort of food to a 'rough' and 'untried' hermit. The story of the gull probably was intended to resonate with the more patristic versions of the topos to be found in the *Vitae* of Saint Cuthbert, but such a connection only highlights the imagery of hermit as peasant. Reginald's earlier account of the gull had employed a different topos, if not genuine anecdote, describing how at meals the gull would 'sit and play and eat' with Bartholomew and any visitors, taking food from their hands. To some this was 'a humorous spectacle of solace' and to others it amounted to a miracle.[5] In either case the Durham writers were presenting the gull in terms of the harmony between animal and saint on Farne, but neither appears in an entirely serious light. Now it may well be that Bartholomew the storyteller created this Elijah topos story, intending it as something of a joke against himself.[6] While this may be the case, neither writer needed to follow the hermit in their tone, or depart from established models for the topos. It may be that the popular character of the cult of Farne encouraged the deviations, but in any case the story demonstrates how established topoi could be adapted to particular social environments.

While the law of Farne is not directly present in the happy tales of the pet gull's mealtimes, the bird's untimely demise does bring forth saintly wrath. One day when the gull came into Bartholomew's cell at mealtime, but while the hermit was absent, a hawk flew in, killed and ate the gull. The two versions of the story show considerable variations from this basic premise. In both versions the hawk is punished for its crime, 'because it had violated the peace of Blessed Cuthbert' in

[2] *Vita Bartholomaei*, ch. 18, pp. 310–11.

[3] Reginald, *Libellus*, ch. 111, p. 247.

[4] *Vita Bartholomaei*, ch. 9, pp. 301–2.

[5] Reginald, *Libellus*, ch. 111, pp. 247–8.

[6] Bartholomew's asceticism was somewhat controversial among the monks of Durham, being considered too harsh. Self-depreciating humour may have disarmed critics; see Dominic Alexander, 'Hermits, Hagiography and Popular Culture: A Comparative Study of Durham Cathedral Priory's Hermits in the Twelfth Century', unpublished Ph.D. thesis, University of London, 2000, chapter 2, pp. 23–7.

Reginald's words, but the *virtus* at work belongs to a different saint in each story.[7] In Reginald it is Cuthbert who takes vengeance, while Geoffrey attributes the power to Bartholomew himself. The story probably originated with the hermit, who would have told it as a miracle of Saint Cuthbert. Geoffrey would certainly have known Reginald's version of the story, yet the stories are significantly different in plot and there are no signs of textual borrowing from Reginald to Geoffrey.

In Reginald's story the hawk, having killed and eaten the gull, flew out of the cell, but was unable to fly away from the island, being blocked by the power of Cuthbert. Flying round and round, the predator became exhausted and returned to the scene of the crime, where it stood in a corner near the altar, with its 'head bowed and wings drooping'.[8] In Geoffrey, by contrast, the hawk remained in the oratorium, unable to find its way out after killing the gull. In both cases, Bartholomew then came to find the scene, but in Reginald's version it seems the hawk has already done its penance, and the hermit's role is to appeal to Cuthbert for mercy for the hawk. In Geoffrey it is the hermit himself who imposes a three-day fast on the bird before allowing it to depart. Geoffrey's version, being less miraculous, may be closer to an original version of the story, which could have been embellished by Reginald in his version, some twenty years before. However, there are reasons to suppose that Bartholomew's original rendition would have been as miraculous and dramatic as the Reginald version. It is equally possible that the hermit himself, and others, told different versions of the story, and that the two monks simply chose between competing oral accounts.

There is a hint that Bartholomew's account of the story may have differed significantly from those of the two Durham writers. Despite the great differences between their two accounts, and the lack of any other overlaps of vocabulary, there is one image they both use, apparently coincidentally. When Bartholomew returns to his cell, he sees the 'bones and feathers' of the gull scattered about his cell.[9] The image appears to have been essential to the story, but it performs no other function than as evidence of the hawk's guilt, which seems unnecessary in such a miracle story. Yet it recalls the images of bones and feathers in the goose resurrection tales. It is possible that the story of Bartholomew's pet gull had a happier ending in the original, one that was suppressed by the monks of Durham. Another connection between this story and the goose resurrections is the image of the penitent hawk, which could echo either of the versions of the Wereburga miracle, as much as it could echo the story of Saint Cuthbert and the penitent ravens. There are also clear

[7] Reginald, *Libellus*, ch. 111, pp. 247–8, and *Vita Bartholomaei*, ch. 19, pp. 311–12.

[8] Reginald may be echoing the penitent ravens of *Vita Cuthberti*, ch. 20, p. 224, in the description of the exhausted hawk, but the vocabulary is in fact closer to the penitent geese of Wereburga; see above, Chapter 5, note 32.

[9] The two writers use different terms for feathers, *pluma* in Reginald, and *pennula* in Geoffrey, further indicating that this coincidence is not a case of textual borrowing. While the standard definition of *pennula* appears to be 'little wing', the sense of 'little feathers' is also possible, and is clearly Geoffrey's meaning here; see *pennula* in Aegidius Forcellini, *Totius Latinitatis Lexicon* (London 1828), 2 vols.

parallels between Bartholomew's pet gull and the story of the pet bird and Saint Kentigern, which the latter resurrected.[10] This later miracle was written, or rewritten, at about the same time as Reginald was writing.

While the peace of Saint Cuthbert on Farne appears often to be observed in the breach and the punishment, if the pet gull story was originally a resurrection story, then it would provide the kind of positive miracle of protection that the goose resurrections and the 'hermit and hunter' stories provided for other saints. A resurrection story would have connected the popular conceptions of Farne with the narratives of death and rebirth found in the goose miracles. This would fit with the whole range of stories about Farne. The ideas of the island as a place outside normal social and natural rules, a purgatory on earth, even a place of supernatural battle between opposing spiritual forces, all would have found expression in the meanings of the popular resurrection story.

Whether or not there was a suppressed resurrection miracle behind the story of Bartholomew's gull, the story itself is best seen as emerging from the popular conception of Farne as a place of peace under the 'law' of Saint Cuthbert. The story is highly unusual in patristic terms, hingeing as it does on the punishment and penance of a wild animal, rather than the reversal and taming of wild nature. Of course, Reginald is able to identify that theme as part of the story, concluding that Saint Cuthbert 'thus punished the wild bird, tamed it, and at the invocation of the name itself, absolved it from the chains of its conscious guilt'.[11] However, there is very little in the story that points to the 'taming' of the hawk being an essential theme in the original narrative. Indeed, in Geoffrey's version there is no trace of such a topos. This is in contrast to the miracle of Saint Kentigern and the pet bird, whose tamed nature is the subject of a few anecdotes. Reginald appears to have added a reference to the standard topos of taming in order to absorb the Farne hermit's popular tale into more conventional monastic conceptions of the saint and animal story.

The gull story could be characterised as a peculiar variant of the 'hermit and hunter' topos. The hawk, taken symbolically, could easily stand for the hunting nobleman, and Cuthbert's protection, although failed in this case, would be analogous to the protection offered to hunted beasts by other saints. At a deeper level, there is a resonance between the logic seen in William of Malmesbury's version of the Wereburga miracle and the law of Farne seen here.[12] Wereburga's protection of animals amounted to a *quid pro quo*, where the saint's miraculous healing was associated with her protection of animals. The same logic appears here on Farne: it is a place of refuge and healing for people, but in return, it is a place of peace, outside the normal patterns of social violence. Hence vengeance is taken even for the natural predation of a hawk upon a gull. With the twelfth-century stories of

[10] Jocelyn of Furness, *Vita Kentigerni*, ch. 5, pp. 170–1, trans. pp. 42–3. The Cistercian hagiographer insists much more on the miraculous domesticity of the bird to Saint Servanus than does either Durham hagiographer. Jocelyn emphasises the ways in which the bird demonstrated its love for the holy man, the latter's contemplation of this wonder, and the power of God.

[11] Reginald, *Libellus*, ch. 111, p. 248.

[12] See above, Chapter 5, p. 94.

Wereburga and Farne, a model of popular understanding of the saint's shrine comes into view: the sacred place demands the suspension of normal social and natural rules. It is not just a wilderness, but a place existing outside both society and the wild. Hence it was natural to associate Farne with problems of the Otherworld, as it was in Bartholomew's story of the boy abducted by elves.[13]

The sacred rules of Farne were most forcibly and repeatedly expressed in the twelfth-century stories of the eiderducks. There is no mention of these birds in either of Cuthbert's *Vitae*, and their first appearance directly linked to the sanctity of Cuthbert and Farne is in Reginald's miracle collection. Yet their holiness appears to have been of long duration: the first miracle concerning an eiderduck involves the hermit Aelric of Farne, who lived there some time before 1150, decades before Reginald was writing. In this story, Reginald explains that God has placed all creation under the command of his servants, and 'in the island of Farne there are animals of several kinds which, from the times of Saint Cuthbert, are domesticated and can be handled by the hands of all inhabitants and visitors'.[14] Reginald describes how the eiderducks will make their nests in houses, in beds, on tables, and will happily sit in your lap. This characterisation of the eiderducks is only partly compatible with the Edenic topos of blissful relations between saints and animals: Reginald gives the impression of wild fecundity and noise overwhelming human habitation during the nesting season. This description is certainly not comparable to the Cistercian lyricism of well-ordered monastic Edens.[15] Nevertheless, Reginald ascribes the eiderducks' behaviour not to 'nature but through grace' as Saint Cuthbert tamed them during his time on Farne: 'Now what their kind received freely in their fathers, the offspring possess and request in heredity of posterity and privilege of dignity'.[16] It seems, despite Reginald's homily on creation and obedience at the beginning of this story, that the eiderducks did not have to perform any miracle of obedience to receive this grace. They received their status through the 'piety and pity of Blessed Cuthbert alone'. These specially blessed wild animals do not seem to have any precedent in hagiographic tradition.

Geoffrey, describing eiderduck habits, including their habit of nesting next to the chapel altar, agrees that this 'prerogative is the dignity of this noble island and if the study of the ancients had learnt of it, would have been diffused in the most beautiful praise throughout the world'.[17] Yet Geoffrey also describes the taking of the young birds to the 'native waves' where 'they regain in wisdom the ancient condition with the sea'. Like Wereburga's geese, outside the presence of the saint, they return to their natural wild state. Their wild behaviour and their grace are intertwined, quite unlike the colonised and obedient nature of Clairvaux. However, Geoffrey is more circumspect about the origin of the eiderducks' grace:

[13] See above, Chapter 7, p. 149.

[14] Reginald, *Libellus*, ch. 27, pp. 60–3. During nesting season the eiderducks today are known to be exceptionally docile: see M. Scott Weightman, *The Farne Islands* (Seahouses 1988), p. 12.

[15] See above, Chapter 3, p. 49.

[16] Reginald, *Libellus*, ch. 27, p. 61.

[17] *Vita Bartholomaei*, ch. 24, p. 315.

> Long tradition maintains that certain birds anciently inhabit this island, of which both the name and kind survives by a miracle. In the time of nesting they assemble there. And by the sanctity of the place or rather by those who sanctified the place in their conversion, they soon accomplished the grace of such gentleness that they were not averse to human gazes and touches.

Unlike Reginald, Geoffrey seems unwilling to advance the notion that Cuthbert was personally responsible for such grace, attributing it to all the hermits of Farne and obliquely referring to oral memory. The two writers' different interpretations are a strong indication that the eiderduck stories were popular legend, rather than a creation of the Durham monks themselves. In this case Reginald was probably accurately reflecting popular belief, while Geoffrey accepted popular legend, but pruned it of the element he knew was unlikely to be true, given that there is no mention of eiderducks in Bede.

As a consequence of this state of grace, the eiderducks could not be harassed or eaten on the Inner Farne itself. Thus each of Durham's three writers relates a miracle of Cuthbert's vengeance upon those who break this law. Reginald comments: 'Blessed Cuthbert offered such quiet of peace to them, that hitherto no man presumed safely to violate it'.[18] But the hermit Aelric was forced to go on an errand and leave his servant Leving unsupervised; the servant was led astray by the devil and his own desire, and he ate an eiderduck. When Aelric returned, the miraculous evidence of the servant's crime, the familiar image of the bones and feathers, appeared washed up on the beach. This was clearly Saint Cuthbert's *virtus* in action. Aelric confronted his servant with the evidence, and the poor sinner promptly vomited up his earlier meal on the doorstep of the hermit's cell. Aelric was then able both to bring the sinner to contrition and forgiveness, and to prevent a more violent vengeance coming from the saint himself. Geoffrey also describes this miracle and other related ones, noting that 'nothing is committed unpunished in this island'.[19] Once again, the similarity in structure between this story and the goose resurrections is notable. In each a servant to the saint consumes a protected animal, or sacred animal perhaps, and is discovered by the saint. As with the miracle of Bartholomew's gull and the hawk, it is possible that this story represents a suppressed resurrection motif.

The anonymous collection of Farne stories details two miracles of vengeance upon men who violated the peace of the 'gulls'.[20] The first was one Roger of

[18] Reginald, *Libellus*, ch. 27, p. 61.

[19] *Vita Bartholomaei*, ch. 23, p. 314.

[20] *Miracles of Farne*, chs. 2 and 3, pp. 10–12. Geoffrey does not give a name to the birds he describes, but they are clearly the eiderducks. Bartholomew's pet 'gull' is described as an *avis parvula* and a *moota* or gull. Reginald refers to the eiderducks as 'the birds of Saint Cuthbert', which are called *lomes* by the English and *eires* by the Flemish: Reginald, *Libellus*, ch. 27. He never uses the term *moota* for them and describes Bartholomew's pet gull as an *avis modica*. The writers seem unsure about what Latin terminology should be used for the eiderducks, and the use of *moota* is probably the result of confusion on the anonymous writer's part. Bartholomew's pet is probably a gull, not an eiderduck. If it was the latter, Geoffrey or Reginald would have given some indication.

Embleton, who came to ask Bartholomew for one of the young eiderducks to eat. Bartholomew replied:

> You know not what you ask. Go rather to the neighbouring islands and take thence what you can. But do not presume to stretch forth your hand against those whom the lodging of this holy place has brought forth. They must enjoy the privilege of that great peace.[21]

But foolish Roger went and disturbed the birds, raising up a great clamour, and bringing the hermit's warning of punishment if he did not desist. The man died three days later. But then his nephew William came to Farne to fish and sneered: 'Do you think Saint Cuthbert cares for gulls?' The young man threw stones at the eiderducks, and subsequently suffered from severe pain in two fingers, but did not die. The writer admits that some may be puzzled at the difference in punishment between the two men, and after some discussion concludes that the second man must have repented in his heart and was thus spared: 'For a just judge does not consider the equality of the crimes, but, in delivering retributive judgement, he assesses the quality of intention'.[22]

Significantly, Bartholomew's speech to Roger indicates that local people were considered free to hunt the eiderducks and other animals on all the other islands. This is not then a case of monastic attempts to monopolise resources, but the singling out of the Inner Farne as a special sacred place, where neither monks nor people exploit the wildlife. Geoffrey is more ambiguous than the anonymous author, apparently stating that eiderduck eggs may be gathered by the monks of Farne or by visitors, if given 'licence'.[23] This seems to contradict the impression of an absolute ban given in the miracle stories, but most likely simply reflects the situation indicated in the anonymous collection, where the eiderducks could be exploited on islands other than the Inner Farne.[24]

A striking element of all three 'vengeance' miracles is their plausibility as genuine events. There is little that is miraculous beyond the bounds of psychological explanation. A culture which interprets day-to-day life in terms of supernatural causation could make individuals react strongly to the perceived threat of the miraculous. Thus the servant of the hermit Aelric vomits his earlier meal under the holy man's harrowing scrutiny.[25] The death of the man Roger, three days after breaking the

21 *Miracles of Farne*, ch. 2, p. 10; trans. Craster, p. 97.

22 *Miracles of Farne*, ch. 3, pp. 11–12; trans. Craster, pp. 98–9.

23 *Vita Bartholomaei*, ch. 24, p. 315.

24 The eiderducks nest on the islands Brownsman, Longstone and Staple as well as Inner Farne itself. On the present-day wild-life of the islands see Peter Hawkey, *Birds of the Farne Islands* (Rothbury 1990), and Raymond A. Cartwright, *The Holy Island of Lindisfarne and the Farne Islands* (Newton Abbot 1976).

25 The third Aelric miracle shows a similar pattern. One of a group of sailors stole a small item of 'necessity' rather than 'beauty or value' from the hermit, and the sailors refused to sail with him aboard until the hermit was informed and forgave the act. Indeed the hermit had to convince the sailors that Saint Cuthbert would not punish them further if they had their fellow on board with

prohibition on hunting animals in this particular sacred place, is a coincidence, but events may have been telescoped in time.[26] Roger's own community very likely interpreted his unexpected death in terms of supernatural explanations for random events. That the next miracle involves a close family member, his nephew, increases the likelihood of that explanation.[27] William threw rocks at the eiderducks, perhaps as an act of rebellion at his community's judgement on his uncle. It is not said that he had any intention of hunting them. William's scepticism concerning Cuthbert's care for ducks is the corollary of his community's belief. It was the hermit Bartholomew who told and in a sense 'created' these miracles. However, someone had to visit Bartholomew and tell him of events, before he could turn the sequence into a story. In the second story, it seems to have been the nephew, in a spirit of repentance, who told Bartholomew of Cuthbert's vengeance upon himself.

The hermit's role, in turning the event into a story, is to confirm and strengthen a community's culture, as reflected in its folklore. A saint's vengeance miracles are usually seen, justifiably, as a kind of historical discourse defending the saint's monastery from its oppressors.[28] However, that model cannot work in these stories of the vengeance of Saint Cuthbert upon those who abuse his eiderducks: monastic interests are not at issue. Instead, the hermit acts as a focus of reconciliation between the saint and the local people. As seen in the previous chapter, Bartholomew frequently appears to have encouraged popular piety and belief in its own terms, rather than through a monastic agenda.

Thus another eiderduck story, while very likely a creation of Bartholomew alone, may well reflect popular religion in the Farne area. Certainly, it does not reflect any typical monastic conception of the animal and saint miracle. Here, a mother duck lost one of her chicks as she led her progeny to the sea: it had fallen into a crevice in the rock. But she 'put on the condition of human reason' and waddled into Bartholomew's cell, roused him from sleep on his bed, and was able to say 'Rise and Follow me'.[29] Bartholomew followed the bird, and rescued her duckling, for which she thanked Bartholomew, just as Wereburga's geese thanked her for a more miraculous service.

them. The miracle was the creation of the sailors' social psychology, and had minimal input by the hermit: Reginald, *Libellus*, ch. 28, pp. 63–5.

[26] On the general problem of time and miracle stories see Finucane, *Miracles and Pilgrims*, pp. 88–9.

[27] Miracles would have had a tendency to run in families in this period: see ibid. pp. 152–4.

[28] Saint Cuthbert is noted for his vengeance miracles, see for example in Symeon, *Libellus de Exordio*, bk 2, ch. 5, pp. 88–91, on the destruction of Lindisfarne: 'But they did not do these things with impunity, for God very soon gave judgment on the injuries which they had inflicted upon St. Cuthbert' (p. 89). This exemplifies the personal interest a saint takes in the house of his monks, and his role in protecting or avenging his own. The litany of disaster and violence continues the moral of Cuthbert's vengeance in Symeon, *Libellus de Exordio*, bk 2, ch. 6, pp. 96–9. See also ibid. bk 2, ch. 14, pp. 126–9, for the privileges of the church of Durham: 'And no one has ever striven with impunity to infringe them'. The vengeance Saint Cuthbert visits on marauders of his church can be seen in somewhat more comical form on Farne in the 'ravaging' of the Norwegian 'king': Reginald, *Libellus*, ch. 29.

[29] *Vita Bartholomaei*, ch. 25, pp. 315–16.

There is an almost blasphemous literary play here: the duck's words echo Christ's words in the Vulgate. Such a command is not unknown in contemporary miracle stories, it occurs in one twelfth-century English Cistercian miracle where the Virgin appears to a monk asleep on his bed.[30] Perhaps this story should be regarded as a *jocus* of Saint Cuthbert, with biblical echo added for the entertainment of a monastic audience, underlining the comically rustic nature of the material.

The idea of animals receiving the gift of reason from a saint begins with patristic writers, but there such grace was in order that the animals could do penance for their crimes against humans. With the stories from Farne and Chester, the ducks and the geese receive that grace purely for their own benefit. The stories are linked by the saint's or hermit's role in protecting animals in the context of a shrine which served local, secular people. If these stories show the influence of popular culture, then it seems a truce between animals and humans at a shrine was a *quid pro quo* for the saint's healing miracles on behalf of humans. The magic of the shrine can heal humans or bestow some sense of reason in animals. The need of weaker members of human society for protection from the more powerful is also paralleled by the animals. While Bartholomew's gull needed protection from the rapacity of the hawk, this hermit was also noted by his hagiographer for condemning the 'savagery' of the rich towards the poor.[31]

Thus the popular cult of Farne may have been idiosyncratic, but it shows clear parallels to other popular miracles where the animal miracle is linked to the healing of women and children, in the same logic of *quid pro quo*.[32] Although there are some possible connections between the Farne stories and ancient strands of folklore embedded in the resurrection miracles and the 'hermit and hunter' topos, predominantly what can be found here is a new complex of folklore, feeding off established Church traditions, but then creating a new stock of stories which satisfied the needs of local rural communities rather than being moulded around Church interests. Indeed it was the monks of Durham who sought to adapt these stories for their own purposes, no doubt in an attempt to direct popular belief into channels useful to their community.

Durham's other hermit, Godric of Finchale, performed a large number of animal miracles, which were also recorded by Reginald of Durham at about the same time as he was writing his collection of Saint Cuthbert's contemporary miracles, after the hermit's death in 1170. At first sight, many of the animal stories attached to Godric may appear relatively traditional, involving control of wild creatures such as snakes and wolves, and the protection of his garden from animal marauders. However, the same logic of the shrine, the protection of animals associated with healing miracles for humans, appears to have operated in this case also. Nonetheless, the animal miracles are framed by a version of the standard journey of the holy hermit into the wilderness, and are accompanied therefore by topoi of colonisation and control of animals.

30 Giles Constable, 'The Vision of a Cistercian Novice', in *Petrus Venerabilis: Studia Anselmiana* 44, ed. Giles Constable and James Kritzeck (Rome 1956), pp. 95–8, particularly p. 97.

31 *Vita Bartholomaei*, ch. 10, p. 303.

32 See above, Chapter 5, p. 94.

Animals first appear in the *Vita Godrici* as apparently demonic figures, wishing to attack the hermit in his lonely wilderness, but in the end it seems that neither snakes nor wolves dared to molest him.[33] Although Godric demonstrates no overtly miraculous power here, Reginald refers to (Vulgate) Psalm 90, noting the saint's ability to trample upon 'the asp and the wandering basilisk' as well as lions and dragons. Reginald is consciously attaching his material to standard hagiographic themes, but even here, patristic hagiography would usually recount a miracle of power. Godric is passive at this point, and Reginald is reluctant to show him wielding miraculous power, since the hagiographer wishes to show the development of the hermit's holiness through an arduous process of ascetic struggle in the wilderness, and eventually through submission to the authority of Durham Priory.[34] Thus, in companionship with an old hermit, Aelric of Wolsingham, the wilderness is a place of fear which deters the less intrepid through 'the rabid madness of wolves gnashing their teeth' with 'an insatiable gluttony'.[35]

However, this wilderness asceticism is not simply a story of spiritual growth, leading to Edenic relations with nature: Godric became 'accustomed [to eating] roots of plants. He was made now not a man but a worm, not rational, but more a brutish beast.'[36] Such images of the hermit as wild man are repeated at several points in the course of Reginald's description of the hermit's wilderness asceticism.[37] Thus Reginald writes that 'in those days he preferred to live with wild beasts, than to have the knowledge of fellowship with men'.[38] Typically in the hagiographic tradition a holy man is presented living in harmony with the wilderness, if in exile from a sinful human society, or is able to transform nature through his virtue. In contrast, Godric at points becomes identified *with* wildness, and his animal miracles therefore carry a different resonance from the patristic types with which they could be compared.

Imagery of the wilderness as a place of horror is continued when Godric reaches Finchale, his final hermitage, which is described as 'a dreadful grave of a multitude of vipers and of squalid solitude'.[39] As Godric made his initial foray into this uncultivated waste, as Reginald repeatedly describes it, 'the ancient enemy, the winding serpent' found it could not bear the hermit's peaceful contemplation, and Godric was attacked by a wolf intending to 'wholly tear to pieces or mangle' him. The hermit made the sign of the cross and invoked the Holy Trinity, while stating that under the 'clemency of God' he had been given leave to live in this place in obedience. Thus defeated, 'having been given licence to depart, the beast raising himself three times to him humbled himself by bowing, and with all gentleness, walked to the wood'.[40] Once again, Reginald has not provided a straightforward miracle in the

33 *Vita Godrici*, ch. 10, pp. 43–4.

34 See Alexander, 'Hermits, Hagiography, and Popular Culture', pp. 70–8.

35 *Vita Godrici*, ch. 11, no. 31, pp. 46–7.

36 Ibid. ch. 10, no. 29, p. 44; Reginald nevertheless calls him the 'Lord's elect' at this point.

37 See particularly ibid. ch. 12, no. 32, p. 47.

38 Ibid. ch. 23, no. 59, p. 71.

39 Ibid. ch. 19, no. 52, p. 65.

40 Ibid. ch. 18, no. 51, pp. 63–4.

patristic tradition: the creature is not tamed, nor like most demonic animals, is it killed. It simply acknowledges Godric's right to the hermitage. In Godric's gradual acquisition of holy grace, he is at once a 'companion of beasts' and superior to them. In all this the wilderness and the saint are both highly ambiguous in their value, appearing at once negative and positive by turns. This ambiguity could be attributed to Reginald's presentation of his material, and the hagiographer certainly uses it to present his argument about the true path to holiness. Nonetheless, Reginald's key point, the need for holy men to be duly obedient to a properly constituted Benedictine monastery, does not require the full scale of the ambiguity, and it is better explained by conceptions embedded in the material Reginald had gathered from others concerning Godric.

Once Godric settles permanently at Finchale, the enormous snakes who inhabited the place present a new barrier to any development of a colonisation topos. Although ultimately expelled as a distraction to prayer, they are for some time the holy man's companions: far from hissing at or attacking Godric they allow themselves to be handled and stroked by the holy man.[41] During the winter they come into the hermitage, and the 'flock' of them lie on one side of the fire, allowing Godric the other, while two of the large ones twist about the hermit in a friendly manner. When they are not cold, they climb about the rafters, or hide in jugs and corners. Reginald, concluding this description of Godric's creepy Eden, comments that the hermit was the 'brother of dragons and companion of ostriches' (Job 30:29), tying the story into the familiar 'companionship of animals' theme.

Reginald's links to hagiographic tradition and his biblical language do not hide the remarkably unusual image of these friendly but poisonous snakes. Reginald specifies that they are gentle only around Godric himself. The patristic theme of the taming of wild animals is therefore specifically not present here. The snakes are neither tamed, nor banished. It is hard to see why Reginald himself would choose to create such an unusual story, when it seems that it is only a conventional hagiographic moral that he draws from the episode.[42] It would seem more likely that the companionship of the snakes was an independent legend about Godric that Reginald had adapted. In a popular context, the story would fit well into the complex of Otherworld legend, with the snakes representative of ambiguous supernatural creatures of the wilderness. Reginald was certainly well aware of beliefs in the supernatural wilderness, and he relates how Godric would tell stories of his encounters with various hairy demonic creatures.[43] Once again, the saint is at home amongst these supernatural forces and is indeed somewhat akin to them.

41 Ibid. ch. 21, no. 55, pp. 67–8.

42 On the use of the quotation from Job by Gregory the Great, which may have been familiar to Reginald, see Straw, *Gregory the Great*, pp. 4, 11, 184–5. Gregory saw the dragons and ostriches as the reprobate amongst whom the righteous must live. The gentleness of many of the snakes towards Godric makes it difficult to see this story within such Gregorian terms.

43 *Vita Godrici*, ch. 90, nos. 187–8, pp. 196–8; Reginald adds 'pygmies' and 'monopods' to the list of demonic illusions, probably from literary sources rather than Godric's report. See also ibid. ch. 144, no. 260, p. 275.

In other stories also, the patterns of patristic tradition do not wholly match the logic of the narratives themselves. In one instance a cow shows its wild nature, tossing Godric's servant upon its horns but, by the command of the hermit, does not actually harm the boy. Rather, the incident is a punishment for the boy's cruelty: thus the cow, a domestic animal, indulges in some violent wildness, while at the same time being obedient to God's will and the hermit's commands.[44] The standard theme of obedience is certainly present in this story, but other elements seem to be turned on their head. While the hagiographic tradition would dictate that a dangerous wild animal becomes tame, here a domestic animal is aggressive. Even where one of the Egyptian fathers has dealings with non-predatory beasts, the theme is the miraculous submission of their wild nature. Thus Abbot Helenus called to a herd of wild asses: '"In the name of Our Lord Jesus Christ, let one out of you come here and take my pack." And one out of the whole herd made its way to him, in all gentleness.'[45] In Godric's story, the power of the saint and of God over nature are not in question, but the behaviour of the animal within that structure contradicts the Edenic model of the gentle submission and domestication of beasts. The story of Godric's cow can be seen in the light of hagiographic tradition, but seems to be obeying a different logic. It would seem more comparable to the tradition of Farne, where those who transgress the special laws of a sacred place are punished.

The bulk of Godric's animal miracles are related to the 'hermit and hunter' topos and the theme of saintly kindness to animals. These miracles need to be placed in the context of the stories of the horror of the wilderness and Godric's kinship with the snakes. Indeed, Reginald is impressed with his hermit's charity towards the lowliest of animals: 'the serenity of his pious heart shone not only to the aid of men, but also his prudent help sometimes cared for reptiles and animals of the earth'.[46] Even within the theme of saintly kindness to animals, Godric's kindliness towards snakes and lizards appears to be unprecedented. A folkloric reading of the stories would, however, suggest an explanation: Godric was identified with chthonic powers by the peasants around Finchale who are so prominent both in his *Vita* and the collection of his posthumous miracles. Godric is so intimately associated with snakes and reptiles because his power was associated with the remains of beliefs about the Underworld.

However, once Godric is installed at Finchale and begins to cultivate a garden, Reginald is able to bring in more conventional images of the colonisation of the wilderness. Thus the wild beasts come in the summer to consume the fruits of his efforts, but like Saint Anthony he drives them off.[47] Yet Godric is exceptionally gentle with the marauding beasts: while chasing the beasts away 'those who were weary, embracing them with his arms, he drew out by lifting them over the enclosures of his hedge'. Once again, Finchale, like Farne, appears to be a place where animals are protected in a manner that would appear extraordinary to any medieval (or

44 *Vita Godrici*, ch. 51, no. 113, and ch. 52, no. 114, pp. 120–2.

45 Rufinus, *Historia Monachorum*, ch. 11, col. 430.

46 *Vita Godrici*, ch. 40, no. 88, p. 98.

47 Ibid. ch. 39, nos. 85–7, pp. 95–8.

later) cultivator of the land. In driving away the beasts Godric states that his food was meant for men rather than beasts: the men were of course the local poor.[48] This is another element which differs from the conventional topos typified by Saint Anthony's keeping his garden clear of beasts. Anthony was only growing food for himself.

Another story later in Godric's *Vita* shows the same pattern: a hare comes to devour the crops Godric is said to grow for the poor, and Godric ties some vegetables on its back and commands it never to return.[49] Thus Godric gives the thief a gift. This could be compared to a patristic topos where human thieves are given what they sought to steal by the saint.[50] However, those stories occurred in a purely monastic context and the remarkable aspect of this chapter is the overwhelming presence of the needs of the local 'rustics'. Godric is defending their rights against the animal, yet nevertheless treating it with the gentleness that befits saint and animal relations in a holy place operating according to the sort of logic found on Farne. There is thus a relationship between Godric's practical charity to the poor of Finchale and the animal stories. From the perspective of the peasants of Finchale, his extraordinary solicitude for small animals is a *quid pro quo* for the aid he gives local people. The details and miracles are different from the details of Farne, but the underlying pattern is directly comparable. Reginald seems to draw two different conclusions, having Godric comment conventionally that if brute animals can so obey the command of the servants of God, then why do not rational men do the same? However, the hagiographer adds that through this example Godric 'kindled the hearts of listeners through the joy of mirth'.[51] This conclusion, that the story is a *jocus* of Saint Godric, may well be a sign that Reginald was aware of the rustic origins of much in these stories.

There is a complex of relationships behind the story of Godric's kind behaviour towards animals during the winter, where he would pick up any animal he found suffering from the cold, and warm it in his arms. In the ensuing passage this image is linked to the 'hermit and hunter' topos: none of his servants are able to snare animals in Finchale without Godric's knowledge. The saint immediately frees the animals upon discovery, and thus 'often brute animals would avoid the snares of the woodland hunters, fleeing to the defences of his cell, because he provided certain refuge to them'.[52]

One last story develops into a version of the 'hermit and hunter' story. Members of the household of Bishop Ranulf Flambard are hunting a stag, which makes for Godric's hermitage, seeming to call on him for help. Godric hides the animal in his cell and persuades the hunters to look for it elsewhere. This they do, although they apparently are well aware of the presence of the stag, as 'they often afterwards

[48] For some examples of Godric's practical aid to the peasants of Finchale, see ibid. ch. 80, no. 171, ch. 84, no. 177, and ch. 130, no. 241.

[49] Ibid. ch. 65, no. 139, pp. 148–9.

[50] See Gregory, *Dialogi*, bk 1, ch. 3, p. 6n.

[51] *Vita Godrici*, ch. 39, no. 87, pp. 97–8.

[52] Ibid. ch. 40, no. 89, p. 99.

related what had happened to them'. The stag itself returns to Godric for years afterwards to give him its thanks.[53] It is notable here that there is no meeting between the hermit and the lord of the hunters, as in so many other examples of the genre. This story is purely about the protection of the hunted animal. Thus as on Farne, an animal may seek refuge in a holy place and be protected from harm. In return for the protection of animals from hunters, the *quid pro quo* in Godric's hermitage is that the animals must not harm humans and their resources either. It is possible that many of the other stories of saintly kindness towards animals may have had contexts in popular understanding similar to that found at Farne and Finchale.[54]

Other stories from twelfth-century Britain follow the same pattern in linking saints' shrines to the protection of animals from predators, human or animal. The miraculous enforcement of the privilege of sanctuary is a notable theme among the miracles in Reginald's collection of miracles of Saint Cuthbert, and animals appear to have the same right of sanctuary as humans.[55] One miracle with no ecclesiastical participation eloquently demonstrates this concept of sanctuary. A group of hunters led by a Scottish knight are chasing a stag, which escapes into a churchyard of Saint Cuthbert's. The hunters give up pursuit, allowing that the animal may not be hunted in the churchyard. In the following miracle there is a breach in the law of sanctuary for the same stag, while a festival is held in the same churchyard. A boy is incited by his father to goad the stag and is killed by the animal. The stag then escapes, only to be killed by the original hunters, who leave the corpse, obviously afraid to become implicated in the breaches of the law of a sacred place. A similar popular conception of the right of animals to sanctuary was thus in operation in Scotland as well as in Northumbria.[56]

Traditions remarkably similar to Cuthbert's Farne are also to be found in an anonymous account of Saint Cuthbert's apocryphal birth in Ireland. This late-twelfth-century work, greatly diverging from the rest of the twelfth-century tradition of Cuthbert, contains a section said to be drawn from 'vulgar traditions'. A hermitage in Scotland associated with Cuthbert 'is a refuge and protection to all living things': both animals and humans within its 'enclosure', are protected from the rapacity of

53 Ibid. (additional), ch. 21, no. 347, pp. 365–6. This story seems to have a low status as far as Reginald is concerned. It occurs as part of an appendix of miracles, many of them posthumous.

54 See above, Chapter 6, p. 128.

55 For the human-related sanctuary miracles, see Reginald, *Libellus*, chs. 60, 61, and 65. One of the animal stories involves an ox, offered as an 'oblation' by a young cleric, in a 'Pictish' church dedicated to Saint Cuthbert. The young cleric does not survive Cuthbert's wrath, although his nemesis, the bull, escapes: ibid. ch. 85; note also ch. 133 concerning a sparrow caught on an altar.

56 Reginald, *Libellus*, chs. 86, 87; ch. 88 details some of the connections of Aelred of Rievaulx with the Cistercian abbot of Melrose, who was the source for the stories in those three chapters. Aelred was thus the source for Reginald. That the stories had passed through a number of ecclesiastical sources does not cast doubt on their popular origins. Contrast these links to the exclusively elite contexts and concerns of some of Caesarius of Heisterbach's stories discussed in McGuire, 'Friends and Tales'.

robbers and wolves.[57] Another odd story comes from the twelfth-century cult of Saint Oswin in Tynemouth. A boy is miraculously punished for killing a small bird which has clearly sought protection within the saint's church. The pattern of this miracle is similar to the eiderduck vengeance stories: the boy dies after the violation of sanctuary and his earlier deed becomes an explanation for his death. Also like Farne, the church of Saint Oswin was the focus of a local healing cult.[58]

Outside northern Britain there are indications of similar attitudes towards saints and animals. A peculiar story in the *Vita* of Wulfric of Haselbury in Somerset may have been remembered locally through the same conceptions of the holy man and the shrine. Wulfric curses a mouse which has been nibbling a cape given to the recluse as a gift. The mouse scuttles across the floor and obediently falls dead at Wulfric's feet. This demonstration of his own power appals the recluse and he confesses the matter to the local priest, Brichtric:

> 'If you would only be good enough to dispatch all the local mice in the same way!' said Brichtric. 'God preserve me', replied the holy man. 'Once with one mouse was a very grave fault. And', he added, 'if I didn't think it would displease my Lord, I would pray to him to bring this mouse to life again.'[59]

The expectation of a holy man's power over nature and protection of creatures within his sphere, in a manner contradictory to normal human practice, explains the origin and the local remembrance of this story. Only through local memory could such a peculiar story be available to John of Ford, who was writing many decades later in the twelfth century. It should also be noted that a muted resurrection motif lurks in this passage: was it in fact the hagiographer, John of Ford, who was displeased with the idea of the resurrection of a mouse?

Other such stories come from Gerald of Wales. He notes a miracle where a boy was trying to steal young pigeons from a nest within a church of Saint David: 'His hand stuck fast to the stone on which he was leaning, this being no doubt a miraculous punishment inflicted by the saint, who was protecting the birds of his own church'.[60] Elsewhere, Gerald describes a local cult in Ireland with startling

[57] *Libellus de Ortu Sancti Cuthberti*, in *Miscellanea Biographica*, ed. James Raine, Surtees Society 8 (1838), pp. 63–87, particularly ch. 28, pp. 84–5, also chs. 24–5, pp. 80–2. See ch. 19, p. 77, for the reference to vulgar traditions. See also Madeleine H. Dodds, 'The Little Book of the Birth of Cuthbert', *Archaeologia Aeliana* 6 (1929), pp. 52–94. It can be argued, largely on the basis of the surviving thirteenth-century manuscripts, which are of Durham origin, that this work originated in Durham. However, it is hard to imagine why the monks there would endorse a tradition which placed Cuthbert as a hermit on a Scottish mountain called Doilweme, now Weem near Dull in central Perthshire, *Libellus de Ortu*, ch. 24, p. 80, over which the convent had no control. Melrose, as Dodds argued, seems much the more likely site for the tradition.

[58] *Vita Sancti Oswini Regis Deiorum*, ed. James Raine in *Miscellanea Biographica*, Surtees Society 8 (1838), pp. 1–59, at ch. 27, pp. 40–1.

[59] *Wulfric of Haselbury, by John, Abbot of Ford*, ed. Dom Maurice Bell, Somerset Record Society 47 (1933), ch. 30; trans. Matarasso, *The Cisterican World*, pp. 247–8.

[60] Gerald of Wales, *Itinerarium Kambriae*, bk 1, ch. 2, pp. 23–4; trans. Lewis Thorpe, *The Journey*

resemblance to Farne and its eiderducks. The ducks of one area were associated with Saint Colman, and were tame enough to take food from the hand. Gerald recounts a few stories of the attempts to eat these ducks, which were invariably unsuccessful, and brought supernatural vengeance down upon the perpetrators. Unlike the eiderducks of Farne, however, these ducks also protected the saint's church. If the church was harmed in any way the ducks would leave the nearby lake, the waters of which would then become too dirty to be used by man or beast.[61] All these examples reveal traditions linking a saint, a shrine and animals, and all are similar to the more developed legends of Farne and Finchale. The popular conception that developed in the cult of Saint Cuthbert on Farne was evidently part of a widespread structure of popular belief by the twelfth century.[62]

It is rare that hagiography provides such an extensive and differentiated corpus of material as the twelfth-century miracles of Farne. The evidence of competing conceptions concerning the nature of the island, together with the popular miracle cult of sailors and secular people seeking healing, provides a context in which to view the animal miracles. Within that context the popular origins of the animal miracles of Farne is clear. In comparison with the miracles of Godric of Finchale and other more isolated stories it is possible to see a consistent logic behind the appearance of animal miracles. In those places where the power of saints was expected to manifest itself to the aid of humans, special rules applied, which were found neither in society nor in the wild. The weak and innocent were protected, or at least avenged, against hunters, whether animal or human.

This logic is likely to have developed and crystallised relatively recently from the point of view of the twelfth century, as it was probably a product of a popular culture that had absorbed much official Christianity and the stories of its saints. Certainly there is no evidence that the eiderduck cult existed before around 1100. In contrast, the goose resurrection miracles and the early appearances of the 'hermit and hunter' miracles relate to quite ancient elements of rural folklore. These stories probably represent a relatively early phase of the absorption of local peasant beliefs and folklore by the Church, even if in written form the goose miracles are mostly late, and, in the case of the Wereburga miracle in particular, show signs of a later phase of development. The popular miraculous logic represented by the cult of Saint Cuthbert's eiderducks represents this later phase of the dialectic between the Church and rural communities, with old elements of both folklore and Christian story now understood in a different context. The eleventh and twelfth centuries are often seen as a crucial watershed in the Christianisation of the mass of the people

through Wales (London 1978), p. 83.

61 Gerald of Wales, *Historia Topographica Hiberniensis*, ch. 29, pp. 117–18.

62 An example of a possibly similar tradition outside Britain and Ireland is an early-thirteenth-century story of Saint Corentin from Brittany, who punished, then forgave, a local man for fishing in his sacred pool, which is otherwise the source of healing miracles. Even fish could receive the protection of the saint: Julia M. H. Smith, 'Oral and Literate: Saints, Miracles and Relics in Brittany, c.850–1250', *Speculum* 65 (1990), pp. 309–43, at pp. 327–8. In the ancient Greek world birds may also have been protected when nesting around sanctuaries: see Herodotus, *The Histories*, bk 1, ch. 159, p. 71.

of western Europe: these popular animal miracles are one manifestation of that process.

The older elements of peasant culture had not been entirely eliminated by the Church: the association between saints and wild supernatural figures remains in evidence, particularly at Finchale. Nonetheless, there is a new dimension of meaning that may have been evident in the original twelfth-century telling of stories of hermits and hunters, or hawks and pet gulls. The folklore of the Otherworld found in the resurrection and hunter stories would have functioned originally in peasant societies relatively free of systematic structures of class dominance and exploitation. This would no longer have been the case for the context of the twelfth-century stories. It was possible to speculate that the occasional dragons or crocodiles in late antique miracles were meant to be understood as symbols of social types.[63] A similar symbolism may have come into operation again in the twelfth-century miracle stories, when, after all, the use of wolves and foxes as social symbols in satirical literature and fable was entirely familiar.[64] Miracle stories may be a different genre, but the symbolic rules of one genre can easily slip into another.[65] Given that the elite hunter was the offender in some stories, other stories, where for example a hawk killed a pet bird, might have been understood in social terms. The whole genre of 'hermit and hunter' and shrine animal sanctuary stories may well have been understood to contain an element of social protest. Outside the shrine, the powerful may be dominant, but inside the shrine a saint could ensure a form of divine social justice which, metaphorically or literally, included all the powerless of Creation.

[63] See Chapter 2, p. 32.

[64] See Ziolowski, *Talking Animals*, p. 9 and pp. 153–97.

[65] Indeed one Irish story seems to have borrowed from the fable genre in its presentation of the antics of the various animal companions of Saint Ciaran. This saint's monks are animals, including a fox, a badger and a boar; see *Vita Sancti Ciarani Episcopi de Saigir* in Plummer, *Vitae Sanctorum Hiberniae*, I, pp. 217–33, at chs. 5–6, pp. 219–20.

CHAPTER 9

Saint Francis and the Thirteenth Century

IT would be possible to classify all the stories of the animal and saint tradition into two emotionally laden categories: those demonstrating power over nature, and those exemplifying empathy with animals. Clearly, this is a very crude dichotomy, but it is a style of thinking into which it is all to easy to slip when discussing this material. The traditional model of literate hagiography could combine the two poles in the Edenic model. The saint's rise to grace allows him, usually, to exercise power over nature, and as a consequence to reveal affective relationships within the hierarchy of man over animals. However, within those stories influenced or created by peasant folklore, the dichotomy of power against affection misses the dynamic altogether. These stories are concerned with human ability to mould and use nature, but the power of nature itself is present also. In the Otherworld motifs the wild requires negotiation, not simply thaumaturgy, and later can even be recognised anthropomorphically as having rights, once a Christian social hierarchy has come to dominate deep levels of rural life. In the stories of Farne, Finchale and elsewhere, there is neither a modern utilitarian attitude towards natural resources nor a sentimental regard for natural life as such. Eiderducks and their eggs were not hunted on the Inner Farne, but they were fair game on the other islands.

The question then arises of where Saint Francis's famous empathy for nature fits into this picture. The answer lies with the very different social context of this saint. By the late twelfth and early thirteenth century, Italy had an economy dominated by towns and cities, and Francis himself was the son of a prosperous merchant. Certainly, agriculture was the occupation of a great majority, but money and trade had vastly more importance here than in the societies considered so far. However, interpretations of Francis have typically focused on the degree to which the saint himself can be shown to have had a particular respect for nature or affinity with animals, and the degree to which his attitude represents something new in Christianity. This approach to Saint Francis is only possible because he left some remarkable writings, in particular the *Canticle of the Sun*, which allow a direct analysis of the saint, rather than simply of his hagiographers. Hence Roger Sorrell has argued that Francis did have a particular affinity for the natural world, which grew directly out of his eremitical tendencies. Francis's 'nature mysticism', including his encounters with animals, was thus a tendency of the eremitical tradition, earlier exemplified by the Cistercians, but much more developed in Saint Francis.[1]

[1] Sorrell, *Francis and Nature*, particularly pp. 8–44, but note the views expressed in a review of

However Francis's spirituality in relation to nature may be characterised, the problem remains of explaining why his hagiographers represented their saint in such a way that he can be read as a 'nature mystic'. Other holy men, Saint Cuthbert for example, could have had some similar sensibility, but their hagiography does not lead so easily to the same interpretation. Perhaps the hagiographers of Saint Francis were responding to a powerful personality and attempting to record faithfully what they saw in him. However, this would be to take a superficial approach to the work of such writers, whose concern would be to adapt their saint to the tradition. In addition the Franciscan hagiographers were concerned to represent Francis to their order, and therefore would be characterising him so as to reflect and mould the character of the friars themselves. The mentality of the order is reflected in Franciscan hagiography as much as Francis himself. Thus it is the hagiographers' choice of topoi and the associated innovations or adaptations in the miracle stories that reveal the degree to which they were adapting the tradition to their saint, or stories about the saint to the existing tradition.

The major themes of hagiographic tradition that appear most often in Franciscan writing are the 'companionship of animals' and the 'hermit and hunter' topoi. Nonetheless, there are some miracles where simple control of nature is the focus, such as the freeing of the town of Greccio from wolves and hail.[2] It is possible that this story arose from the context of popular belief: Francis is also said to have built a nativity scene one Christmas at Greccio, and the hay from this holy installation cured animals of their illnesses, and eased difficult births for women who lay upon it.[3] However, the hagiographic moral of the wolves and hail story is that freed from these scourges, the people grew prosperous and complacent, a situation inevitably leading to a fall back into sin. They are duly punished by the return of even greater natural scourges, ending with fire. The key Franciscan theme of penitence is thus worked into this story. The rough side of nature is revealed to have a purgatorial function, while the value of the harsh Franciscan life is revealed.

A similar penitential reflection can be found in one of the stories of the *Legenda Perugia* of the end of Saint Francis's life. Tormented by illness, the saint was unable to rest as 'there were so many mice running around here and there, around him and even on him, that they prevented him from taking a rest; they even hindered him greatly in his prayer'.[4] This demonic persecution leads to the *Legenda* account of Francis's *Canticle of the Sun*, where the harmonious unity of creation under God

Sorrell by Derk Visser in *Church History* 59 (1990), pp. 394–6.

[2] Thomas of Celano, *Vita Secunda Sancti Francisci*, in *Analecta Franciscana* 10 (1926), pp. 129–260; nos. 35–6, p. 152; trans. in Habig, *Omnibus*, pp. 392–4.

[3] Thomas of Celano, *Vita Prima Sancti Francisici*, in *Analecta Franciscana* 10 (1926), pp. 3–115, at no. 87, p. 65.

[4] *Scripta Leonis, Rufini et Angeli, Sociorum S. Francisci*, ed. and trans. Rosalind Brooke (Oxford 1970), ch. 43, pp. 162–7. The Greccio story appears not long before this in the *Legenda* account, ibid. ch. 34, pp. 146–51, and its spiritual message is not greatly different from that of the *Vita Prima*. Sorrell, *Francis and Nature*, p. 44, sees the story of the mice as part of a traditional element in Francis's ascetic experience.

is reaffirmed. The harsh reality of nature as it appears in these two stories is exceptional within the Franciscan corpus. However, while relatively traditional in hagiographic terms, they both serve to exemplify values of the early order. Thus even the joyous *Canticle* is given a penitential context through its introduction with the story of the demonic mice.

More typical animal miracles also respond to hagiographic tradition while exemplifying the values of the early order. One noted miracle is his power to silence the 'chattering' swallows when he is preaching to the people of Alviano. He addresses the birds as 'my sisters, swallows', telling them 'it is now time for me to speak'. Duly they are silent 'to the astonishment and wonder of the people standing by'.[5] There is no question of equality between Francis and animals: the hierarchy is always clear in this saint's miracles, unlike those of Bartholomew of Farne, who is ordered off his bed by a mother eiderduck.[6] Moreover, silencing noisy birds is by no means a unique act. The Irish Saint Cainnech commanded noisy birds to be silent, while the recluse, Sigar, in twelfth-century St Alban's, prevailed upon God to banish the nightingales which annoyed him during his prayers.[7]

Apart from Francis's singular mode of addressing animals, it is the context which sets the miracle apart from tradition. Thomas of Celano places the miracle just after Francis preached to the birds near Bevagna. In this famous incident, Celano relates that the saint, 'being a man of very great fervour and great tenderness toward lower and irrational creatures', ran towards the birds, and found them waiting for him rather than flying off as birds normally would do. This prompts Francis to preach to them: 'praise your Creator very much and always love him'.[8] The story is part of a small group of animal stories which occur just after Francis's failed expeditions to Syria are described.[9] Following this group, Celano refers again to Francis's preaching to the birds, as an introduction to his preaching to the people in Ascoli. Here it is said that 'almost all the people were filled with such great grace and devotion' that thirty men accepted the habit from him.[10] The placement makes it clear that the 'preaching to the birds' story is an inversion of those miracles of the desert fathers grouped into the 'companionship of animals' theme.[11]

Jerome's Saint Anthony cried out against the world that 'the beasts speak of Christ and you worship monsters instead of God'.[12] In comparison to this cry, Francis's preaching to the birds excuses his failures to convert Muslims, since he was able to do something even more wondrous: rouse birds to worship. This also then reflects negatively on rational human beings, who do not worship the 'correct' God,

[5] Celano, *Vita Prima*, no. 59, pp. 45–6; Habig, *Omnibus*, pp. 278–9.

[6] See above, Chapter 8, p. 159.

[7] Heist, *Vita Cainnechi*, ch. 30, pp. 189–90; *Gesta Abbatum Monasterii Sancti Albani*, ed. Henry Thomas Riley, Rolls Series 28 (1867), 3 vols, at I, p. 105.

[8] Celano, *Vita Prima*, no. 58, pp. 44–5; Habig, *Omnibus*, pp. 277–8.

[9] Celano, *Vita Prima*, nos. 55–7, pp. 42–4.

[10] Ibid. no. 62, p. 47; Habig, *Omnibus*, pp. 280–1.

[11] See above, Chapter 2, p. 36.

[12] Jerome, *Vita Pauli Eremitae*, ch. 8, col. 24, trans. Waddell, *Lives of the Fathers*, p. 33.

in contrast to irrational creatures. The desert fathers found companionship in wild animals when a fallen humanity rejected Christian morals. Francis's preaching to the birds is a mirror image of such spiritual solace, since rather than being marked by pessimism about the redemption of the mass of humanity, the incident spurs him on again to redeem and convert in Italy. In this sense, while preaching to birds may be original, it is clearly linked to traditional themes.[13] Celano no doubt intended the inverted meaning of the traditional theme to be a signal of the redemptive powers of his saint and a symbol of the role of the Franciscan order itself. In this context it is difficult to use the story as a reflection of Francis's own spirituality. If a real event is assumed to have existed beneath the story, Francis himself may have felt or intended a more traditional reading of his avian preaching, but it was perhaps his companions who interpreted the event differently at a later point. Be that as it may, stories of Francis and animals have to be taken as a reflection of the early Franciscan order itself, not simply as a record of the saint's spirituality.

While the companionship of animals theme is the major traditional theme to which most of Francis's animal miracles can be compared, the 'hermit and hunter' topos is reflected in a few stories. One, recounted by Celano in the same group as the preaching to the birds, is of a rabbit caught in a trap. The rabbit was brought to Francis by one of the brothers, and when it was released through the saint's pity, 'it fled to the saint, and, without being forced by anyone, it lay quiet in his bosom as the safest place possible'.[14] This story uses the basic motif of the hunted animal protected by the saint, but puts the emphasis on the animal's attachment to Francis. Every time the rabbit was freed, it jumped back into the saint's bosom. Celano effectively extends the story of the rabbit by relating Francis's 'tender affection toward fish'. When given a large fish, the saint put it back into the water and prayed while the fish swam alongside until it was given permission to leave.[15] In the traditional Edenic topos animals are tame and obedient around the saint, but here that motif is exaggerated into grateful attachment.

The image of small animals nesting in a saint's bosom is familiar from Saint Columban, Godric of Finchale and William Firmat.[16] In the case of Godric of Finchale and some other saints, the combination of these sentimental motifs with the 'hermit and hunter' legend seems to have been the result of hagiographic adaptation of popular stories. Where the underlying 'hermit and hunter' story places the saint in the position of an ambiguous wild man, the sentimental topoi replace that popular understanding with a more acceptably Christian example of the extraordinary expression of charity. The question arises therefore whether there is any similar popular understanding of sanctity underlying the Francis stories, or whether the stories of Francis's affection for animals had a different genesis altogether. The topoi used in Franciscan hagiography were largely well established by the thirteenth

[13] On the preaching to the birds see also Sorrell, *Francis and Nature*, pp. 47, 62–4, who sees the story in terms of Francis's eremitical asceticism and evangelical fervour.

[14] Celano, *Vita Prima*, no. 60, p. 46; Habig, *Omnibus*, pp. 279–80.

[15] Celano, *Vita Prima*, no. 61, pp. 46–7; Habig, *Omnibus*, p. 280.

[16] See above Chapter 3, p. 47, and Chapter 6, p. 129.

century and do not demand in themselves an explanation in popular folklore. Indeed there is, for example, little trace of wild-man imagery associated with Francis and his early companions, suggesting the absence of that layer of folklore in the creation of this part of the Franciscan legend. The only hint of wild-man imagery comes in an anecdote where the lord of Ostia notices that the brothers' beds 'might be taken for the lairs of wild beasts', because of their great poverty, and is greatly edified.[17] Perhaps more significant is Francis's disapproval of some brothers who 'pretended great contempt for themselves by letting their beards grow long'.[18] Oddly, considering that long beards were clearly part of the general image of the holy hermit, Francis dismisses the practice as a novelty and condemns it as a 'bad example'.

It is not entirely clear what Francis is objecting to here, but in effect he, or Thomas of Celano at least, is rejecting a sign of popular sanctity. Celano would have been aware of and concerned about the possibly heretical implications of some signs of popular sanctity. It may be suspected as a consequence that he was concerned to keep the image of Francis free from associations with popular folklore. Godric of Finchale's compassion for creatures extended to snakes and reptiles, but the context revealed the hermit to have popular chthonic associations. The same associations cannot be found in a parallel story of Saint Francis, where he removed from the road little worms so that they would not be crushed.[19] Here this is part of Francis's extraordinary concern for all parts of creation, including candles, which he would not snuff out, seeing them as symbols of 'Eternal Light'.

There is no particular reason to suspect that there might once have been some popular influence on any of these Franciscan anecdotes, yet the absence of folkloric elements is persistent. This is surprising, if only because it would have been likely for some elements of popular folklore to be shared by many of the brothers themselves, even when they were themselves from prosperous backgrounds. However, the context was greatly complicated by the existence of ascetic heretics, particularly Cathars. Even as they worked against heresy, and with the patronage of powerful ecclesiastics, Francis and his early companions would have had to walk a fine line to avoid the wrong associations. This problem would have remained for much of the thirteenth century and early hagiographers might well have been careful to avoid any ambiguous elements in their stories of Francis.[20] Celano would have been equally concerned with internal problems of the order, and those who were radically committed to the principle of poverty might well have been attracted to such eremitical habits as the wearing of long beards. In the context of internal and

[17] Celano, *Vita Secunda*, no. 63, pp. 168–9; Habig, *Omnibus*, p. 415. Note also the absence of wilderness rhetoric associated with Franciscan hermitages: see for example Celano, *Vita Prima*, nos. 91–6, pp. 69–74.

[18] Celano, *Vita Secunda*, no. 156, p. 220; Habig, *Omnibus*, p. 487.

[19] Celano, *Vita Secunda*, no. 165, pp. 225–6; Habig, *Omnibus*, p. 494. The same anecdote can be found in Celano, *Vita Prima*, no. 80, pp. 59–60, where the reference is made to Psalm 21:7, and the contrast lies between contemplation of the sun, stars and firmament, and the worms on the ground. This can be read in terms of exaggerated humility.

[20] On the Franciscans and heresy see Malcolm Lambert, *The Cathars* (Oxford 1998), pp. 171–4.

external threats to the coherence and stability of the friars, if elements of popular folklore were present in any early oral versions of the stories, it may have been deemed sensible to suppress them.

The hagiographic motivation for the abundance of sentimental topoi in Franciscan hagiography remains therefore obscure. There could have been folkloric elements in the stories as they grew among the early Franciscans, and these could have been removed by Celano and other writers. Equally, the topoi could have been culled from the hagiographic corpus for the purpose of representing Francis's great compassion and love. Nonetheless, there is a series of stories which resemble the 'sanctuary' logic of Farne and Finchale to some degree. Two birds were allowed crumbs from the table to feed their young, and were then given grains by the saint. The birds offer their 'little ones' to the brothers, 'as having been reared at their expense', and the friars thus acquire two pets, in a curiously feudal Edenic bargain. However, one of the young birds became greedy and began to persecute the smaller ones, thus 'greed broke up the peace'. Francis predicted the bully's demise, and swiftly it met an accident and died.[21] The peace of the saint is restored through the punishment of the aggressor animal. In another incident at Gubbio, a 'wicked sow' killed a newborn lamb. Francis compared the lamb to Christ and cursed the cruel sow which immediately began to sicken and die. Once dead, it was cast into a ditch, where its body shrivelled and dried as no creature would eat it.[22] It would be possible to detect a certain 'sanctuary' logic here where an Edenic peace is enforced by the saint's virtue.

However, while the comparison can be drawn, the extent to which a popular 'sanctuary logic' operated here is questionable. Firstly, there is no immediate context of rural belief in these stories, so the 'sanctuary logic' would have had to come from the brothers' own conceptions. This would not be impossible: it has already been remarked that many of the early friars would likely have shared some elements of popular belief. Secondly, however, both miracles have at their core a moralistic purpose. The providentially punished animals represent a sin, whether greed or anger, for which the stories act as parables. The early Franciscans probably used these stories as warnings about the behaviour of brothers amongst themselves: individuals damaging the collective life would find themselves facing damnation. Just as lambs could represent Christ, or innocence, so other animals could symbolise other virtues or vices, from obedience to greed. Thus, rather than reflecting Francis himself, it is possible that many of the animal miracles were created for the purpose of shaping internal behaviour. In the early days, the absence of a detailed rule might have made parables such as these necessary for the internal discipline of the order. The extent to which they represented any aspect of popular culture is perhaps to be found in the almost Aesopian character of the greedy bird and cruel sow stories.

Another incident related to the 'hermit and hunter' theme may reveal more clearly the specific social context of Franciscan animal stories. On one occasion

21 Celano, *Vita Secunda*, no. 47, p. 160; Habig, *Omnibus*, pp. 404–5.

22 Celano, *Vita Secunda*, no. 111, p. 196; Habig, *Omnibus*, p. 454.

Francis and a companion came across a man taking two lambs, 'hanging bound over his shoulder' to the market.[23] Francis is naturally filled with pity, particularly finding that the animals would be sold and eaten, and gave his mantle in return for the lambs. The core of this story lies in symbolism: it is preceded by stories concerning Francis's love for lambs through their symbolic link to Christ.[24] The lambs over the peasant's shoulder thus recall Christ crucified, or perhaps innocent souls destroyed by the necessary but cruel ways of the fallen world. This story contains the familiar theme of the saint protecting the weak, but it is not created by any folkloric logic. Rather, at the heart of it is the rejection of the secular world, as part of the early Franciscans' commitment to the ethic of poverty. The man's act of taking the innocent lambs to be sold in the marketplace is the real sin here, and redemption comes from an exchange which proceeds from charity, rather than one based on money.

To focus on the rescue of the lambs as a literal event would imply that Francis was a kind of radical vegetarian, and sentimental, unable to bear the killing of any animal, particularly not lambs. However, Francis was not such a figure. Once when recovering from illness, he noted to his companion that he would eat a bird if he had one. A horseman appears with a 'fine bird', which he gives to Francis, who welcomes it as a sign that Christ 'was taking care of him'.[25] Here the gift exchange apparently involves killing a creature, but that is not a problem. Hence, the incident of the lambs should be read in symbolic terms, not primarily as a rescue of small animals, but as part of the Franciscan rejection of the normal structures and practices of a commercial society.[26]

Money occupies a notable place within Francis's ascetic values, and is also linked to the only creature that does not seem to have been valued by the saint. A brother who refuses to beg is called 'brother fly' and is expelled from the order. Others, who failed to find anything to buy in a poor village, were rebuked by the saint: 'You find nothing because you trust more in your flies than in God'.[27] They are instructed to go and beg door to door instead. Here it seems that the brothers were used to operating in the context of a money economy, and in this instance Francis knew better than they that a very poor village would lie outside such a commercial context. However, Francis's angry rejection of money goes deeper than any such practical consideration. Among other miracles where an absolute rejection of money can be found, a purse full of money turns out to be a diabolical illusion. Francis's companion wishes to retrieve it and give the money to the poor, but the purse is revealed by the

[23] Celano, *Vita Prima*, no. 79, p. 59; Habig, *Omnibus*, p. 295.

[24] Celano, *Vita Prima*, nos. 77–8, pp. 57–8.

[25] Thomas of Celano, *Tractatus de Miraculis B. Francisci*, in *Analecta Franciscana* 10 (1926), pp. 271–330, at no. 34, p. 285; Habig, *Omnibus*, pp. 548–9.

[26] On commercial exchange, as opposed to gift exchange, being seen as a source of pollution in the twelfth century, particularly by religious reformers, see Lester K. Little, *Religious Poverty and the Profit Economy* (London 1978), pp. 31–2, 64–9, 72–3. For a discussion of the same problem in relation to holy men in twelfth-century England, see D Alexander, 'Hermits and Hairshirts', pp. 210–17.

[27] Celano, *Vita Secunda*, no. 75, no. 77, p. 177; Habig, *Omnibus*, p. 427.

saint to contain a snake rather than coin.[28] Thus in the right spiritual circumstances, creatures can directly symbolise sin and evil. This should be borne in mind when considering the saint's fondness for animals and creation in general: it is a symbolic nature that is praised, one that is free from the contamination of human sin.

The praise of nature is therefore connected to the rejection of money and commercial exchange: where nature is presented negatively, it is often through association with money. The Franciscan miracles are therefore marked with a different consciousness of nature and society than found in earlier saint and animal stories. Unlike many of the stories found in the 'hermit and hunter' tradition, or the hermitages of Farne or Finchale, there is little sense of the ambiguity of nature in Saint Francis. A highly lyrical Edenic conception of the relationship between the saint and nature is almost always dominant. Even if there are some instances where nature induces suffering, it is not presented as thorny, foul or worm-ridden, as it is with Godric in his hermitage. Nor are Francis's relations with animals part of his asceticism, as it was with Saint Cuthbert and the otters, and so many other saints. The closest Francis approaches to such a connection occurs in a story where the saint is on the way over a lake to the hermitage of Greccio. A fisherman offered Francis a waterfowl. The saint took it in his hands and told the bird it was free to fly away, but it preferred to stay with the saint. Francis then prayed for a while and finally commanded it to fly away. This story somewhat recalls the story of Saint Kevin and the blackbird, but does not have any of the sense of ascetic trial, where the Irish saint suffered in stillness while the bird nested in his hands.[29]

The presence of the fisherman in this miracle highlights another difference between the Francis stories and the general tendencies of the 'hermit and hunter' topos. The fisherman, whose livelihood was to capture creatures for food, found his gift to the saint effectively rejected, if he had assumed he was supplying a holy man with food. Francis rescues fish from fishermen and lambs from peasants. The pattern serves to draw a sharp distinction between the behaviour of the saint and the ways of the secular world. Rather than focusing on the cruel or arrogant behaviour of lords and hunters, the equivalent tales of Saint Francis contrast the saint's behaviour towards animals with the necessary actions of peasants and fishermen. This social bias certainly removes any hint of criticism of social hierarchy from the picture the early Franciscans give of Saint Francis. It also redirects the 'hermit and hunter' topos firmly back to a traditional Edenic portrayal of the saint and animal relationship.

Indeed, other stories, however picturesque, simply demonstrate the Edenic obedience and affection animals have for the saint. A falcon would call during the night at the exact time when Francis was accustomed to rise for prayer, but when Francis was ill and needing respite, the bird refrained from making a noise until dawn.[30] A pheasant given to the saint became so entirely attached to him that it refused to eat unless it was near the saint. On another occasion the saint called a cricket to him to

[28] Celano, *Vita Secunda*, no. 68, pp. 171–2; see also nos. 65–7, pp. 170–2.

[29] Ibid. no. 167, pp. 227–8, and for Saint Kevin, see above, Chapter 1, p. 17.

[30] Ibid. no. 168, p. 228.

sing in praise of God, which it did, until told to leave by the saint. The insect never returned, for as Francis said, 'we do not want our flesh to glory vainly over things of this kind'.[31]

Francis himself, and many of the early companions, were wealthy citizens of a relatively commercially developed, urban-centred society. Francis's ascetic rejection of secular life involved the rejection of a world where new economic rhythms had significantly displaced natural ones. Thus 'nature' appeared as the structural opposite of a fallen human society in the minds of those who joined Saint Francis. An economic life revolving almost entirely within the agricultural cycle would not give rise to a sense of 'nature' as a thing separate from human culture. An economic life that is dependent upon monetary exchange, local markets and regional and international exchange is one in which economic patterns have become alienated, to one degree at least, from 'nature'. Central Umbria around 1200 was not a fully exchange-based society alienated from a natural economy like an industrialised society. Yet the structural separation of urban and mercantile people from the natural economy was advanced. The position of Saint Francis's family stands, for example, in marked contrast to such women and men as Brigit or Ailbe, who are presented as fully immersed in an agricultural economy.[32]

Thus the use of rural resources does not provide stories for Saint Francis's interactions with nature. Godric of Finchale cuddled small creatures to his bosom in the winter, but there are also many stories of his miraculous supply of salmon from the adjacent river.[33] Francis is not presented in the context of agricultural labour or natural resources and it is notable how rarely key domesticated animals, such as cows or pigs, or game animals, such as stags or boars, appear in his miracles. The saint is materially separated from productive nature and human labour in nature, whilst at the same time he is spiritually associated with symbolic nature.[34] Francis's material separation from nature allowed him to experience nature as a spiritually symbolic creation that could praise its Creator alongside himself. In contrast, for medieval peasants the natural was a fluid context, full of potential dangers and resources, both evil and good. The Otherworld figures which overlapped with holy men like Godric of Finchale appear in stories full of the ambiguity of the natural world. Over a century later, a different but equally ambiguous attitude towards nature could be found in the Pyrennean village of Montaillou. Peasants here found it natural that

[31] Celano, *Vita Secunda*, nos. 170–1, pp. 228–9; Habig, *Omnibus*, pp. 498–500.

[32] See above, Chapter 4, pp. 58–60 and 75.

[33] See for example, *Vita Godrici*, ch. 71, no. 150, pp. 160–1.

[34] This analysis here lies in contrast to Sorrell's, *Francis and Nature*, p. 44, where he argues that the saint's reverence for 'Sister Earth' and his 'humble compliments' to various creatures in the *Canticle* 'reflect a life which was closely attached to the earth' and that Francis 'deeply valued the simple experiences amid the natural world'. Francis, in rejecting the values of the urban world (see Sorrell, pp. 56–7), certainly adopted a new valuation of 'nature' as a deliberate contrast. However, adopting a moral regard for the natural as a contrast to society is the privilege of those who have been economically separated from it. In fact as Sorrell himself points out, pp. 64–71, Francis anthropomorphises nature as a whole by seeing creatures as participants in a spiritually transformed courtly code.

God created useful animals and helpful aspects of nature, while the devil clearly created 'wolves, snakes, toads, flies and all harmful and poisonous beasts'.[35] This attitude was neither Cathar heretic nor orthodox Catholic, but could, in the right circumstances, be assimilated to either with some adjustment.

Francis, despite 'Brother Fly', betrays no such ambiguous departures from orthodoxy. This is a consequence of his social background, which led people like himself to define nature as conceptually separate from society. Indeed, Sorrell argues that a medieval ascetic ambivalence towards creation prevented 'nature mysticism' on Francis's model from emerging before him.[36] This analysis should be reversed: the social-economic context for Francis's attitude towards nature did not exist before him. Thus the character of the saint and animal stories to be found in early Franciscan literature is marked by a new social context, and the older layers of rural folklore have much less importance here. The confidence with which a highly idealised Edenic virtue is presented as shining forth in Francis's person, the manner in which creation *loves* Saint Francis, as he loves all manifest symbols of God, is born of the spiritual intensity with which the Franciscans mounted their penitential rebuke to the ways of the newly complex, commercial world of the thirteenth century.

The different interpretations of the proper way of life for the Franciscans in the course of the thirteenth century led to the leaders of the order requiring a revised account of Francis. Certain compromises, particularly concerning poverty, needed to be made for the good of the order. The animal stories in Celano were edited by Bonaventure in the context of these internal problems. The changes that were made were thus likely related to the internal political problems of the Franciscan order. In the main the central tales remain, although they are almost entirely grouped together in a single chapter. There are a few losses: Francis's care for worms appears not to have appealed to Bonaventure, even while he does note the saint's affection for 'even the most insignificant creatures'.[37] Such a detail may have appeared too grotesque for the more orderly saint which Bonaventure required.

The animal section opens with the explanation that it was compassion which enabled Francis 'to return to the state of primeval innocence by restoring man's harmony with the whole of creation'.[38] Bonaventure notes that 'he often rescued lambs, which were being led off to be slaughtered, in memory of the Lamb of God who willed to be put to death to save sinners'.[39] But he does not recount the story of the lambs tied up over a peasant's shoulder to be taken to the market: this incident revealed some of the connections between Francis's attitude towards money and towards nature. That connection is broken in Bonaventure's rendition of the stories. Grouping the stories together and relating them in abbreviated form also affects the

35 Emmanuel Le Roy Ladurie, *Montaillou, village occitan de 1294 à 1324* (Paris 1975), p. 453, and generally pp. 451–64; *Montaillou*, trans. Barbara Bray (London 1978), p. 291.

36 Sorrell, *Francis and Nature*, pp. 79–89.

37 Bonaventure, *Legenda Maior*, in *Analecta Franciscana* 10 (1926), pp. 557–653, at ch 8, no. 6, p. 594.

38 Ibid. ch. 8, no. 1, p. 592; Habig, *Omnibus*, p. 688.

39 Bonaventure, *Legenda Maior*, ch. 8, no. 6, p. 594.

meaning. The Edenic value of the stories becomes the exclusive message. The possibility is minimised that those Franciscans dedicated to the strictest poverty could find justifications for radical interpretations of the apostolic life.

The tradition of the saint and animal story is thus expressed in uncomplicated form in Bonaventure's Francis: the saint obedient to God and the Church is able to regain in himself prelapsarian conditions, and thus nature is obedient to him. Neither in Celano nor Bonaventure are the animal stories in any way used as an appeal to the people as the story of the hare was used in the *Vita* of Saint Anselm. Where particularly through the tenth to twelfth centuries the animal and saint story often marked a certain level of engagement between the Church and popular belief and concerns, this relationship is absent from the Franciscan corpus. This is not accidental, but is connected to larger developments in the ecclesiastical and political structures of Europe. The carefully pruned simplicity of Bonaventure reflects the concern of the thirteenth-century Church to control and standardise practice and belief, in a new rational, bureaucratic conformity.[40]

There was less room in the thirteenth century for local and regional churches to respond to conditions, cultures and circumstances particular to their areas, and the newly coherent clerical elite was much less likely to respond flexibly to local traditions than their predecessors. The growing population of literate clerics, merchants and others would find a universal and consistent religion far more appealing than eccentric local traditions. The key hagiographic work of the thirteenth century, the *Golden Legend*, was the sign of the newly standardised form in which the cult of the saints would be propagated.[41] This work summarised the main and best-known legends of the saints, with their narratives stripped of the local significance which many of them would have had. The author was suspicious, as in the case of Margaret of Antioch, of the stranger legends, as most well-educated scholars of the thirteenth century would have been.[42]

The peculiar instance of the thirteenth-century holy greyhound, Guinefort, illuminates how clerical culture now interacted with peasant folklore. This dog was honoured as a martyr by peasants near Lyon and children were taken to his 'shrine' to be cured. The core of the cult, the loyal dog killed by its owner in the false belief that it had killed rather than protected his child, may have been a 'vulgarisation' of a literary story, but the cult was the creation of peasant folklore, using the cultural materials that lay at hand. Unsurprisingly, the cult was condemned by the Dominican Friar, Stephen of Bourbon, as a curiosity of ignorant belief and it was firmly suppressed.[43] As it stands this story would never have found its way into a hagiographic corpus, yet in an earlier context perhaps it could have been altered and adapted until, however strange, it was acceptable to official Christian belief. This

[40] See Moore, *First European Revolution*, 'Order Restored', particularly pp. 160–73, 188–92.

[41] While the form of the compendium of saint's *Lives* was not unprecedented, its wide popularity is a mark of the new literate culture.

[42] See Head, *Medieval Hagiography*, pp. 676–7.

[43] Jean-Claude Schmitt, *The Holy Greyhound*, trans. Martin Thom (Cambridge 1983), pp. 4–5 and 159–60.

adaptation probably had happened in cases such as the goose resurrections. This is not to say that local traditions and peasant folklore did not persist, and no doubt in some cases were newly incorporated into official culture after 1200.[44] Nonetheless, the dominant tendency had decisively shifted against the tolerance and adaptation of peasant folklore embodied in non-Christian local traditions.

Much of this peasant folklore, practice and belief would remain in existence beneath official culture, to re-emerge later in new forms, but the next major European-wide interaction between clerical and popular culture would produce the horrifying spectacle of witch persecutions.[45] The development of the saint and animal story reflects therefore the evolution of wider society over the thousand years encompassing the collapse of one highly organised, bureaucratic and literate empire, through to the emergence of one successor civilisation in the form of western Christendom.

[44] There are, for example, some later appearances of the goose miracles; see above, Chapter 5, note 92.

[45] Compare the accounts in Ginzberg, *Ecstasies*, and Norman Cohn, *Europe's Inner Demons* (London 1993).

BIBLIOGRAPHY

Primary sources

Acta Sanctae Margaritae seu Marinae, *AASS* 20 July, pp. 33–9.

Acta Sanctae Pharaildis, ed. Édouard Hautcœur, *Actes de Sainte Pharailde* (Lille 1882).

Acta Sancti Blasii II, Auctore Anonymo, *AASS* 3 February, pp. 339–44.

Acta Sancti Georgii, *AASS* 23 April, pp. 117–22.

Adomnán, *Adomnán's Life of Columba*, ed. and trans. A. O. and M. O. Anderson (Edinburgh 1961).

Adso, *Vita Sancti Waldeberti Abbatis Luxoviensis*, *AASS* 2 May, pp. 274–82, also printed in *Miracula SS. Waldeberti et Eustasii Auctore Adsono*, MGH SS 15 (2) (1887), ed. O. Holder-Egger, pp. 1170–6.

Baudonivia, *Vita Sanctae Radegundis*, MGH SSRM 2 (1888), ed. B. Krusch, pp. 377–95; trans. in Joan M. Peterson, *Handmaids of the Lord* (Kalamazoo 1996), pp. 400–24.

Bede, *Historia Ecclesiastica*: *Bede's Ecclesiastical History of the English People*, ed. and trans. Bertram Colgrave and R. A. B. Mynors (Oxford 1969).

Bede, *Vita Sancti Cuthberti*, in *Two Lives of Saint Cuthbert*, ed. and trans. Bertram Colgrave (Cambridge 1940), pp. 141–307.

Benedict, *The Rule of Saint Benedict*, ed. Timothy Fry (Collegeville, Minnesota, 1981).

Bethu Brigte, ed. Donncha Ó hAodha (Dublin 1978).

Bieler, Ludwig, ed., *Four Latin Lives of Saint Patrick* (Dublin 1971).

Bonaventure, *Legenda Maior*, in *Analecta Franciscana* 10 (1926), pp. 557–653.

Bradshaw, Henry, *Life of Saint Werburge of Chester*, ed. Carl Horstmann, Early English Text Society os 88 (London, 1887).

Caesarius of Heisterbach, *Dialogus Miraculorum*, ed. Joseph Strange (London 1851, reprinted 1966), 2 vols; *Dialogue on Miracles*, trans. Henry Scott and Charles Bland (London 1929).

Chrétien de Troyes, *Yvain*, in *Oeuvres complètes*, ed. Daniel Poiron (Paris 1994), pp. 339–503.

Cogitosus, *Vita Sanctae Brigidae*, *AASS* 1 February, pp. 129–41; 'Cogitosus: Life of Saint Brigit', trans. Sean Connolly and J.-M. Picard, *Journal of the Royal Society of Antiquaries of Ireland* 117 (1987), pp. 5–27.

Constantius, *Vita Sancti Germani Episcopi Autissiodorensis*, MGH SSRM 7 (1920), eds B. Krusch and W. Levison, pp. 247–83.

Craster, H. H., ed., 'The Miracles of St. Cuthbert at Farne', in *Analecta Bollandiana* 70 (1952), pp. 5–19; trans. H. H. Craster, in 'The Miracles of Farne', *Archaeologia Aeliana* 29 (1951), pp. 93–107.

Descriptio: Positionis seu Situationis Monasterii Clarae-Vallensis, PL 185, cols. 570–4; trans. in Pauline Matarasso, *The Cistercian World* (London 1993), pp. 287–92.

Dugdale, William, *Monasticon Anglicanum* (London 1817–30), 6 vols.

Eadmer, *Vita Anselmi: The Life of St Anselm, Archbishop of Canterbury by Eadmer*, ed. and trans. R. W. Southern (Oxford 1962).
Elliott, J. K., ed., *The Apocryphal New Testament* (Oxford 1993).
Evagrius, *Vita Beati Antonii Abbatis*, PL 73, cols. 125–94.
Felix, *Vita Sancti Guthlaci*, in *Felix's Life of Saint Guthlac*, ed. and trans. Bertram Colgrave (Cambridge 1956).
Florence of Worcester, *Chronicon ex Chronicis*, ed. Benjamin Thorpe, English Historical Society, no. 10 (1848–9), 2 vols.
Forbes, Alexander P., ed. and trans., *Lives of St. Ninian and St. Kentigern* (Edinburgh 1874).
Garmondsway, G. N., ed. and trans., *The Anglo-Saxon Chronicle* (London 1953).
Geoffrey of Coldingham, *Vita Sancti Bartholomaei Farnensis*, in *Symeonis Monachi Opera Omnia*, ed. Thomas Arnold, Rolls Series 75 (London 1882–5), 2 vols, I, pp. 295–325.
Geoffrey of Coldingham, *Vita Sancti Godrici Eremitae, AASS* 5 May, pp. 68–85.
Geoffrey Grossus, *Vita Beati Bernardi Tironiensis*, PL 172, cols. 1362–1446.
Geoffrey of Monmouth, *Historia Regum Britannie*, ed. Neil Wright (Cambridge 1984).
Geoffrey of Monmouth, *Vita Merlini*, ed. John Jay Parry, University of Illinois Studies in Language and Literature 10 (1925).
Gerald of Wales, *Historia Topographica Hiberniensis*, ed. James F. Dimock, Rolls Series 21 (1867), vol. 5; trans. John O'Meara, *Gerald of Wales: The History and Topography of Ireland* (London 1951).
Gerald of Wales, *Itinerarium Kambriae*, ed. James F. Dimock (London 1868), Rolls Series 21, vol. 6; trans. Lewis Thorpe, *The Journey through Wales* (London 1978).
Gerontius, *Vitae Sanctae Melaniae Junioris*, in *Analecta Bollandiana* 8 (1889), pp. 16– 23.
Gesta Abbatum Monasterii Sancti Albani, ed. Henry Thomas Riley, Rolls Series 28 (1867), 3 vols.
Goscelin of Saint Bertin, *Vita Sanctae Edithae Virginis*, ed. Andre Wilmart, in *Analecta Bollandiana* 56 (1938), pp. 5–101 and 265–307.
Gregory the Great, *Dialogi*, ed. and trans. Adalbert de Vogüé (Paris 1978–80), 3 vols.
Gregory of Tours, *Gloria Confessorum*, MGH SSRM 1(2) (1885), ed. B. Krusch, pp. 744–820.
Gregory of Tours, *Liber Vitae Patrum*, MGH SSRM 1(2) (1885), ed. B. Krusch, pp. 661–744; *Life of the Fathers*, trans. Edward James (Liverpool 1985).
Guthrie, K. S., *The Pythagorean Sourcebook and Library* (Michigan 1987).
Habig, Marion A., ed., *St. Francis of Assissi: Writings and Early Biographies* (Chicago 1972).
Heist, W. W., ed., *Vitae Sanctorum Hiberniae* (Brussels, 1965).
Herodotus, *The Histories*, trans. Aubrey de Sélincourt, revised John Marincola (London 2003).
Henry of Huntingdon, *Historia Anglorum*, ed. and trans. Diana Greenway (Oxford 1996).
Heraclidis Paradisus, PL 74, cols. 251–342.
Hilary of Arles, *Sermo de Vita Sancti Honorati, Episcopi Arelatensis*, PL 50, cols. 1249–73.
Historia Brittonum, ed. David N. Dumville (Cambridge 1985).
Historia Divae Monacellae, in Huw Price, '*Historia Divae Monacellae*', *Montgomeryshire Collections* 82 (1994), pp. 23–40.
Hoare, F. R., *The Western Fathers* (London 1954).
Jackson, Kenneth Hurlstone, *A Celtic Miscellany* (London 1951).
Jacobus de Voragine, *Legenda Aurea*, ed. T. Graesse (Dresden 1846); *The Golden Legend: Readings on the Saints*, trans. William Granger Ryan, 2 vols. (Princeton 1993).
James, M. R., ed. and trans., *The Apocryphal New Testament* (Oxford 1942).

Jerome, *Ad Eustochium*, PL 22, vol. 1, cols. 394–425.
Jerome, *Vita S. Hilarionis Eremitae*, PL 23, cols. 29–54.
Jerome, *Vita S. Pauli Primi Eremitae*, PL 23, cols. 18–30.
Jocelyn of Furness, *Vita Sancti Kentigerni*, in *Lives of St. Ninian and St. Kentigern*, ed. and trans. Alexander P. Forbes (Edinburgh 1874), pp. 159–253.
John of Ford, *Vita Beati Wulfrici Anachoretae*, in *Wulfric of Haselbury, by John, Abbot of Ford*, ed. Dom Maurice Bell, Somerset Record Society 47 (1933); partial trans. in Pauline Matarasso, *The Cistercian World* (London 1993), pp. 235–73.
John Moschus, *Pratum Spirituale*, PL 74, cols. 123–240.
John of Tynemouth, *Nova Legenda Anglie*, ed. Carl Horstman (Oxford 1901).
Jonas, *Vitae Sanctorum Columbani, Vedastis, Iohannis*, MGH Scriptores Rerum Germanicarum 37 (1905), ed. Bruno Krusch.
Karl, Louis, 'La légende de Saint Jehan Paulus', *Revue des langues romanes* 56 (1913), pp. 425–45.
Laurence of Durham, *Vita V Sanctae Brigidae*, *AASS* 1 February, pp. 172–85.
Libellus de Ortu Sancti Cuthberti, in *Miscellanea Biographica*, ed. James Raine, Surtees Society 8 (1838), pp. 63–87.
Liber Eliensis, ed. Ernest O. Blake, Royal Historical Society 92 (1962).
Liber Landavensis, ed. and trans. W. J. Rees (Llandovery 1840).
Liber Miraculorum Sancte Fides, ed. Luca Robertini (Selestat 1994); *The Book of Sainte Foy*, trans. Pamela Sheingorn (Philadelphia 1995).
Mabinogion, trans. Gwyn Jones and Thomas Jones (London 1974).
Miracula de Translationibus Sancti Cuthberti, in *Symeonis Monachi Opera Omnia*, ed. Thomas Arnold, Rolls Series 75 (1885), 2 vols, I, pp. 333–62.
Muirchú, *Vita Sancti Patricii*, in A. B. E. Hood, ed. and trans., *St Patrick: His Writings and Muirchu's 'Life'* (London 1978), pp. 61–77.
Musurillo, Herbert, ed. and trans., *The Acts of the Christian Martyrs* (Oxford 1972).
Navigatio Sancti Brendani Abbatis, ed. Carl Selmer (Notre Dame 1959).
Paladius, *Historia Lausiaca*, PL 73, cols. 1085–1218.
Paphnutius, *Histories of the Monks of Upper Egypt and the Life of Onnophrius*, trans. T. Vivian (Kalamazoo 1993).
Plummer, Charles, *Vitae Sanctorum Hiberniae* (Oxford 1910), 2 vols.
Plummer, Charles, *Lives of Irish Saints* (Oxford 1922), 2 vols.
Prima Acta Sancti Blasii, *AASS* 3 February, pp. 336–9.
Reginald of Durham, *Libellus de Admirandis Beati Cuthberti Virtutibus quae Novellis Patratae sunt Temporibus*, ed. James Raine, Surtees Society 1 (1835).
Reginald of Durham, *Libellus de Vita et Miraculis Sancti Godrici, Heremitae de Finchale*, ed. Joseph Stephenson, Surtees Society 20 (1847).
Rhigyfarch, *Vita Beati Davidis Archiepiscopi et Confessoris*, in *Rhigyfarch's Life of Saint David*, ed. and trans. J. W. James (Cardiff 1967), pp. 1–28.
Rufinus, *Historia Monachorum*, PL 21, cols. 387–462; *The Lives of the Desert Fathers* (Oxford 1981), trans. N. Russell, intro. B. Ward.
Scripta Leonis, Rufinus et Angeli, Sociorum S. Francisci, ed. and trans. Rosalind Brooke (Oxford 1970).
Seinte Katerine, ed. S. R. T. O. d'Ardenne and E. J. Dobson, Early English Text Society ss 7 (Oxford 1981).
Sicotière, L. de la, *Légende de Sainte Opportune, abbesse d'Almeneshes au diocèse de Seez en Normandie* (Rouen 1966).

Sigebert of Gembloux, *Vita S. Maclovii sive Machutii*, PL 160, cols. 729–46.

Snorri Sturluson, *The Prose Edda of Snorri Sturluson*, trans. Jean I. Young (Cambridge 1954).

Stokes, Whitley, ed., *Tripartite Life of Saint Patrick*, Rolls Series 89 (1887).

Stokes, Whitley, ed., *Lives of the Saints from the Book of Lismore* (Oxford 1899).

Sulpicius Severus, *Dialogi*, PL 20, cols. 183–222.

Sulpicius Severus, *Vita Beati Martini*, PL 20, cols. 159–76.

Symeon of Durham, *Libellus de Exordio atque Procursu istius hoc est Dunelmensis Ecclesie*, ed. and trans. David Rollason (Oxford 2000).

Tait, J., ed., *The Chartulary or Register of the Abbey of St. Wereburga, Chester*, Chetham Society 79 and 82 (1920, 1923).

Talbot, Charles H, *The Anglo-Saxon Missionaries in Germany* (London 1954).

Thomas of Celano, *Tractatus de Miraculis B. Francisci*, in *Analecta Franciscana* 10 (1926), pp. 271–330.

Thomas of Celano, *Vita Prima Sancti Francisici*, in *Analecta Franciscana* 10 (1926), pp. 3–115.

Thomas of Celano, *Vita Secunda Sancti Francisci*, in *Analecta Franciscana* 10 (1926), pp. 129–260.

Translatio Sancti Arnulphi, ed. C. de Smedt, in *Analecta Bollandiana* 8 (1889), pp. 97–8.

Translatio Sancti Eugenii, ed. R. P. Morin, in *Analecta Bollandiana* 5 (1886), pp. 385–95.

Venantius Fortunatus, *Vita Sanctae Radegundis*, MGH SSRM 2 (1888), ed. B. Krusch, pp. 364–77.

Verba Seniorum, PL 73, cols. 855–1062.

Vita Sanctae Amelbergae Virginis, *AASS* 10 July, pp. 89–103.

Vita Sanctae Balthildis, MGH SSRM 2 (1888), ed. B Krusch, pp. 475–508.

Vita I Sanctae Brigidae, *AASS* 1 February, pp. 118–34.

Vita IV Sanctae Brigidae, *AASS* 1 February, pp. 141–71.

Vita Sanctae Genovefae Virginis, *AASS* 3 January, pp. 137–53.

Vita Sanctae Geretrudis, MGH SSRM 2 (1888), ed. B. Krusch, pp. 447–74.

Vita Sanctae Mariae Aegypticae Meretricis, PL 73, cols. 671–90.

Vita Sanctae Opportunae Abbatissae, *AASS* 22 April, pp. 61–72.

Vita Sanctae Scaribergae, *AASS* 18 July, pp. 417–21.

Vita Sanctae Wereburgae Virginis, *AASS* 3 February, pp. 384–90.

Vita Sancti Aegidii, *AASS* 1 September, pp. 284–304.

Vita Sancti Aventini Presbyteri, *AASS* 4 February, pp. 474–80.

Vita Sancti Aviti Eremitae, *AASS* 17 June, pp. 360–4.

Vita Sancti Bassiani, Episcopi Laudensis, *AASS* 19 January, pp. 221– 6.

Vita Prima Sancti Bernardi Abbatis Clarevallensis, PL 185, vol. 1, cols. 225– 68, and trans. Pauline Matarasso *The Cistercian World* (London 1993).

Vita Sancti Brioci, ed. R. P. Plaine, in *Analecta Bollandiana* 2 (1883), pp. 161–90.

Vita Sancti Carilefi Presbyteri, *AASS* 1 July, pp. 85–99.

Vita Sancti Carileffi Sacerdotis et Abbatis, MGH SSRM 3 (1896), ed. Bruno Krusch, pp. 386–94.

Vita Sancti Cuthberti Auctore Anonymo, in *Two Lives of Saint Cuthbert*, ed. and trans. Bertram Colgrave (Cambridge 1940), pp. 59–139.

Vita Sancti Galmier, *AASS* 27 February, pp. 683–4.

Vita Sancti Gamelberti, sive Amelberti, *AASS* 27 January, pp. 783–7.

Vita Sancti Gudwali, *AASS* 6 June, pp. 728–48.

Vita Sancti Guenaili, *AASS* 3 November, pp. 669–79.

Vita Sancti Guilielmi Firmati, *AASS* 24 April, 334–42.

Vita Sancti Mariani, *AASS* 20 April, pp. 758–61.
Vita Sancti Norberti, MGH SS 12 (1856), ed. Roger Williams, pp. 663–706.
Vita Sancti Oswini Regis Deiorum, in *Miscellanea Biographica*, ed. James Raine, Surtees Society 8 (1838), pp. 1–59.
Vita Sancti Pachomii, PL 73, cols. 229–72.
Vitae Sancti Roberti Knaresburgensis, Vitae Antiquioris Fragmenta, ed. Paul Grosjean, in *Analecta Bollandiana* 57 (1939), pp. 365–74.
Vitae Sancti Roberti Knaresburgensis, Vita Recentior, ed. Paul Grosjean, in *Analecta Bollandiana* 57 (1939), pp. 375–400.
Vita Antiqua Samsonis, ed. R. P. Plaine, in *Analecta Bollandiana* 6 (1887), pp. 77–150.
Vita Sancti Samsonis, *AASS* 28 July, pp. 568–91.
Vita Sancti Simeonis Stylitae, PL 73, cols. 325–34; trans. Robert Doran, *The Lives of Saint Simeon Stylites* (Spencer, Mass., 1992).
Vita Sancti Vigoris, *AASS* 1 November, pp. 287–306.
Waddell, Helen, trans., *Beasts and Saints* (London 1934).
Waddell, Helen, trans., *Lives of the Fathers* (London 1936).
Wade-Evans, A. W., *Vitae Sanctorum Hiberniae* (Cardiff 1944).
Ward, Benedicta, *The Sayings of the Desert Fathers* (London 1975).
William of Canterbury, *Miracula Gloriosi Martyris Thomae Cantuariensis Archiepiscopi*, ed. James C. Robertson, Rolls Series 67 (London 1875), vol. 1, pp. 173–546.
William of Malmesbury, *De Gestis Pontificum Anglorum*, ed. N. E. S. A. Hamilton, Rolls Series 52 (London 1870), 2 vols; *William of Malmesbury, The Deeds of the Bishops of England*, trans. D. Preest (Woodbridge 2002).
William of Malmesbury, *De Gestis Regum Anglorum*, ed. William Stubbs, Rolls Series 90 (London 1887–9), 2 vols.
William of Newburgh, *Historia Rerum Anglicarum*, in *Chronicles of the Reigns of Stephen, Henry II and Richard I*, ed. Richard Howlett, Rolls Series 82 (London 1964), vol. 1.
Williams, Hugh, ed. and trans., *Two Lives of Gildas by a Monk of Ruys and Carador of Llancarfan* (1899, reprinted 1990).
Wolters, Mathais Joseph, *Notice historique sur l'ancien chapitre de chanoinesses nobles de Munsterbilsen dans la province actuel de Limbourg* (Ghent 1849).
Wormonoc, *Vita Sancti Pauli Episcopi Leonensis*, ed. R. P. Plaine, in *Analecta Bollandiana* 1 (1882), pp. 208–58.
Wrdisten, *Vita S Winwaloei Abbatis*, *AASS* 3 March, pp. 245–54.
Ysengrimus, ed. Jill Mann (Leiden 1987).

Secondary sources

Alexander, Dominic, 'Hermits, Hagiography and Popular Culture: A Comparative Study of Durham Cathedral Priory's Hermits in the Twelfth Century' (unpublished PhD thesis, University of London 2000).
Alexander, Dominic, 'Hermits and Hairshirts: The Social Meanings of Saintly Clothing in the *Vitae* of Godric of Finchale and Wulfric of Haselbury', *Journal of Medieval History* 28 (2002), pp. 205–26.
Anti, Elisa, *Santi e animali nell' Italia padana secoli IV–XII* (Bologna 1998).
Aubourg, G., 'Saint Vigor, évêque de Bayeux, VI siècle', in *Bulletin de la Société des Antiquaries de Normandie*, part 1, vol. 57, pp. 317–75, part 2, vol. 58, pp. 127–73 (1965–6).
Barrow, G. W. S., *Glasgow Cathedral: King David I and the Church of Glasgow* (Glasgow 1996).

Bates, D. R., 'The Character and Career of Odo, Bishop of Bayeux', *Speculum* 50 (1975), pp. 1–20.

Borsje, Jacqueline, 'The Monster in the River Ness in the *Vita Sancti Columbae:* A Study of a Miracle', *Peritia* 8 (1994), pp. 27–34.

Borst, Karen Gail, 'A Reconsideration of the *Vita Sancti Cadoci*', in *Celtic Folklore and Christianity: Studies in Memory of William W. Heist*, ed. Patrick K. Ford (Santa Barbara 1983), pp. 1–15.

Bouquet, Alan C., *Comparative Religion* (New York 1941).

Brand, J., *Faiths and Folklore: A Dictionary*, ed. W. Carew Hazlitt (London 1905), 2 vols.

Bray, Dorothy Ann, *A List of Motifs in the Lives of the Early Irish Saints* (Helsinki 1992).

Brown, Peter, 'Rise and Function of the Holy Man in Late Antiquity', *Journal of Roman Studies* 61 (1971), pp. 80–101.

Burne, Charlotte Sophia, ed., *Shropshire Folk-Lore* (London 1883).

Butler, Dom Cuthbert, *The Lausiac History of Palladius*, vol. 6 of *Texts and Studies: Contributions to Biblical and Patristic Literature*, ed. J. Armitage Robinson (Cambridge, 1904).

Carey, John, 'Varieties of Supernatural Contact in the Life of Adamnán', in *Saints and Scholars: Studies in Irish Hagiography*, ed. John Carey, Máire Herbert and Pádraig Ó Riain (Bodmin 2001), pp. 49–62.

Cartwright, Raymond A., *The Holy Island of Lindisfarne and the Farne Islands* (Newton Abbot 1976).

Clark, Francis, *The Pseudo-Gregorian Dialogues*, 2 vols (Leiden 1987).

Cohn, Norman, *Europe's Inner Demons* (London 1993).

Connolly, S., and J.-M. Picard, 'Cogitosus: Life of Saint Brigit', *Journal of the Royal Society of Antiquaries of Ireland*, 117 (1987), pp. 5–27.

Constable, Giles, 'The Vision of a Cistercian Novice', in *Petrus Venerabilis: Studia Anselmiana* 44, ed. Giles Constable and James Kritzeck (Rome 1956), pp. 95–8.

Constable, Giles, *The Reformation of the Twelfth Century* (Cambridge 1996).

Coon, Lynda L., *Sacred Fictions: Holy Women and Hagiography in Late Antiquity* (Philadelphia 1997).

Corbet, Patrick, *Les saints ottoniens: sainteté dynastique, sainteté royale et sainteté feminine autour de l'an mil* (Sigmaringen 1986).

Cross, Tom Peete, *Motif-Index of Early Irish Literature* (New York 1968).

Cubitt, Catherine, 'Sites and Sanctity: Revisiting the Cult of Murdered and Martyred Anglo-Saxon Royal Saints', *Early Medieval Europe* 9 (2000), pp. 53–83.

Cusack, P. A., 'Some Literary Antecedents of the Totila Encounter in the Second Dialogue of Pope Gregory I', *Studia Patristica* 12 (1975), pp. 87–90.

Dagens, Claude, *Saint Gregoire le grand* (Paris 1977).

Destombes, C.-J., *Les Vies de saints de Cambrai et Aras* (Lille 1887), 4 vols.

Doble, Gilbert H., *Saint Gudwal or Gurval: Bishop and Confessor* (Truro 1933).

Doble, Gilbert H., *Saint Paul (Paulinus) of Léon: Bishop and Confessor* (Lampeter 1941).

Doble, Gilbert H., *Lives of the Welsh Saints* (Cardiff 1971).

Dodds, Madeleine H., 'The Little Book of the Birth of Cuthbert', *Archaeologia Aeliana* 6 (1929), pp. 52–94.

Donatus, Mary, *Beasts and Birds in the Lives of the Early Irish Saints* (Philadelphia 1934).

Doucet, Marc, 'Pedagogie et théologie dans la "Vie de Saint Benoit" par Saint Gregoire le grand', *Collectanea Cisterciensia* 38 (1976), pp. 158–73.

Duine, F., *Questions d'hagiographie et vie de S. Samson* (Paris 1914).

Ehrman, Bart D., *Lost Christianities* (Oxford 2003).

Elkins, Sharon K., *Holy Women of Twelfth Century England* (London 1988).
Elliott, Alison Goddard, *Roads to Paradise: Reading the Lives of the Early Saints* (London 1987).
Essen, Leon J. van der, *Étude critique et littéraire sur les Vitae des saints merovingiens de l'ancienne Belgique* (Paris 1907).
Fawtier, Robert, *La Vie de Saint Samson* (Paris 1912).
Filotas, Bernadette, *Pagan Survivals, Superstitions, and Popular Cultures* (Toronto 2005).
Finucane, Ronald C., *Miracles and Pilgrims: Popular Beliefs in Medieval England* (London 1977).
Forcellini, Aegidius, *Totius Latinitatis Lexicon* (London 1828), 2 vols.
Ford, Patrick K., 'Aspects of the Patrician Legend', in *Celtic Folklore and Christianity: Studies in Memory of William W. Heist*, ed. Patrick K. Ford (Santa Barbara 1983), pp. 29–49.
Fournée, Jean, 'Le culte populaire de l'iconographie de sainte Opportune', in *L'abbaye d'Olmenèches-Argentan et Saint Opportune: sa vie et son culte*, ed. Y. Chaussy (Paris 1970), pp. 237–84.
Frazer, James George, *The Golden Bough: A Study in Magic and Religion* (London 1936), 12 vols.
Ginzburg, Carlo, *Ecstasies: Deciphering the Witches' Sabbath*, trans. Raymond Rosenthal (London 1990).
Ginzburg, Carlo, *The Cheese and the Worms: The Cosmos of a Sixteenth-Century Miller*, trans. John and Anne Tedeschi (Baltimore 1992).
Glacken, Clarence J., *Traces on the Rhodian Shore: Nature and Culture in Western Thought from Ancient Times to the End of the Eighteenth Century* (Berkeley 1967).
Goff, Jacques le, 'Ecclesiastical Culture and Folklore in the Middle Ages: Saint Marcellus of Paris and the Dragon', in Jacques Le Goff, *Time, Work and Culture in the Middle Ages*, trans. Arthur Goldhammer (Chicago 1980), pp. 159–88.
Goff, Jacques le, *The Birth of Purgatory*, trans. Arthur Goldhammer (London 1984).
Goff, Jacques le, 'Levi-Strauss in Broceliande: A Brief Analysis of a Courtly Romance', in *The Medieval Imagination*, trans A. Goldhammer (Chicago 1988), pp. 107–31.
Goff, Jacques le, 'The Wilderness in the Medieval West', in *The Medieval Imagination*, trans. Arthur Goldhammer (Chicago 1988), pp. 47–59.
Golding, Brian, 'The Hermit and the Hunter', in *The Cloister, The World: Essays in Medieval History in Honour of Barbara Harvey*, ed. John Blair and Brian Golding (Oxford 1996).
Goody, Jack, *The Logic of Writing and the Organisation of Society* (Cambridge 1986).
Goody, Jack, *The Interface between the Oral and the Literate* (Cambridge, 1987).
Gotfredsen, Lise, *The Unicorn* (London 1999), trans. Anne Born.
Gurevich, Aron, *Categories of Medieval Culture*, trans. G. L. Campbell (London 1972).
Gwynn-Jones, T., *Welsh Folklore and Folk-Custom* (Cambridge 1930).
Hardy, T. D., *Descriptive Catalogue of Materials Relating to the History of Great Britain and Ireland*, Rolls Series 26 (1862–71), 3 vols.
Hawkey, Peter, *Birds of the Farne Islands* (Rothbury 1990).
Head, Thomas, *Hagiography and the Cult of the Saints: The Diocese of Orleans, 800–1200* (Cambridge 1990).
Head, Thomas, *Medieval Hagiography* (London 2001).
Hen, Yitzhak, *Culture and Religion in Merovingian Gaul* (New York 1995).
Hill, Rosalind, *Both Small and Great Beasts* (London 1953).
Holdsworth, Christopher, 'Christina of Markyate', in *Medieval Women*, *Studies in Church History: Subsidia 1*, ed. Derek Baker (Oxford 1978), pp. 185–204.
Holdsworth, Christopher, 'Hermits and the Power of the Frontier', in *Saints and Saints' Lives*, ed. Keith Bate *et al.*, Reading Medieval Studies 16 (1990), pp. 55–76.

Howe, John, 'The Date of the *Life* of Saint Vigor of Bayeux', *Analecta Bollandiana* 102 (1984), pp. 303–12.
Husband, Timothy, *The Wild Man: Medieval Myth and Symbolism* (New York 1980).
Jarmon, A. O. H., 'The Welsh Myrddin Poems', in *Arthurian Literature in the Middle Ages*, ed. Roger S. Loomis (Oxford 1959), pp. 20–30.
Jobes, Gertrude, *Dictionary of Mythology, Folklore and Symbols* (New York 1962), 2 vols.
Johnston, Elva, 'The "Pagan" and "Christian" Identities of the Irish Female Saint', in *Celts and Christians*, ed. Mark Atherton (Cardiff 2002), pp. 60–78.
Kelly, John N. D., *Jerome, His Life, Writings and Controversies* (London 1975).
Klingender, Francis, *Animals in Art and Thought* (London 1971).
Krappe, Alexander H., 'Saint Patrick and the Snakes', *Traditio* 5 (1947), pp. 323–30.
Ladurie, Emmanuel le Roy, *Montaillou, village occitan de 1294 à 1324* (Paris 1975); trans. Barbara Bray, *Montaillou* (London 1978).
Lambert, Malcolm, *The Cathars* (Oxford 1998).
Leach, Maria, ed., *Dictionary of Folklore, Mythology and Legend* (London 1975).
Leclercq, Jean, *The Love of Learning and the Desire for God*, trans. Catherine Misrahi (London 1961).
Leclercq, Jean, '*Eremus* et *eremita*: pour l'histoire du vocabulaire de la vie solitaire', *Collectanea Ordinis Cistercensium Reformatorum* 25 (1963), pp. 8–30.
Lemmens, Joseph, *La mémoire des monastères: une histoire de la Belgique du VIIe au XVIIIe siècle* (Brussels 1999).
Little, Lester K., *Religious Poverty and the Profit Economy* (London 1978).
Locatelli, René, 'Luxeuil aux XIIe et XIIIe siècles', *Revue Mabillon* 60 (1981), pp. 77–102.
Loomis, R. S., *White Magic: An Introduction to the Folklore of Christian Legend* (Cambridge, Mass., 1948).
Love, Rosalind C., *Three Anglo-Latin Saints' Lives* (Oxford 1996).
Low, Mary, 'The Natural World in Early Irish Christianity: An Ecological Footnote', in *Celts and Christians*, ed. Mark Atherton (Cardiff, 2002), pp. 169–203.
McCann, Philip J., *St. Benedict* (London 1937).
McCone, Kim, 'Brigit in the Seventh Century: A Saint with Three *Lives?*', *Peritia* 1 (1982), pp. 107–45.
McCone, Kim, 'An Introduction to Early Irish Saint's Lives', *The Maynooth Review* 11 (1984), pp. 26–59.
McCone, Kim, *Pagan Past and Christian Present in Early Irish Literature* (Maynooth 1990).
McCready, William D., *Signs of Sanctity: Miracles in the Thought of Gregory the Great* (Toronto 1989).
McGuire, Brian P., 'Written Sources and Cistercian Inspiration in Caesarius of Heisterbach', *Analecta Cisterciensia* 35 (1979), pp. 227–82.
McGuire, Brian P., 'Friends and Tales in the Cloister: Oral Sources in Caesarius of Heisterbach's *Dialogus Miraculorum*', *Analecta Cisterciensia* 36 (1980), pp. 167–247.
Macquarrie, Alan, 'The Career of Saint Kentigern of Glasgow: *Vitae, Lectiones* and Glimpses of Fact', *Innes Review* 37 (1986), pp. 3–24.
Mahler, Maximillien, 'Evocations bibliques et hagiographiques dans la Vie de St. Benedict', *Revue bénédictine* 83 (1973), pp. 398–429.
Mead, G. R. S., *Apollonius of Tyana* (London 1901).
Melia, Daniel, 'Law and the Shaman Saint', in *Celtic Folklore and Christianity: Studies in Memory of William W. Heist*, ed. Patrick K. Ford (Santa Barbara 1983), pp. 113–28.
Meyvaert, Paul, 'Bede and Gregory the Great', in Paul Meyvaert, *Benedict, Gregory, Bede and*

Others (London 1977), pp. 1–26.
Micha, Alexandre, 'The Vulgate Merlin', in *Arthurian Literature in the Middle Ages*, ed. Roger S. Loomis (Oxford 1959), pp. 319–24.
Michel, Édouard, *Abbayes et monastères de Belgique* (Brussels 1923).
Millinger, Susan, 'Humility and Power: Anglo-Saxon Nuns in Anglo-Norman Hagiography', in *Distant Echoes: Medieval Religious Women*, ed. John A. Nichols and Lillian T. Shank (Kalamazoo 1984), pp. 115–29.
Montalembert, Charles F. R. Count de, *The Monks of the West: From St. Benedict to St. Bernard* (London 1896), 6 vols.
Moore, R. I., *The First European Revolution* (Oxford 2000).
Morvannou, F., 'Guénolé et Guénaël', *Annales de Bretagne* 81 (1974), pp. 25–42
Moyse, Gérard, 'Les origins du monachisme sans le diocèse de Besançon (V^{e}–X^{e} siécles)', *Bibliothèque de l'école de Chartres*, 131 (1973), pp. 21–104, 369–485.
Northumberland County History Committee, *History of Northumberland* (London 1895–1940), 15 vols.
Norwich, John Julius, *Byzantium: The Early Centuries* (London 1988).
Ó Briain, Felim, 'Saga Themes in Irish Hagiography', in *Féilscríbhinn Torna*, ed. Séamus Pender (Cork 1947), pp. 33–42.
O'Neill, Paul, *Upon this Rock: The Story of the Roman Catholic Church in Newfoundland and Labrador* (St John's 1984).
Oury, D. Guy, 'Saint Opportune, sa vie et ses reliques', in *L'abbaye d'Olmenèches-Argentan et Saint Opportune: sa vie et son culte*, ed. Y. Chaussy (Paris 1970), pp. 221–36.
Partner, Nancy F., *Serious Entertainments: The Writing of History in Twelfth-Century England* (Chicago 1977).
Peers, C. R., 'Finchale Priory', *Archaeologia Aeliana* 4 (1927), pp. 193–220.
Petersen, Joan M., *Handmaids of the Lord: Holy Women in Late Antiquity and the Early Middle Ages* (Kalamazoo 1996).
Picard, J.-M., 'Structural Patterns in Early Hiberno-Latin Hagiography', *Peritia* 4 (1985), pp. 67–82.
Pollard, John, *Birds in Greek Life and Thought* (Plymouth 1977).
Poncelet, A., 'Les saints de Micy', *Analecta Bollandiana* 24 (1905), pp. 5–104.
Poncelet, A., 'Les biographies de Sainte Amelberge', *Analecta Bollandiana* 31 (1912), pp. 401–9.
Richards, Jeffrey, *Consul of God: The Life and Times of Gregory the Great* (London 1980).
Riches, Samantha, *Saint George: Hero, Martyr and Myth* (Stroud 2000).
Ridyard, Susan J., *The Royal Saints of Anglo-Saxon England* (Cambridge 1988).
Rollason, David, *The Mildrith Legend: A Study in Early Medieval Hagiography in England* (Leicester 1982).
Rollason, David, *Saints and Relics in Anglo-Saxon England* (Oxford 1989).
Rosenthal, Constance L., *The Vitae Patrum in Old and Middle English Literature* (Philadelphia 1936).
Round, Steve, *The Penguin Guide to the Superstitions of Britain and Ireland* (London 2003).
Rousseau, Philip, *Ascetics, Authority and the Church* (Oxford 1978).
Salisbury, Joyce E., *The Beast Within: Animals in the Middle Ages* (London 1994).
Schmitt, Jean-Claude, *The Holy Greyhound*, trans. Martin Thom (Cambridge 1983).
Sharpe, Richard, '*Vitae S. Brigitae*: The Oldest Texts', *Peritia* 1 (1982), pp. 81–106.
Sharpe, Richard, 'Some Problems concerning the Organisation of the Church in Early Medieval Ireland', in *Peritia* 3 (1984), pp. 230–70.

Sharpe, Richard, *Medieval Irish Saints Lives: An Introduction to Vitae Sanctorum Hiberniae* (Oxford 1991).

Smith, Julia M. H., 'Oral and Literate: Saints, Miracles and Relics in Brittany, c.850– 1250', *Speculum* 65 (1990), pp. 309–43.

Smith, Julia M. H., 'The problem of female sanctity in Carolingian Europe c780–920', *Past and Present* 146 (1995) pp. 3–37.

Snieders, Irène, 'L'influence de l'hagiographie irlandais sur les *vitae* des saints irlandais de Belgique', *Revue d'histoire ecclésiastique* 24 (1928), pp. 596–627, 828–67.

Sorrell, Roger D., *Saint Francis and Nature: Tradition and Innovation in Western Christian Attitudes to the Environment* (Oxford 1988).

Stancliffe, Clare, *St Martin and His Hagiographer* (Oxford 1983).

Straw, Carole, *Gregory the Great: Perfection in Imperfection* (University of California 1988).

Swainson, Charles, *The Folk Lore and Provincial Names of British Birds* (London 1886).

Talbot, Charles H., 'The *Liber Confortatorius* of Goscelin of St Bertin', *Studia Anselmiana* 37 (Rome 1955), pp. 1–118.

Tchouhadjian, Armand, *Saint Blaise: évêque de Sébaste* (Paris 2004).

Thacker, Alan, '*Loca Sanctorum*: The Significance of Place in the Study of the Saints', in *Local Saints and Local Churches in the Early Medieval West*, ed. Alan Thacker and Richard Sharpe (Oxford 2002), pp. 1–43.

Thompson, Stith, *Motif-Index of Folk Literature* (Copenhagen 1957), 6 vols.

Tillery, Maureen A., 'Martyrs, Monks, Insects and Animals', in *The Medieval World of Nature*, ed. Joyce Salisbury (London 1993), pp. 93–108.

Tudor, Victoria, 'The Cult of St. Cuthbert in the Twelfth Century: The Evidence of Reginald of Durham', in *St. Cuthbert, His Cult and His Community to A.D. 1200*, ed. Gerald Bonner, David Rollason and Clare Stancliffe (Woodbridge 1989), pp. 447–67.

Turner, Victor, *The Ritual Process* (London 1974).

Victoria History of the County of Durham, ed. William Page (London 1893–1940), 3 vols.

Visser, Derk, Review of Roger D. Sorrell, *Saint Francis and Nature*, in *Church History* 59 (1990), pp. 394–6.

Vogüé, Adalbert de, 'Benoit, modèle de vie spirituelle d'après le deuxième livre des *Dialogues* de Saint Gregoire', *Collectanea Cisterciensia* 38 (1976), pp. 147–57.

Voisenet, Jacques, *Bestiaire chrétien: l'imagerie animale des auteurs du haut moyen âge* (Toulouse 1994).

Wallace-Hadrill, David S., *The Greek Patristic View of Nature* (Oxford 1968).

Ward, Benedicta, *The Spirituality of Saint Cuthbert* (Oxford 1992).

Ward, H. L. D., 'Lailoken (or Merlin Silvester)', *Romania* 22 (1896), pp. 504–26.

Weightman, M. Scott, *The Farne Islands* (Seahouses 1988).

Wickham, Chris, *Framing the Early Middle Ages: Europe and the Mediterranean, 44– 800* (Oxford 2006).

Williams, Charles Allyn, 'Oriental Affinities of the Legend of the Hairy Anchorite', *University of Illinois Studies of Language and Literature* 10 (1925), pp. 9–56, and 11 (1926), pp. 57–119.

Wood, Ian, 'The *Vita Columbani* and Merovingian Hagiography', *Peritia* 1 (1982), pp. 63–80.

Ziolowski, Jan, *Talking Animals: Medieval Latin Beast Poetry* (Philadelphia 1993).

INDEX